Communications
in Computer and Information Science 551

Commenced Publication in 2007
Founding and Former Series Editors:
Alfredo Cuzzocrea, Dominik Ślęzak, and Xiaokang Yang

More information about this series at http://www.springer.com/series/7899

Leszek A. Maciaszek · Joaquim Filipe (Eds.)

Evaluation of Novel Approaches to Software Engineering

9th International Conference, ENASE 2014
Lisbon, Portugal, April 28–30, 2014
Revised Selected Papers

 Springer

Editors
Leszek A. Maciaszek
Wroclaw University of Economics
Wroclaw
Poland

Joaquim Filipe
INSTICC
Polytechnic Institute of Setúbal
Setúbal
Portugal

ISSN 1865-0929   ISSN 1865-0937   (electronic)
Communications in Computer and Information Science
ISBN 978-3-319-27217-7   ISBN 978-3-319-27218-4   (eBook)
DOI 10.1007/978-3-319-27218-4

Library of Congress Control Number: 2015955869

Springer Cham Heidelberg New York Dordrecht London

Springer International Publishing AG Switzerland is part of Springer Science+Business Media
(www.springer.com)

Preface

The present book includes extended and revised versions of a set of selected papers from the 9th International Conference on Evaluation of Novel Approaches to Software Engineering (ENASE 2014), held in Lisbon, Portugal, during April 28–30 2014, which was sponsored by the Institute for Systems and Technologies of Information, Control and Communication (INSTICC) and technically co-sponsored by the IEEE Computer Society and IEEE Computer Society's Technical Council on Software Engineering (TCSE).

The mission of ENASE is to be a prime international forum for discussing and publishing research findings and IT industry experiences related to the evaluation of novel approaches to software engineering. By comparing novel approaches with established traditional practices and by evaluating them against software quality criteria, ENASE conferences advance the knowledge and research in software engineering, identify the most promising trends, and propose new directions for consideration by researchers and practitioners involved in large-scale software development and integration.

We received 58 submissions, from 28 countries in all continents, of which 33 % were orally presented and 16 % presented as posters, and their authors were invited to submit extended versions of their papers for this book. In order to evaluate each submission, double-blind reviewing was performed by the Program Committee. Finally, only the best 11 papers were included in this book.

We would like to highlight that ENASE 2014 included five plenary keynote lectures, given by internationally distinguished researchers, namely: Kecheng Liu (University of Reading, UK), Jan Dietz (Delft University of Technology, The Netherlands), Antoni Olivé (Universitat Politècnica de Catalunya, Spain), José Tribolet (INESC-ID/Instituto Superior Técnico, Portugal) and Hans-J. Lenz (Freie Universität Berlin, Germany). We must acknowledge the invaluable contribution of all keynote speakers who, as renowned researchers in their areas, have presented cutting-edge work, thus contributing toward enriching the scientific content of the conference.

We especially thank the authors, whose research and development efforts are recorded here. The knowledge and diligence of the reviewers were essential to ensure the quality of the papers presented at the conference and published in this book. Finally, a special thanks to all members of the INSTICC team, whose involvement was fundamental for organizing a smooth and successful conference.

April 2015

Joaquim Filipe
Leszek Maciaszek

Organization

Conference Chair

Joaquim Filipe   Polytechnic Institute of Setúbal/INSTICC, Portugal

Program Chair

Leszek Maciaszek   Wroclaw University of Economics, Poland and
Macquarie University, Sydney, Australia

Organizing Committee

Marina Carvalho	INSTICC, Portugal
Helder Coelhas	INSTICC, Portugal
Bruno Encarnação	INSTICC, Portugal
André Lista	INSTICC, Portugal
Andreia Moita	INSTICC, Portugal
Raquel Pedrosa	INSTICC, Portugal
Vitor Pedrosa	INSTICC, Portugal
Cátia Pires	INSTICC, Portugal
Susana Ribeiro	INSTICC, Portugal
Mara Silva	INSTICC, Portugal
José Varela	INSTICC, Portugal
Pedro Varela	INSTICC, Portugal

Program Committee

Guglielmo de Angelis	CNR - IASI, Italy
Marko Bajec	University of Ljubljana, Slovenia
Alexandre Bergel	Pleiad Lab, University of Chile, Santiago, Chile
Maria Bielikova	Slovak University of Technology in Bratislava, Slovak Republic
Wojciech Cellary	Poznan University of Economics, Poland
Rebeca Cortazar	University of Deusto, Spain
Massimo Cossentino	National Research Council, Italy
Bernard Coulette	University of Toulouse 2- Le Mirail/IRIT Laboratory, France
Mariangiola Dezani	Università di Torino, Italy
Angelina Espinoza	Universidad Autónoma Metropolitana, Iztapalapa (UAM-I), Spain
Vladimir Estivill-Castro	Griffith University, Australia

Joerg Evermann	Memorial University of Newfoundland, Canada
Maria João Ferreira	Universidade Portucalense, Portugal
Maria Ganzha	SRI PAS and University of Gdansk, Poland
Juan Garbajosa	Technical University of Madrid, UPM, Spain
Cesar Gonzalez-Perez	Institute of Heritage Sciences (Incipit), Spanish National Research Council (CSIC), Spain
Philipp Haller	Typesafe, Switzerland
Mahmoud EL Hamlaoui	University of Med V Souissi, ENSIAS, SIME Laboratory, IMS Team, Morocco
Rene Hexel	Griffith University, Australia
Benjamin Hirsch	EBTIC/Khalifa University, UAE
Robert Hirschfeld	Hasso-Plattner-Institut, Germany
Charlotte Hug	Université Paris 1 Panthéon-Sorbonne, France
Zbigniew Huzar	Wroclaw University of Technology, Poland
Slinger Jansen	Utrecht University, The Netherlands
Monika Kaczmarek	Poznan University of Economics, Poland
Diana Kirk	Auckland University of Technology, New Zealand
Robert S. Laramee	Swansea University, UK
George Lepouras	University of the Peloponnese, Greece
Pericles Loucopoulos	Harokopio University of Athens, Greece
Jian Lu	Nanjing University, China
André Ludwig	University of Leipzig, Germany
Ivan Lukovic	University of Novi Sad, Serbia
Leszek Maciaszek	Wroclaw University of Economics, Poland and Macquarie University, Sydney, Australia
Lech Madeyski	Wroclaw University of Technology, Poland
Sascha Mueller-Feuerstein	Ansbach University of Applied Sciences, Germany
Johannes Müller	University of Leipzig, Germany
Andrzej Niesler	Wroclaw University of Economics, Poland
Janis Osis	Riga Technical University, Latvia
Mourad Oussalah	University of Nantes, France
Marcin Paprzycki	Polish Academy of Sciences, Poland
Dana Petcu	West University of Timisoara, Romania
Naveen Prakash	MRCE, India
Elke Pulvermueller	University of Osnabrück, Germany
Rick Rabiser	Johannes Kepler University, Linz, Austria
Lukasz Radlinski	University of Szczecin, Poland
Radoslaw Rudek	Wroclaw University of Economics, Poland
Francisco Ruiz	Universidad de Castilla-La Mancha, Spain
Krzysztof Sacha	Warsaw University of Technology, Poland
Motoshi Saeki	Tokyo Institute of Technology, Japan
Ioana Sora	Politehnica University of Timisoara, Romania
Jakub Swacha	University of Szczecin, Poland
Stephanie Teufel	University of Fribourg, Switzerland
Rainer Unland	University of Duisburg-Essen, Germany
Olegas Vasilecas	Vilnius Gediminas Technical University, Lithuania

Krzysztof Wecel   Poznan University of Economics, Poland
Igor Wojnicki   AGH University of Science and Technology, Poland
Kang Zhang   The University of Texas at Dallas, USA

Additional Reviewers

Amine Benelallam   AtlanMod Inria Mines Nantes, France
Jessica Diaz Fernandez   Universidad Politécnica de Madrid, Spain
Marko Jankovic   University of Ljubljana, Slovenia
Patrizia Ribino   ICAR- CNR, Italy
Luca Sabatucci   National Research Council - Italy, Italy
Sergiusz Strykowski   Poznan University of Economics, Poland
Javier Tuya   University of Oviedo, Spain
Slavko Žitnik   University of Ljubljana, Slovenia

Invited Speakers

Kecheng Liu   University of Reading, UK
Jan Dietz   Delft University of Technology, The Netherlands
Antoni Olivé   Universitat Politècnica de Catalunya, Spain
José Tribolet   INESC-ID/Instituto Superior Técnico, Portugal
Hans-J. Lenz   Freie Universität Berlin, Germany

Contents

Reducing the Level of Complexity of Working with Model Transformations

Iván Santiago[(✉)], Juan M. Vara, Valeria de Castro, and Esperanza Marcos

Grupo de Investigacin Kybele, Universidad Rey Juan Carlos,
Avda. Tulipán S/N, 28933 Móstoles, Madrid, Spain
{ivan.santiago,juanmanuel.vara,valeria.decastro,esperanza.marcos}@urjc.es
http://www.kybele.es

Abstract. Valuable information can be obtained from the relationships that hold between the elements involved in any Model-Driven Engineering (MDE) process. This information can be then used to support impact change analysis, validation of requirements, etc. However, dealing with traceability is a complex and error-prone task if no tool support is provided to that end. The adoption of MDE can definitely alleviate such complexity. For instance, MDE techniques such as models transformations, matching or weaving, can be used to automate the production and management of traceability, without requiring an extra effort from any of the stakeholders involved in the project. In this line, this work presents the different visualization mechanisms for traceability information supported by iTrace, a framework for the management of traceability in the context of MDE. They provide insights into how the elements of a given project relate to each other, offering simple and intuitive representations of such relationships with different granularity levels. These visualizations help to reduce the inherent complexity of dealing working with model transformations, making it possible for instance to understand the typology of the elements processed by a particular mapping rule without mastering the entire transformation language or even the transformation under study.

Keywords: Model-driven engineering · Traceability · Program comprehension

1 Introduction

Traceability [1] has always been a relevant topic in Software Engineering [2]. Maintaining links from requirement to analysis, design artifacts, working-code or test cases has been acknowledged as one of the best ways to perform impact analysis, regression testing, validation of requirements, etc. Likewise, the appropriate management of traceability information is key to control the evolution of the different system components during the software development life cycle [3].

Unfortunately, maintaining links among software artifacts is a tedious, time-consuming and error-prone task if no tooling support is provided to that end

© Springer International Publishing Switzerland 2015
J. Filipe and L. Maciaszek (Eds.): ENASE 2014, CCIS 551, pp. 1–17, 2015.
DOI: 10.1007/978-3-319-27218-4_1

[4]. As a consequence, traceability data use to become obsolete very quickly during software development. Even sometimes it is completely omitted. Nevertheless, the advent of Model-Driven Engineering [5] can drastically change this landscape. The key role of models positively influences the management of traceability since the traces to maintain are simply the links between the elements of the different models handled along the process. Furthermore, such traces can be collected in other models to process them using any model processing technique, such as model transformation, model matching or model merging [6].

One of the areas where appropriate management of traceability has been acknowledged to help decisively is software comprehension [7]. This statement gains strength in the context of Model-Driven Engineering [5], where software (in the shape of model transformations) is responsible for driving forward the development process. In fact, any MDE project consists basically of a chain of model transformations that consume input models to produce output models [8]. Being able to keep trace of the relationships between the elements of such models implies complete control over the transformations that implemented them and thus over the development process itself [9].

Therefore, in previous works [10] a systematic review was conducted to assess the state of the art on traceability management in the context of MDE. The review showed that despite the maturity reached by MDE tools for some specific tasks, such as model edition or transformation [11], the area of traceability management presents some serious limitations, like the absence of proposals to support the analysis of the information produced when traceability is considered or the lack of appropriate tooling to visualize traceability data. Regarding the latter, the review revealed that there are very few tools providing ad-hoc mechanisms to deal with trace models AMW [12], ModeLink [13], MeTaGeM-Trace [14] and none of them supports both model-to-model (m2m) traces and model-to-text (m2t) traces. Besides, the huge amount of data collected during an MDE project where the production of traceability information is enabled, makes it very convenient to provide some kind of aggregated view over such data.

To deal with these issues, this work introduces the visualization mechanisms supported by iTrace [15], a framework for traceability management in MDE projects. On the one hand, it bundles an editor for trace models that supports both m2m and m2t traces. On the other hand, it leans on Business Intelligence (BI) [16] tools to provide a set of dashboards for traceability data[1] that can be used to produce high-level overviews of the relationships between the artefacts involved in the development process.

The rest of this paper is structured as follows: Sect. 2 introduces existing works in the field, highlighting the contributions of this work. The running example used to illustrate the proposal can be found in this URL[2]. Section 3 illustrates the production of trace models from legacy projects, while Sect. 4 presents our proposal for the visualization of the data collected in such models.

---

[1] A dashboard is a visual interface that provides at-a-glance views into key measures relevant to a particular objective or business process [17].

[2] http://www.kybele.etsii.urjc.es/itracetool/publications/lncs-2015/.

Finally, Sect. 5 summarizes the main conclusions derived from this work and provide some directions for further work.

2   Related Works

It is worth noting that there are several works dealing with the use of traceability matrix or reports to present the traceability information gathered during an MDE project. However, this work focuses on more elaborated visualizations based on some kind of graphical abstraction, such as graphs, editors or dashboards.

First of all, most of the existing works in the context of MDE lean on the Eclipse Modeling Framework (EMF) [18] to implement their proposals [19]. One of the main features of EMF is the ability to generate simple yet fully functional tree-based editors from a given metamodel. These editors are consequently widely used by MDE tools. Nevertheless, their generic nature do not always fit with the specific nature of some scenarios. For instance, trace models are eminently *relational* models, i.e. models whose main purpose is to collect the relationships between the elements of some other models [20].

A few works have previously addressed this issue by providing multi-panel editors for EMF models. This is the case of AMW, ModeLink, MeTaGeM-Trace or iTrace [21]. However, although they improve the capabilities of the generic EMF editors to display relational models, they still own some generic nature that results in some limitations when used to display trace models.

The main limitation of AMW when it is used to display trace models is that it hampers the distinction between source and target models when dealing with more than two related models. This results in related models being misplaced regarding their role in the traceability relationship. For instance, contrary to the most intuitive idea, source models would be placed on the right of the traces model.

ModeLink in turn just supports the visualization of two/three models, including the relationships (traces) model. Therefore, the user can only define relationships between the elements of one source and one target model. As a consequence, a limitation arises when traces between elements of several source and/or target models are needed.

Finally, although MeTaGeM-Trace overcame these limitations, it does not support the definition of traces between model elements and source-code (blocks), i.e. m2t traces.

By contrast, Acceleo [22] provides a solution to the last issue. In fact, it is a m2t transformation language which support traces generation. Every time an Acceleo transformation is run, a traces model between the input model and the code generated is produced. Unfortunately, due to its functionality, it is obviously limited to work with m2t trace models. Besides, such models are just transient models. They can only be used for debugging purposes but they are not persisted when the IDE is closed.

From the visual point of view, the graph-based visualizations supported by GEF3D [23], TraceViz [24] or TraVis [25], are probably more appealing. However, while GEF3D is mainly a extension to support 3D diagramming atop of Eclipse-GEF, TraceViz and TraVis are general-purpose tools for traceability management. That is, none of them were devised to work with models, what results in a number of issues when used in the context of MDE. The most immediate is the need to serialize the trace models produced in MDE projects according to the input format required by such tools.

Regarding iTrace its editor for trace models solve the different issues of the multi-panel editors mentioned before: it displays n models that are correctly placed regarding their role in the traceability relationship. Besides, it supports m2m or m2t trace models. Nevertheless, the most outstanding feature of iTrace regarding existing works is the use of BI tools to provide a set of dashboards for traceability data. They support the tracking of traces from high-level models to source-code and the selection of different granularity levels, either showing or abstracting from technical details. As a result, simpler and more intuitive visualizations are provided.

To summarize the main findings of this section, Table 1 compares the main features of iTrace regarding visualization of traceability data against those of reviewed proposals. In particular, the following features are reviewed:

- Nature of the traced artifacts (*NaT*): the tool can be used to display (m2m) traces, (m2t) traces or both.
- Cardinality (*#Art*): the tool supports *(Sim)*ple traces, which can reference elements from just two artifacts (either models or source-code files) or *(Mul)*tiple traces, which can reference elements from more than two artifacts.
- Type of Visualization supported (*Vsl*): graph-based (G), tree-like editor (TL), multipanel editor (M), dashboard (D).
- MDE-oriented (*MDE*): either the tool was developed to work in the context of MDE (✓) or not (✗).
- Aggregated views (*AGG*): either the tool provides aggregated views of traceability data (✓) or not (✗).

3   Generation of Trace Models

First step towards the appropriate management of traceability is to dispose of traceability data. Unfortunately many projects do not collect such data.

Table 1. Tools supporting traces visualization.

Tool	NaT	#Art	Vsl	MDE	AGG
Acceleo	m2t	Sim	TL	✓	✗
AMW	m2m	Sim	M	✓	✗
GEF3D	m2m	Mul	G[a]	✗	✗
ModeLink	m2m	Sim	M	✓	✗
TraceViz	m2t	Sim	G	✗	✗
TraVis	m2m	Mul	G	✗	✗
MeTaGeM-Trace	m2m	Mul	M	✓	✗
iTrace	Both	Mul	M/D	✓	✓

[a] *GEF3D models*

However, one of the advantages of MDE is the ability to run the project any number of times since it is mostly automated. `iTrace` takes advantage from this feature to gather traceability data from legacy MDE projects. These data are persisted in trace models which conform to the `iTrace` metamodel, which is briefly introduced in the following.

3.1 The `iTrace` Metamodel

The `iTrace` metamodel, shown in Fig. 1, is defined to support the modeling of the low-level traceability information obtained from transformations and weaving models.

An `iTraceModel` (root class) contains (software) `Artifacts`, `TraceLinks` and/or `SpecificFeatures`. The latter serve to collect the ad-hoc features of the project under study which might be of interest for the subsequent analysis. Since the information to gather about each project might be completely different, each particular feature is a simple key-value pair, thus leaving complete freedom to the storage of any type of data considered relevant.

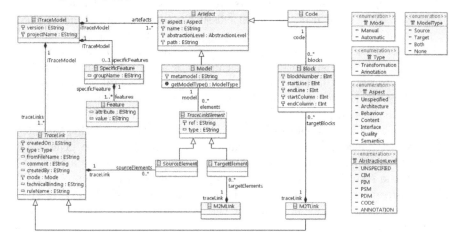

Fig. 1. The iTrace metamodel.

The class `Artifacts` represents the building blocks of the MDE project, i.e. models and source-code, while the `TraceLink` class represents the traces between them. Actually, such traces connect their components, represented by `TraceLinkElement` objects in the case of models and `Blocks` in the case of source-code. `TraceLinkElement` objects own an `EObject` reference to point to a particular model element.

Each `TraceLink` owns a `type` property whose value defines how was the trace produced: either from a model `Transformation` or from an `Annotation` model. Each `TraceLink` is in turn a `M2MLink` or a `M2TLink`. While the former relates two or more model elements (at least a `TraceLinkSourceElement` and a `TraceLinkTargetElement`), the latter relates one or more model elements with source-code blocks (`M2TLink.codeTarget.blockCode`).

3.2 Generation Process

`iTrace` supports the production of trace models in two different scenarios. On the one hand, it supports the enrichment of model transformations that were developed with model transformation languages which do not support the generation of traces. On the other hand, it bundles a set of transformations to normalize existing traces models to a common metamodel: the `iTrace` metamodel. In this paper, only the first scenario is considered, i.e., the production of trace models by enriching existing model transformations. More specifically, we focus on the generation of trace models from enriched ATL transformations.

ATL provides limited access to the target elements generated by running a transformation, e.g. in the current version of the ATL virtual machine (ATL-VM), target elements cannot be selected according to their type. Besides, the ATL-VM discards the tracing information after the transformation is run. This implies that ATL model transformations should be refactored to support the production of trace models [26]. However, such refactoring can be automated by using High-Order Transformations (HOT) [27], i.e. *"a model transformation such that its input and/or output models are themselves transformation model"*.

This way, HOTs are used to enrich existing m2m transformations so that they are able to produce not only the corresponding target models, but also trace models. This idea was first proposed by Jouault in [28] that introduced an initial prototype to support the enrichment of ATL transformations. The enrichment process bundled in `iTrace` is a little bit more complex than the one from [28], due to the increased complexity of `iTrace` metamodels.

Figure 2 depicts graphically the enrichment process for m2m transformations supported by `iTrace`: first, the TCS [29] injector/extractor for ATL files bundled in the AMMA platform[3] produces a transformation model from a given ATL transformation (a); next, such transformation model is enriched by a HOT (b) and finally the resulting transformation models is again serialized into an ATL model transformation (c). As mentioned before, the execution of such enriched transformation will produce not only the corresponding target models, but also a traces model.

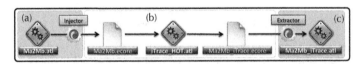

Fig. 2. Adding traceability capabilities in ATL transformations - adapted from [28].

The result of this enrichment process is partially illustrated by Listings 1.1 and 1.2 which show a transformation rule and its refactored version. More concretely, Listing 1.1 shows the `MemberEnd2NotNullOnTT` mapping rule while Listing 1.2 shows the version of such rule produced by the enrichment process. Note that LOC 1–15 (in both versions) and 16–19 (original) and 42–47 (refactored) remain invariant.

---

[3] The Atlas Model Management Architecture Platform. Available in: http://www.sciences.univ-nantes.fr/lina/atl/AMMAROOT/.

By contrast, lines 16–41 in the refactored correspond to the statements incorporated with the aim of producing iTrace objects. More concretely, lines 17–26 correspond to the generation of a TraceLink; next, mirror source (27–36) and target (37–41) objects are also generated and latter related with the target objects produced by the mapping rule (44–46).

Listing 1.1. Original version of MemberEnd2NotNullOnTT transformation rule.

```
1   rule MemberEnd2NotNullOnTT {
2       from
3           prop : UML!Property,
4           c : UML!Class
5           (
6               (prop.isAssociationLowerMoreThanZero()) and
7               (c.generatesTypedTable()) and
8               (c.ownsMemberEnd(prop)) and
9               (not c.isAbstract)
10          )
11      to
12          notNull : SQL2003!NotNull (
13              table <- thisModule.resolveTemp(c, 'tt'),
14              columns <- prop
15          )
16      do {
17          prop.name.debug('rule_MemberEnd2NotNullOnTT_');
18      }
19  }
```

Listing 1.2. Refactored version of MemberEnd2NotNullOnTT transformation rule.

```
1   rule MemberEnd2NotNullOnTT {
2       from
3           prop : UML!Property,
4           c : UML!Class
5           (
6               (prop.isAssociationLowerMoreThanZero()) and
7               (c.generatesTypedTable()) and
8               (c.ownsMemberEnd(prop)) and
9               (not c.isAbstract)
10          )
11      to
12          notNull : SQL2003!NotNull (
13              table <- thisModule.resolveTemp(c, 'tt'),
14              columns <- prop
15          )
16  -- -------- Begin Added by iTrace --------
17          ,TraceLink : iTrace!M2MLink (
18              ruleName <- 'MemberEnd2NotNullOnTT',
19              comment <- 'Automatic_generation_by_iTrace',
20              createdOn <- '15-02-2013',
21              mode <- 'Automatic',
22              technicalBinding <- 'ATL',
23              createdBy <- 'iTrace_Tool',
24              type <- 'Transformation',
25              iTraceModel <- thisModule.getTraceModelRoot
26          ),
27          elementSource_prop : iTrace!SourceElement (
28              type <- prop.oclType().toString(),
29              traceLink <- TraceLink,
30              model <- thisModule.getModel_UML
31          ),
32          elementSource_c : iTrace!SourceElement (
33              type <- c.oclType().toString(),
34              traceLink <- TraceLink,
35              model <- thisModule.getModel_UML
36          ),
37          elementTarget_notNull : iTrace!TargetElement (
38              type <- notNull.oclType().toString(),
39              traceLink <- TraceLink,
40              model <- thisModule.getModel_SQL2003
41          )
42      do {
43          prop.name.debug('rule_MemberEnd2NotNullOnTT_');
44          elementSource_prop.refSetValue('object', prop);
45          elementSource_c.refSetValue('object', c);
46          elementTarget_notNull.refSetValue('object',
47                                            notNull);
48      } }
```

4   iTrace Visualization Mechanisms

Once traceability data has been persisted in the shape of trace models, being able to visualize such links is valuable, at least as an exploratory aid [30]. However, the development of tool support to that end is a non-trivial task and considerable effort is needed to recover, browse and maintain traces [24].

In the following, the visualization mechanisms for traceability data supported by iTrace are introduced. A multipanel editor for trace models is first presented and then the use of dashboards providing aggregated and non-aggregated views of traceability data is described. The former can be seen as a tool for low-level management of traces whereas the latter provides high-level information from such traces.

4.1   Multipanel Editor for Trace Models

iTrace bundles an *ad-hoc* EMF-based multipanel editor for trace models. Such editor supports the management (visualization and edition) of the EMF trace models generated from the execution of model transformations. Note that such transformations are previously enriched by iTrace to support the generation of traces.

Figure 3 provides a high-level overview of the planned structure for the editor. In order to overcome the limitations described in Sect. 2 the editor was devised to support the following set of functionalities:

- It should bundle three different panels to show separately the source models, the trace model and the target models. If there are several source or target models, they should be co-located vertically in their corresponding panel. Even the same model could appear in both panels if it is referenced both as source and target model by any set of traces.
- The panel for target models should be adapted to the nature of the models displayed, i.e. a proper set of models or source-code files. Note that, in the end, a source-code file is another model, this one with the lowest level of abstraction. Thus, the term models might be used as well to refer to source-code files in the following.
- The user should be able to drag elements from source and target models and drop them on the traces model to create new trace-link objects.
- If the user selects a trace-link object, the editor has to highlight automatically the elements referenced by the selected link, either model elements or source-code blocks, in the corresponding model or source-code file.
- If the user selects a source or target element, the editor must highlight the trace-link objects that reference it.

In the following, two of the traces models produced in the running example are displayed in the multipanel editor bundled in iTrace to illustrate the final result.

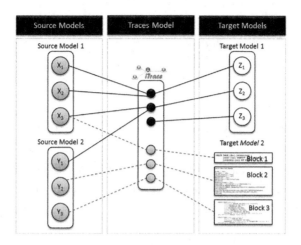

Fig. 3. Desired behavior for the iTrace multipanel editor.

Fig. 4. UML2SQL2003 m2m traces model displayed in the iTrace multipanel editor.

Running Example. When the UML2SQL2003 model transformation is run using the OMDB class diagram as input, an SQL:2003 ORDB model plus a traces model between both models are generated.

Figure 4 shows an excerpt of such traces model displayed in the multipanel editor of iTrace. Note that as the Property persons source element is selected, the trace-links referencing it are automatically highlighted: M2M Link generate-AtributteRef. The target elements referenced by those traces are highlighted as well in the SQL2003 model: attribute persons, Reference Type Ref_Person_Type y MULTISET Ref_Person_Type.

To illustrate the visualization of m2t traces models, Fig. 5 shows an excerpt of the traces model produced by the ORDB4ORA2CODE transformation in the running example. In this case, the right panel shows the SQL script generated to implement the ORDB schema modeled in the source model (ORDB4ORA model). The selection of the first trace-link (M2T Link generateAttribute) results in the automatic highlighting of the corresponding source elements (Attribute country) and associated source-code (country column in line 6 of the SQL script).

Fig. 5. ORDB4ORA2CODE m2t traces model displayed in the **iTrace** multipanel editor.

Notice for instance the utility of the editor for change impact analysis since it eases enormously tracking dependencies between source and target elements and the other way round.

4.2 Dashboards for Traceability Data

A quick look at the traces model shown in the previous section serves to give an idea of the number of traces that can be generated by any MDE project. The multipanel editor introduced supports efficiently edition of such traces. Nevertheless, working at this level of abstraction might not fit to all the stakeholders involved in the project. Aggregated views providing with high-level information of the raw data (trace-links) would be welcome in this context.

To address this issue, **iTrace** leans on BI tools to support the multidimensional analysis of traces models. The aim is to elicit knowledge from the trace-links gathered during the project. To that end, traces models are first denormalized and then used to populate QlikView [31] dashboards. As a result, high-level overviews of the relationships between the artefacts involved in the development process are obtained. In the following, three particular dashboards produced in the running example are used to illustrate the proposal.

Running Example: Project Overview Dashboard. The Project overview dashboard shows all the model elements involved in the project under study (including source-code blocks), as well as their relationships. Besides, it allows assessing the contribution of each element to the project by identifying the #LOC directly related with it. Figure 6 shows an screen capture of the dashboard which is divided into two main blocks:

Upper part allows tracking all the relationships of a given element along the project. To that end, it shows all the model elements so that when a given element is selected, related elements in the rest of models are automatically highlighted while the rest of elements are greyed-out. For instance, the figure shows that the selection of a UML element results in the highlighting of related elements in the SQL2003 and ORACLE models, as well as the corresponding source-code blocks. Currently the framework uses the unique identifier of every model element to display them in the dashboard. However, more intuitive identifiers will be used in future versions.

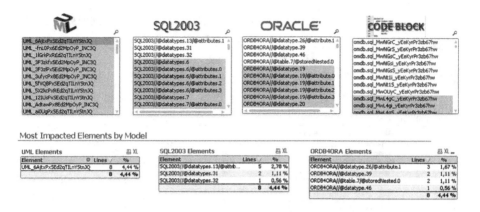

Fig. 6. Project overview dashboard.

Lower part of the dashboard (*Most Impacted Elements by Model*) shows the elements of each model which are associated with the highest #LOC. In this case, the UML is related to 4.44 % of the total #LOC generated in the project.

Model transformations are inherently complex [32]. They get even more complex when they aim at lowering the level of abstraction at which software is modelled to support code generation since the semantic gap between the models involved implies making assumptions and adding extra machinery to consider all the possible scenarios. In this context, the Project overview dashboard abstracts from such complexity providing a quick overview of the relationships between the different elements of the project without having to look at the source code that implements the model transformations connecting them.

Running Example: Mapping Rules Overview Dashboard. The Mapping rules overview dashboard shown in Fig. 7 goes a step further, since it provides a closer look at the transformations involved in the project. In particular, it allows identifying which are the rules involved in a given transformation and which is their role in the project. The latter refers to the workload of such rules, i.e. the amount of objects effectively mapped by the mapping rule under consideration. To that end, upper side of the dashboard bundles a set of controls to define high-level criteria for the analysis. This way, the traces that will be analyzed can be filtered according to:

– Transformations: only traces produced by the select model transformations will be considered.
– Type: only model-to-model or model-to-text traces will be considered.
– Mapping Rules: only traces produced by the selected mapping rules will be considered.

Likewise, the model elements that will be object of consideration can be filtered according to another set of criteria:

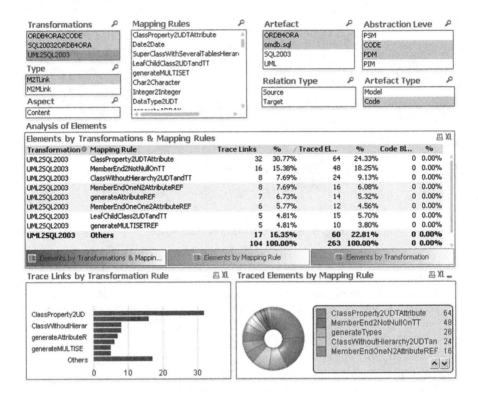

Fig. 7. Mapping rules overview dashboard.

- Artefact: only elements included in the selected models or source-code files will be considered.
- Relation Type: depending on the selection, only model elements used that were either as source or target objects of the selected transformations will be considered.
- Abstraction Level: only model elements belonging to models defined at the selected abstraction levels will be considered.
- Artefact Type: depending on the selection, only model elements or source-code blocks will be considered.

Obviously, none of the criteria above are mandatory. That is to say, the user might set no values for any of them. If so, no filtering is applied and every trace (respectively model element) is considered in the analysis.

Once the criteria have been fixed (if any), the central and lower part of the dashboard collects aggregated data regarding the number of traces, model elements (referred to as `traced elements`) and source-code blocks, which fulfill the criteria. In this case, the table in the middle shows which are the mapping rules producing more traces. In particular, it shows the top 8 rules, while the rest are blended into the `Others` row.

First and second columns show respectively the transformations and mapping rules under consideration (those that meet the filtering criteria). Next columns show the number of trace links produced by each mapping rule and the percentage over total number of traces produced by the mapping rules selected. Following columns show also the number of model elements and source-code blocks referenced by each mapping rule.

For instance, second row of the table states that the `MemberEnd2Not-Null-OnTT` of the `UML2SQL2003` transformation generates 16 trace links (15.38 % over the total number of trace links produced by the selected mapping rules) and such links refer to 48 model elements (note that not every trace link represents a one-to-one relationship).

Finally, lower side of the dashboard provides different views of these data. The bar graph on the left summarizes the number of trace links produced by each transformation rule, while the pie chart on the right represents the distribution of traced elements by transformation rule.

The information collected in this dashboard could be used by model-transformation developers to locate candidates for refining. For instance, the data presented in Fig. 7 highlights the importance of the `ClassProperty2UDTAttribute` mapping rule, which generates more than 30 % of the trace links produced by the `UML2SQL2003` transformation. Thus, this rule might be object of study if transformation developers aims at optimizing the overall performance of the transformation.

Running Example: Mapping Rules Detail Dashboard. Model transformations are inherently complex [32]. Therefore, dealing with legacy transformations might be even more complex. The analysis of trace models can be used to raise the abstraction level at which we think about model transformations. In addition, it allows the developer to abstract from the particular model transformation language used and provide him with simple and comprehensible information regarding the mapping rules that compose the different transformations.

For instance, Listing 1.1 showed a code excerpt from the `UML2SQL2003` transformation. In particular, it shows the `MemberEnd2NotNullOnTT` mapping rule. To understand the functionality of this rule and what type of elements it maps, a minimum knowledge of ATL is needed.

By contrast, a quick look at the dashboard shown in Fig. 8 let us know at first sight which the purpose of the mapping rule is. Indeed, no previous knowledge of ATL is needed. The information displayed on the upper side of the dashboard reveals that the rule is part of the `UML2SQL2003` transformation and it maps UML objects into SQL2003 objects (recall that the name of the transformations are now always as intuitive as here). More revealing is a look at the lower side of the dashboard which shows that the rule is responsible for mapping pairs of `Class` and `Property` objects into `NotNull` objects.

Note that the dashboard provides this type of information for all the transformations bundled in the project under study. To move through them, the upper side of the dashboard provides a set of filters that allow the user to select a

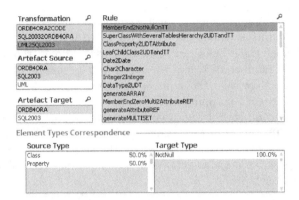

Fig. 8. `Mapping rules detailed` dashboard.

particular transformation, source model, target model or mapping rule/s (non-selected filtering values are greyed-out). The bottom part of the dashboard shows the type of elements transformed by the mapping rules that meet the criteria established by the user. Note also that this analysis may be useful in order to document not only m2m transformations, but also m2t ones.

To sum up, `iTrace` supports a number of different visualizations with different granularity levels: transformations, transformation rules and model (elements). For the sake of space just some of them have been introduced here to illustrate the utility and potential of the proposal.

5   Conclusion and Future Works

Despite the prominent role played by traceability in SE has been widely acknowledged, it is commonly omitted since dealing with traceability is a task inherently complex. The main principles of MDE, where models, model transformations and automation act as main actors, might contribute to boost the actual usage of traceability data [10]. In this sense, huge effort is still needed to recover, browse and maintain trace-links [24]. Nevertheless, even though MDE tooling has reached certain levels of maturity during the last years [11] the management of traceability leaves still much room for improvement [33].

In particular, this work has first introduced the main issues related with the visualization of traceability data to later introduce the solutions provided by `iTrace` an EMF-based framework for the management of traceability data in MDE projects. On the one hand, the framework bundles a multipanel panel editor for trace models (both m2m or m2t trace models) that can be used to support low-level management of traceability data. On the other hand, such data is denormalized in order to populate different dashboards that provide high-level views of the traceability information.

The dashboards from the running example have shown that the information provided can be used to produce a high-level overview of the transformations involved in a project, to explain the purpose of a particular mapping rule or to identify the rules that should be optimized in order to improve the execution of a given transformation. Besides, it is worth noting that, once the data has been denormalized, ad-hoc dashboards can be defined at will for different purposes.

Three main lines are distinguished regarding directions for further work. First, we are working to support the *extraction of partial* trace models. The idea is to produce trace models attending to the criteria previously defined by the user by selecting a number of trace-links from a given trace model. Besides, support for text-to-model transformations is also being integrated in the framework, so that Model-Driven Reverse Engineering projects can be also object of study. Therefore, the visualization of text-to-model traces will be tackled as well. Finally, we would like to emphasize the fact that we are currently working on the evaluation of the tool with *external* MDE developers.

Acknowledgements. This research has been partially funded by the Regional Government of Madrid under project SICOMORo-CM (S2013/ICE-3006), in the framework of the MASAI project (TIN-2011-22617) and the Technical Support Staff Subprogram (MICCINN-PTA-2009), which are partially financed by the Spanish Ministry of Science and Innovation.

References

1. IEEE: IEEE Standard Glossary of Software Engineering Terminology. Technical report, Institute of Electrical and Electronics Engineers (1990)
2. Asunción, H.U.: Towards practical software traceability. In: Companion of the 30th International Conference on Software Engineering, ICSE Companion 2008, pp. 1023–1026. ACM, New York (2008)
3. Ramesh, B., Stubbs, C., Powers, T., Edwards, M.: Requirements traceability: theory and practice. Ann. Softw. Eng. **3**, 397–415 (1997)
4. Oliveto, R.: Traceability management meets information retrieval methods - strengths and limitations. In: 12th European Conference on Software Maintenance and Reengineering (CSMR'2008), pp. 302–305 (2008)
5. Schmidt, D.: Model-driven engineering. IEEE Comput. **39**, 25–31 (2006)
6. Bernstein, P.: Applying model management to classical meta data problems. In: 1st Biennial Conference on Innovative Data Systems Research, Asilomar, CA, USA, pp. 1–10 (2003)
7. De Lucia, A., Oliveto, R., Zurolo, F., Di Penta, M.: Improving comprehensibility of source code via traceability information: a controlled experiment. In: Proceedings of the 14th IEEE International Conference on Program Comprehension (ICPC 2006), pp. 317–326. IEEE (2006)
8. Sendall, S., Kozaczynski, W.: Model transformation: the heart and soul of model-driven software development. IEEE Softw. **20**, 42–45 (2003)
9. Mohagheghi, P., Dehlen, V.: An overview of quality frameworks in model-driven engineering and observations on transformation quality. In: Workshop on Quality in Modeling, pp. 3–17 (2007)
10. Santiago, I., Jiménez, A., Vara, J.M., De Castro, V., Bollati, V., Marcos, E.: Model-driven engineering as a new landscape for traceability management: a systematic review. Inf. Softw. Technol. **54**, 1340–1356 (2012)

11. Volter, M.: From programming to modeling - and back again. IEEE Softw. **28**, 20–25 (2011)
12. AMW: Atlas Model Weaver. http://www.eclipse.org/gmt/amw/ (2008). Accessed 28 January 2013
13. ModeLink: ModeLink Project. http://www.eclipse.org/epsilon/doc/modelink/ (2010). Accessed 26 October 2013
14. MetagemTrace: Metagem-Trace Website. http://www.kybele.etsii.urjc.es/metagem-trace/ (2012). Accessed 26 April 2013
15. Santiago, I., Vara, J.M., de Castro, M.V., Marcos, E.: Towards the effective use of traceability in model-driven engineering projects. In: Ng, W., Storey, V.C., Trujillo, J.C. (eds.) ER 2013. LNCS, vol. 8217, pp. 429–437. Springer, Heidelberg (2013)
16. Kimball, R.: The Data Warehouse Lifecycle Toolkit. Wiley, New York (1998)
17. Alexander, M., Valkenbach, J.: Excel Dashboards and Reports. Wiley Publishing, Inc., Hoboken (2010)
18. Gronback, R.C.: Eclipse Modeling Project: A Domain-Specific Language (DSL) Toolkit. Eclipse Series. Addison-Wesley Professional, Boston (2009)
19. Vara, J.M., Marcos, E.: A framework for model-driven development of information systems: technical decisions and lessons learned. J. Syst. Softw. **85**, 2368–2384 (2012)
20. Jiménez, A., Vara, J.M., Bollati, V., Marcos, E.: Developing a multi-panel editor for EMF traces models. In: 1st Workshop on ACademics Modelling with Eclipse (ACME), Kgs. Lyngby (Dinamarca) (2012)
21. iTrace: iTrace Tool. http://www.kybele.etsii.urjc.es/itracetool/ (2012). Accessed 17 January 2014
22. Obeo: Acceleo. http://www.obeo.fr/pages/acceleo/en (2008). Accessed 17 April 2013
23. von Pilgrim, J.: Graphical Editing Framework 3D (GEF3D). http://gef3d.org (2008). Accessed 26 April 2013
24. Marcus, A., Xie, X., Poshyvanyk, D.: When and how to visualize traceability links? In: 3rd International Workshop on Traceability in Emerging Forms of Software Engineering, TEFSE 2005, pp. 56–61. ACM, New York (2005)
25. de Souza, C.R.B., Hildenbrand, T., Redmiles, D.F.: Toward visualization and analysis of traceability relationships in distributed and offshore software development projects. In: Meyer, B., Joseph, M. (eds.) SEAFOOD 2007. LNCS, vol. 4716, pp. 182–199. Springer, Heidelberg (2007)
26. Yie, A., Wagelaar, D.: Advanced traceability for ATL. In: 1st International Workshop on Model Transformation with ATL (MtATL 2009), Nantes, France, pp. 78–87 (2009)
27. Tisi, M., Cabot, J., Jouault, F.: Improving higher-order transformations support in ATL. In: Tratt, L., Gogolla, M. (eds.) ICMT 2010. LNCS, vol. 6142, pp. 215–229. Springer, Heidelberg (2010)
28. Jouault, F.: Loosely coupled traceability for ATL. In: 1st European Conference on Model-Driven Architecture: Traceability Workshop (ECMDA 2005), Nuremberg, Germany, vol. 91, pp. 29–37 (2005)
29. Jouault, F., Bézivin, J., Kurtev, I.: TCS: a DSL for the specification of textual concrete syntaxes in model engineering. In: 5th International Conference on Generative Programming and Component Engineering, GPCE 2006, pp. 249–254. ACM, New York (2006)
30. Kerren, A.: Information Visualization: Human-Centered Issues and Perspectives, 1st edn. Springer, Heidelberg (2008)

31. QlikTech International AB: QlikView. http://www.qlikview.com (1993). Accessed 15 Febrary 2013
32. Bollati, V., Vara, J.M., Jiménez, A., Marcos, E.: Applying MDE to the (semi-) automatic development of model transformations. Inf. Softw. Technol. **55**, 699–718 (2013)
33. Kuhn, A., Murphy, G.C., Thompson, C.A.: An exploratory study of forces and frictions affecting large-scale model-driven development. In: France, R.B., Kazmeier, J., Breu, R., Atkinson, C. (eds.) MODELS 2012. LNCS, vol. 7590, pp. 352–367. Springer, Heidelberg (2012)

Learning from the Current Status
of Agile Adoption

Georgia M. Kapitsaki[✉] and Marios Christou

University of Cyprus, University Avenue 1, 2109 Aglantzia, Cyprus
gkapi@cs.ucy.ac.cy, marios_2c@hotmail.com

Abstract. Software processes have evolved significantly since the first formal appearance of software engineering. The academia and the industry have introduced, embraced or rejected various methodologies that are more or less efficient in theory and in practice. A current popular trend can be found in Agile methodologies widely adopted in the last decade. Since software processes are constantly evolving, it is vital to see how they evolve over time. This work presents the current state of the adoption of Agile methodologies with an emphasis on Scrum development method. Study results from 44 different countries were collected during the months of March and April 2012. The results are enlightening in order to understand how Agile development and Scrum are viewed today, to see where their success factors lie, discover if they offer benefits in comparison to heavyweight approaches and discuss their future evolution.

Keywords: Agile · Software process · Adaptive development · Scrum

1 Introduction

As organizations become global and modular new software paradigms derive with some being embraced from the software community and others still lacking wider acceptance. The most widely adopted processes that have gained a strong momentum in the last years can be found in Agile development. Agile methodologies have been adopted by many industry leaders worldwide including Yahoo, Microsoft, Oracle, HP, IBM, Motorola, Xerox, Federal Reserve Bank and Capital One [6]. Adaptive methodologies are generally considered to perform better in terms of increase in productivity, quality improvement, cost reduce, maintainable and extensible code, collaboration and customer satisfaction. Nevertheless, since nothing comes without drawbacks, in Agile methodologies these are usually found in the need for constant customer participation, the difficulty to scale in large projects and the need for training on the use of Agile methodologies [15].

This paper presents a field study conducted on the current adoption of Agile methodologies in the software industry with a specific focus on Scrum [18]. Motivated by this global spread of adaptive software development and our personal experience in a Scrum industrial environment it is interesting to see where Agile

© Springer International Publishing Switzerland 2015
J. Filipe and L. Maciaszek (Eds.): ENASE 2014, CCIS 551, pp. 18–32, 2015.
DOI: 10.1007/978-3-319-27218-4_2

and more specifically Scrum stand in the software engineering world today. The main objectives of the survey we conducted were to:

- Demonstrate where Agile adoption lies today globally in terms of quantities.
- Discover the success or failure rate of and Agile- and Scrum-driven projects.
- Perform a comparison among the results of using Scrum- or Agile-based techniques and of following traditional development approaches (i.e., heavyweight, such as the waterfall model).
- Study development aspects relevant today (e.g., team geographical distribution).

The third point indicated was the most important, since many software engineering books and research works [13] enumerate the differences between Agile and traditional ways of development, in terms of advantages and disadvantages. Since theory may not reflect the real situation, a view in the state of our days is necessary and useful. Although many Agile-related surveys have been conducted, since the introduction of Agile in the industry (the first one dates back in 2003), the reality in the software industry is constantly evolving. Moreover, to the best of our knowledge this is the first survey with an emphasis on Scrum. The initial goal was to concentrate solely on Scrum with its backlog, the burndown chart, the retrospective, the customer review process and the Scrum Master. However, in order to keep contact with the big picture viewing Scrum in the framework of Agile, we decided to study both perspectives: (1) Agile in general and (2) Scrum more specifically. Participants were informed that some questions would concern only Scrum. Those with experience with more than one Agile methodologies were asked to base their answers on Scrum. The majority of participants (76.9 %) indicated Scrum as the employed Agile methodology, which makes the results obtained more applicable on this specific case of Scrum.

The rest of the paper is structured as follows. Section 2 analyzes the motivation and execution of the survey, whereas Sect. 3 presents the survey results in detail: the participants views concerning Agile and its comparison with traditional heavyweight methodologies are demonstrated and discussed. In Sect. 4 information specific to Scrum is given, whereas Sect. 5 presents an overview of previous Agile studies Sect. 6 indicates limitations of the study, and, finally, Sect. 7 concludes the paper discussing briefly the future trends observed through the survey.

2 Research Methodology

For the survey management and execution a procedure typical followed for conducting surveys was used [9] with decisions taken at each step:

1. *Formulation of the Statement of Objectives:* The survey motivation was determined, the objectives were set and the following research questions were identified: *R1.* Does Agile or Scrum adoption provide better results in software development? *R2.* Do people follow strictly the guidelines? *R3.* Have companies tried to think out-of-the-box by experimenting with Agile and Scrum variants? *R4.* Do engineers like Scrum?

2. *Selection of a Survey Frame and Determination of the Determination of Sample Design:* A request for participation was distributed to employees of various organizations and individual Agile practitioners. The potential sample members were selected among Agile practitioners instead of targeting software engineering companies in general. We searched for companies of various sizes with an active role in the software industry, sent email requests to over 200 companies with an Agile profile including personal emails to specific employees and requests for distribution within the organization through Human Resources departments. We also sent notifications to members of Agile-related groups (e.g., Scrum Alliance) exploiting relevant mailing lists and exploited Online Social Networks (OSNs) with announcements on the Facebook group of Scrum alliance and LinkedIn contacts.

3. *Questionnaire Design:* In order to keep the time necessary for the completion of the questionnaire to a minimum, the majority of questions were of closed type. However, there were some open questions and the possibility of general comments, in order to allow the participants to express their opinion more freely. Indeed this proved useful as we gained useful insights from these comments. The length of the questionnaire was restricted to 35 questions. In order to increase the validity of our results attentions was paid on the survey design making sure that we are asking questions that measure what we want to measure referring here mainly to the research questions posed. In particular, these were divided into the following groups with group (a) covering questions R2 and R3 and group (b) reflecting questions R1 and R4.
   (a) Agile questions including a set of Scrum-specific questions
   (b) Comparison of Agile and traditional development approaches
   (c) Organization profile (e.g., organization type, location, size) and demographics

4. *Data Collection:* The web-based survey was open for a period of two months (March-April 2012). All potential participants were informed that approximately 10 min would be required to complete the survey.

5. *Data Capturing and Coding, Editing and Imputation:* The survey management was done through SurveyMonkey[1].

The preliminary version of the study analysis with an emphasis on Scrum can be found in a previous publication [11]. This paper focuses on the presentation of the results for drawing useful conclusions on Agile adoption in general. Detailed results of the study along with the complete set of questions are also available online (website of first author).

3   Results

We gathered a total of 335 responses during the months of March and April 2012. The initial questions on demographics were completed by all participants, but from the point on where the questions concerned development methodologies

---

[1] http://www.surveymonkey.com.

many participants skipped the remaining questions. As a result not all participants completed all survey steps, which resulted to a total number of 233 complete questionnaires.

3.1 Organization Profile

We obtained answers from more than 126 companies distributed geographically in 44 different countries: North and South America (40 %), Europe (35 %), companies with a global presence, i.e., presence in more than one continent (4 %), Africa, Asia and Australia (total of 13 %), while in 8 % of the cases no country was specified. The participants are working in enterprises of different sizes: one third is coming from enterprises with over 1000 employees (30.6 %), one quarter with 101 to 1000 employees (25.5 %), whereas the rest is employed in smaller companies.

When it comes to new technologies and methods most of the participating organizations do not hesitate to adopt new technologies (62.4 %), some are more conservative (30.3 %), since they follow the approach only when the technology is proven, and a smaller percentage prefers more traditional approaches (7.3 %). We calculated that the ones open to new technologies follow in most cases Agile techniques (62.4 %), whereas the adopters of traditional approaches follow in most cases the waterfall model (91.7 %). This observation supports the fact that Agile development is usually embraced by innovative people [14].

3.2 Demographics

Most of our participants were between the age of 30 and 40 (41.1 %), 28.1 % between 40 and 50, 14.3 % between 50 and 60, 12.1 % between 18 and 30 and 4.5 % above 60. Men mostly responded to the survey (90.5 %) opposed to women (9.5 %). The education level of the participants was high with the majority possessing masters degree (42.5 %), bachelor or diploma (38.9 %) and others in possession of technical degree (8.0 %), PhD (4.4 %) or college degrees (2.2 %).

The results cover a wide range of practitioners. 27 % indicated themselves as software engineers, 25.2 % as IT managers, 23.0 % as project managers, while the remaining 23.8 % of the participants are active in other roles, such as quality assurance engineers (or testers), business stakeholders, data professionals and analysts. The fact that the majority of participants have a direct involvement in the development process is an advantage for the accuracy of the results. Concerning the participants specific experience in teams working with Agile techniques most are quite experienced with their involvement ranging from 3 to over 10 years.

3.3 Popularity Among Agile

Participants were asked about their choice on both heavyweight and lightweight approaches. Our survey showed that the most popular among heavyweight alternatives is, as expected, the waterfall model (36.5 %), whereas enterprises tend

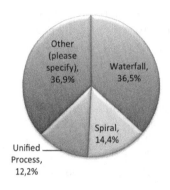

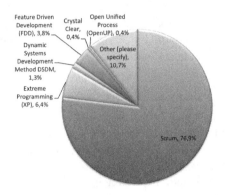

Fig. 1. Traditional methodology mostly used.

Fig. 2. Agile methodology mostly used.

to adopt also hybrid approaches or reject traditional methodologies completely heading directly for adaptive techniques (36.9 %) (Fig. 1). Among Agile methodologies the big winner is Scrum (76.9 %), whereas Agile combinations are also to be found (Fig. 2). In these combinations increasing importance is given to Kanban, which is based on building the production of software on customer demand. Scrum was the most popular Agile methodology also in a Forrester Research survey of 2010. Earlier back in 2003 XP had the dominant role (the majority of the 131 survey participants in the survey of the Australian Shine Technologies [19] were referring to adoption of XP and around 8 % to the adoption of Scrum).

These results constitute an indication of a tendency moving from XP to Scrum. Scrum is also the preferred way of the participants for constructing software systems: 64.9 % indicated Scrum, 14.9 % chose XP, 4.4 % FDD, 1.8 % DSDM, 0.9 % Open Unified Process, 0.4 %, Crystal Clear and the remaining 12.7 % hybrid approaches.

3.4   How Big Is the Team, How Long Is the Iteration

According to Agile practices the team size should be relatively small (less than 10 members). For Scrum it is often indicated that teams larger than 7 members should be split into more Scrum teams resulting to Scrums of Scrums, for XP ideal teams range between 3 and 20 members, whereas for Crystal Clear even smaller teams comprising of up to 6 developers are suggested [1]. The most famous answer we received from participants is 6–10 team members (45.4 %), whereas some have successfully used larger teams of 11–20 members (22.7 %) (Fig. 3). Dr. Dobbs Journal survey conducted with 168 participants in 2011 also indicated small teams: 63.1 % of successful teams had less than 11 members [3].

Iteration duration is also an important issue. Many factors affect the ideal duration including team experience and time devoted to reviews and planning. Iterations are also relevant to the time the customer has defined in order to assess the progress of the development of the system. Agile iterations usually have a duration of 2–3 weeks. Scrum iterations range from 2 to 4 weeks, while

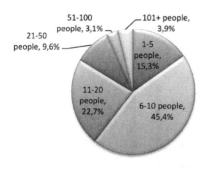
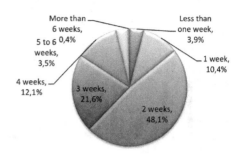

Fig. 3. Largest team size used with success.

Fig. 4. Length of most recent project iteration.

XP iterations are 1 or 2 weeks long [7]. Having iterations that are longer than one month is generally very random. This was also verified in our case: for most Agile adopters iterations are restricted to 2 weeks (48.1 %), whereas it is usual to have longer ones of 3 (21.6 %) or 4 weeks (12.1 %) (Fig. 4).

3.5   Where Do Teams Work

Team collocation is very important in Agile development. One of the twelve principles of the Agile manifesto states that: *"The most efficient and effective method of conveying information to and within a development team is face-to-face conversation."* As organizations become global, it is usual for distant teams to collaborate despite being placed in different cities, countries or even continents; this is applied even on Agile projects [16]. Offshore development with engineers operating from different countries, is gaining on importance lately mainly due to the significant cost reduce. At a previous survey on the geographical distribution of Agile teams with 642 participants it was observed that teams are generally collocated [2]. In our survey success rates are very high for collocated teams, while the possibility for a successful project reduces significantly for offshore development (Fig. 5).

3.6   Agile and Tradition

Agile focuses on four main principles found in the Agile manifesto published 11 years ago:

1. Individuals and interactions over processes and tools
2. Working software over comprehensive documentation
3. Customer collaboration over contract negotiation
4. Responding to change over following a plan

The principle that is valued most by practitioners is 4, while many are intrigued by 1 and 2 (Fig. 6). Indeed adaptation to change is one of the main

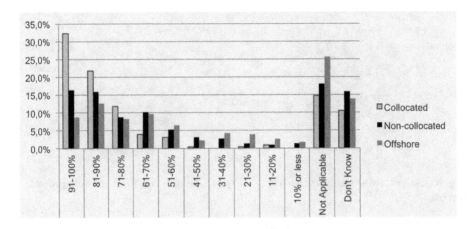

Fig. 5. Overall success rate for different types of distributed Agile teams.

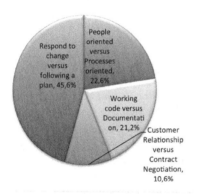

Fig. 6. Appealing Agile aspects compared to heavyweight methodologies.

Fig. 7. Most common problem experienced while practicing Agile methodologies.

characteristics of Agile [13]. However, there are also elements that people dislike in Agile as the lack of project structure given as the most typical answer (38.2 %), the low documentation (35.2 %), although some see it as an advantage, the low planning (16.6 %) and the less management control (10.1 %).

Agile adoption is not always easy and seamless within an organization. Agile drawbacks are usually found in the need for constant customer participation, the difficulty to scale in large projects and the need for training on the Agile use [15]. This lack of experience with Agile methods and the company culture are indicated as project failure reasons in previous surveys [20]. The lack of skilled people who can follow Scrum is one important reason for failure according to our survey answers (Fig. 7). Indeed motivated people are needed, since Agile in general requires discipline in order to be successful. In order to motivate their employees organizations undertake educational activities; for instance IBM has introduced an Agile night school program in order to educate staff members on the use of Agile [22]. Project size/complexity is also a problem. It is true that as project size grows, so does the need for people participation, which introduces more complexity in communication among team members. Other participants see the lack of customer collaboration as a major problem. Customers may find it hard to comply with Agile principles that state the importance of the active participation of the customer throughout the development process. Customer involvement is, however, vital in order to have guarantees that the correct product will be delivered. Other problems noted are the lack of top management support and the project team size. Team size is also linked with project complexity, although in many cases Agile teams are structured hierarchically when large projects are considered. With large team sizes used to cover the needs of large projects non-neglecting communication overhead is added to the software process.

In comparison to traditional approaches adaptive methodologies are considered to perform better in terms of increase in productivity, quality improvement, cost reduce, maintainable and extensible code, collaboration and customer satisfaction. Companies have seen positive results of Agile over Heavyweight, such as in the adoption of XP by Motorola that led to a significant increase in engineer productivity [8]. We also wanted to see whether there was an improvement in the four elements of: productivity, quality, cost of development and stakeholder satisfaction. The majority of participants indicated a more or less significant increase in productivity, much higher or somewhat higher quality of the product, much lower or somewhat lower development cost and much higher or somewhat higher stakeholder satisfaction (Table 1). The percentages of users that found Agile techniques less effective than heavyweight methodologies were significantly low. The rest of the participants did not provide any answer, which may indicate that they did not have access to this kind of information (e.g., software engineers may not have a view of the overall development cost). The only point, where Agile methodologies may be problematic was from the perspective of cost, which appeared slightly increased in many cases (22.4%). This is justifiable for organizations that adopted Agile for the first time, since any changes come with time needed for the transition, training activities and the general learning curve. All these aspects increase the costs and may also affect the development procedure.

Table 1. Outcome of Agile techniques in comparison with traditional approaches.

Project measure	Higher	No change	Lower	No answer
Productivity	89.6%	6.12%	4.1%	0.18%
Quality	84.8%	11.7%	3.2%	0.3%
Development cost	22.4%	23.3%	54.2%	0.1%
Stakeholder satisfaction	86.5%	9.2%	4.3%	0%

The earlier survey of Shine Technologies [19] shares more or less the same views (49% of the participants stated that costs were reduced, 93% that productivity was better, 83 % that business satisfaction was better and 88 % that the quality of the software was better). Also in a 2008 survey [21] the increased productivity, job satisfaction, improved predictability of costs and quality and the knowledge transfer were the main benefits observed, whereas the lack of Agile knowledge and the individual resistance were seen as the main challenges.

4   Scrum-Specifics

As aforementioned the Agile practitioners of the survey employ mostly Scrum. More specifically, most of them were quite experienced with its use: Scrum is either the normal way the organization uses to build software (32.5 %), one of the standard ways (27.3 %) indicating that it is usually employed in combination with other techniques, the method that has just been adopted for development across the organization (14.7 %) or a method that has been piloted without taking any adoption decision yet (10.8 %). Some are currently piloting Scrum (9.5 %), whereas only 5.2 % have not used Scrum. This last result provides a rough estimation on the non-Agile practitioners contacted during the distribution of the questionnaire. Regarding the specific use of Scrum in the organization development projects, Scrum is generally used a lot (61.1 % answered that Scrum is used for a percentage around 50 % and higher) (Fig. 8) showing a tendency of applying Scrum organization wide.

As aforementioned the Scrum Master is one of the main players in Scrum. Many participants indicated themselves as Scrum Masters. The Scrum Master does not have a pure technical role but provides rather guidance assisting in problem solving in the Scrum team. We wanted to see how people see the Scrum Master: most find the role useful (73.7 %) or useful to some extend (19.2 %),

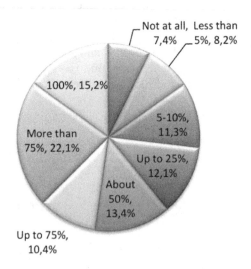

Fig. 8. Development work performed by Scrum.

Table 2. Overall satisfaction with Scrum.

Answer options	Response percentage (%)
Very pleased with Scrum	38.0
Scrum exceeds my expectations	10.9
Scrum is adequate for my needs	38.0
Disappointing outcome	3.1
Not at all pleased with Scrum	3.9
I don't know yet	2.6
Not applicable	3.5

Table 3. Outcome of Scrum in comparison with traditional approaches.

Project measure	Higher	No change	Lower	No answer
Productivity	87.5%	6,8%	5.5%	0.18%
Quality	84,3%	13,1%	2.5%	0.3%
Development cost	26%	25.4%	48.5%	0.1%
Stakeholder satisfaction	85.4%	9,5%	5.15%	0%

whereas some find it redundant (4.2 %) or not useful (2.8 %). It might be that the role cannot be fully perceived by players involved in the Scrum development process that are not, however, part of the development team that is in constant contact with the Scrum Master.

Investigating how practitioners see Scrum in general most appear satisfied, whereas a small percentage is not sure or does not find Scrum suitable for their needs (Table 2). Roughly 1 out of 10 is either not satisfied or has not made up his/her mind yet Regarding the comparison of the Scrum development success in comparison with traditional approaches, Table 3 presents the results on productivity, quality, cost of development and stakeholder satisfaction as exported for the case of Scrum adopters from the general results (i.e., Agile vs. traditional). The results are very close to the general observations on Agile versus heavy-weight processes. The increase in quality and productivity was also observed in the adoption of Scrum in Primavera [17]: it resulted in an increase of 30 % in quality in terms of number of customer defects compared to the traditional software process and an improvement in time to market with the product delivered in 10 months instead of the original plan of 14 months. Similar improvements were indicated by Yahoo [5], Amazon [4] and Microsoft [23], where the impressive productivity increase of 250 % was observed (measured by the number of lines produced in each Scrum Sprint). Many of the above experience reports indicated the importance of the organization culture for the successful adoption of Scrum. The adoption constitutes a big challenge for companies that are rather traditional than Agile-oriented. Unsuccessful Scrum adoption cases are also to be found proving that Scrum is not a priori successful in any environment [10].

In summary, the main Scrum characteristics in comparison to traditional techniques as collected can be found in the following points:

- *Respond to Change Rather than Following a Plan:* 47.1 % of the Scrum practitioners believe that this is the main asset of Scrum. Scrum can assist in rapid reorganization, allowing sudden project changes without introducing significant losses in time and cost management.
- *People-Centric and Not Process-Centric:* The most significant advantage of Scrum for 22.4 % of the participants.
- *Emphasis on Code Writing Instead of Documentation:* The most important aspect for 21.3 % of the participants.
- *Increase in Team Productivity* was observed for 87.5 % of the participants.
- *Product Quality:* The quality has been increased for 84.3 % of the cases.
- *Decrease in Project Cost:* This is considered true for 48.5 % of the participants, although cost increase was also observed in many cases.
- *Stakeholder Satisfaction:* An increased customer satisfaction is considered true for 85.4 % of the participants. Another positive aspect of Scrum that was not verified directly through the survey concerns the personal relation with the customer. Despite the above, Scrum comes with flaws sharing the ones indicated for Agile in general (Fig. 7).

5   Related Surveys

Apart from the ones aforementioned in the analysis of the previous section (e.g., [2,3,19,21]), various other surveys have been conducted on Agile development processes or software processes in general after the formal appearance of adaptive processes in 2001 expressed through the Agile manifesto. We are interested in global surveys and not cases applicable in specific countries, which can also be found in the literature. One of the earliest surveys on Agile, already mentioned, was conducted by the Australian Shine Technologies in 2003 [19]. Although a rather early survey, when Agile experience had not been not gained yet, the results from the Agile use are in accordance with the outcome of the survey presented in this work. However, as aforementioned XP was much more popular than Scrum. The survey of Digital Focus of 2006 was based on responses from 136 executives across 128 organizations and showcased the main advantages and disadvantages of adaptive software processes.

A survey of 2008 focusing again on Agile adoption indicated among others the benefits and problems of adopting Agile techniques [21]. However, this survey approaches Agile from the perspective of individuals view within the team focusing on knowledge and data exchange opposed to the survey presented in this work. The adoption of Agile methods and on the applicability degree of the Agile principles is also discussed in [12]. From this survey it is interesting to see that the majority of employees and customers are satisfied with the adoption of Agile practices. The most recent survey on Agile adoption and success or failure project results was published by Version One in 2013 [20]. Among the main failure reasons the lack of experience with Agile methods and the company philosophy or culture were indicated by the participants with higher percentage.

A more specialized survey on the degree of adoption of Scrum was announced to be performed in Carnegie Melon University in 2011, but its results or whether it was conducted were never reported. The questions used in the questionnaire concerned only the adoption of Scrum and were not referring to any comparisons to other approaches.

In summary, many Agile studies have been conducted in the last decade. In contrast to those, the focus of our work is to give an emphasis on Scrum, present the view of technical users and view whether improvements in comparison to heavyweight processes were observed.

6   Threats to Validity

In terms of threats to validity encountered in case study research [24] the main issues of our study were detected in relation to external validity; related specifically to what extent we can generalize our findings. The communication on the emphasis on Scrum to the participants may have affected the outcome giving less accuracy to the obtained results for general Agile: participants may have responded based only on Scrum even if they also adopted other Agile techniques (e.g., XP, Dynamic Systems Development Method/DSDM, FDD). The number of incomplete questionnaires poses an additional threat (233 questionnaires were complete out of the 335 that were partially answered). This was an observed disadvantage of the procedure selected for the collection, since the survey would allow participants to skip some questions. The high number of incomplete questionnaires is attributed to either the lack of adoption of Agile methodologies from the specific participant or the inadequacy of the participants organization as a representative case for the survey goals. This lack of adoption of Agile techniques was an undesirable characteristic of the potential participants that we tried to avoid from the beginning through the selected dissemination to practitioners with wide or limited Agile expertise. Judging from the survey results the questionnaire apparently reached also non-agile practitioners; it is unfortunate that it was impossible to determine their exact number. Lastly, we did not perform any analysis on the participants distribution among the companies, i.e., if there was a higher participation rate of employees inside specific companies.

Despite these remarks, the conclusions validity is not largely affected. The number of responses and comments we gathered can be considered representative of the current state on the use of Agile methodologies. Regarding reliability validity related with whether the study can be replicated we have made the study results available online (website of first author).

Construct validity refers to whether the explanation provided for the results is indeed the correct one. In our study one threat is linked with whether we are asking the correct questions (in terms of Research Questions). In order to increase the validity attention was paid on the survey design making sure that we are asking questions that measure what we want to measure.

7 Where We Are and Conclusions

In this paper a field study on the effectiveness Agile methodologies in the industry with an emphasis on Scrum was presented. The study was conducted through an online questionnaire and gathered 233 participants from organizations spread in different countries around the globe. The survey indicated a significant increase in the adoption of Scrum with many successful project executions in small-sized teams. Agile projects in general are used in teams of 6–10 people with iterations of 2 weeks for most cases, whereas highest project success rates appear with collocated teams. The participants valued the main characteristics of Agile processes that generally assist in achieving increased productivity and products of higher quality.

The participants answers in the survey were indicative of the current state of Agile compared to traditional approaches, whereas the opinions or experience on Agile development expressed by many participants through dedicated comments were useful for drawing further conclusions on software engineering practice. The most useful outcome was the wide adoption of Kanban or the combination of Kanban with Scrum, namely Scrumban. This hybrid method is indicative of the future trends in software process evolution, whereas the combination of Scrum with other Agile practices, such as XP, is also usual [20]. A general observation is that the efficiency from the adoption of Agile and Scrum depends heavily on the nature of the software product and the organization culture that can assist in the transition from waterfall to Agile. When it comes to specific techniques the adherence degree to the defined principles comes also to play.

In terms of initial research questions introduced the field study assists in expressing the following remarks:

R1. Does Agile or Scrum Adoption provide better Results in Software Development?

The general answer is yes. In addition to our results it has been observed in specific case studies that Agile assists in the quality and productivity increase, but this cannot be identified in the short term, i.e. in a pilot Agile adoption. The problematic part is this initial cost required for investing time on learning Scrum and getting used to Agile processes in general integrating them in coding activities.

R2. Do People follow Strictly the Guidelines?

Although not a direct result of the survey, many companies adopt Agile in a wider sense: they follow its principles (i.e., Agile manifesto) without adhering to a specific Agile methodology. Many Agile processes leave some degrees of freedom and may not be adopted strictly but rather in a more flexible way, however, it is important to adhere to the principal rules.

R3. Have Companies tried to think out-of-the-box by experimenting with Scrum and Agile Variants?

Companies do experiment (the survey showed that 62.4 % do not hesitate to adopt new technologies). When it comes to Agile they mainly experiment with large engineering teams, distributed environments, different sprint durations. All these are vital in order to understand which is the most ideal choice for each environment supported by the fact that the software process lifecycle is closely related to the organizational culture, the management structure and the adopted business processes.

R4. Do Engineers like Scrum?

In principle they do. Of course the answer depends also on the personality, the organization and its effect on the execution of the daily activities of the engineer. Another issue is specific roles as the Scrum Master introduced in Scrum that is not present in other lifecycle models. Is the Scrum master a manager or can a manager become a Scrum master? The answer is no. Indeed one of the participants indicated for Scrum that *"You need a team that is open minded with a strong scrum master who does not over-manage."* The way roles are viewed depends again on the daily interaction of the engineer; interpersonal relationships are also relevant here.

References

1. Abrahamsson, P., Salo, O., Ronkainen, J., Warsta, J.: Agile Software Development Methods: Review and Analysis. VTT Publications, Espoo (2002)
2. Ambler, S.W.: The distributed agile team (2008). http://www.drdobbs.com/architecture-and-design/the-distributed-agile-team/212201434. Accessed 18 January 2015
3. Ambler, S.W.: Agile Adoption Strategies: Survey Results (2011). http://www.ambysoft.com/surveys/agileStateOfArt201111.html. Accessed 18 January 2015
4. Atlas, A.: Accidental adoption: the story of scrum at amazon.com. In: Agile Conference, AGILE 2009, pp. 135–140. IEEE (2009)
5. Benefield, G.: Rolling out agile in a large enterprise. In: Proceedings of the 41st Annual Hawaii International Conference on System Sciences, pp. 461–461. IEEE (2008)
6. Bhardwaj, D.: Scrumming it up, A Survey on current software industry practices (2010)
7. Biju, S.M.: Agile software development methods and its advantages. In: Elleithy, K., Sobh, T., Iskander, M., Kapila, V., Karim, M.A., Mahmood, A. (eds.) Education and Automation Technological Developments in Networking, pp. 603–607. Springer, Heidelberg (2010)
8. Drobka, J., Noftz, D., Raghu, R.: Piloting XP on four mission-critical projects. IEEE Softw. **21**(6), 70–75 (2004)
9. Franklin, S., Walker, C.: Survey Methodology. Statistics Canada, Ottawa (2003)
10. Hajjdiab, H., Taleb, A.S., Ali, J.: An industrial case study for scrum adoption. J. Softw. **7**(1), 237–242 (2012)
11. Kapitsaki, G.M., Christou, M.: Where is scrum in the current agile world? In: Proceedings of the 9th International Conference on Evaluation of Novel Approaches to Software Engineering, ENASE 2014, Lisbon, Portugal, 28–30 April 2014, pp. 101–108 (2014). http://dx.doi.org/10.5220/0004867701010108
12. Kurapati, N., Manyam, V.S.C., Petersen, K.: Agile software development practice adoption survey. In: Wohlin, C. (ed.) XP 2012. LNBIP, vol. 111, pp. 16–30. Springer, Heidelberg (2012)

13. Leau, Y.B., Loo, W.K., Tham, W.Y., Tan, S.F.: Software development life cycle agile vs traditional approaches. In: International Conference on Information and Network Technology, vol. 37, pp. 162–167 (2012)

14. Moore, G.: Crossing the Chasm: Marketing and Selling Disruptive Products to Mainstream Customers (rev. edn.). HarperBusiness Essentials, New York (2002)

15. Petersen, K., Wohlin, C.: A comparison of issues and advantages in agile and incremental development between state of the art and an industrial case. J. Syst. Softw. **82**(9), 1479–1490 (2009)

16. Phalnikar, R., Deshpande, V., Joshi, S.: Applying agile principles for distributed software development. In: International Conference on Advanced Computer Control, ICACC 2009, pp. 535–539. IEEE (2009)

17. Schatz, B., Abdelshafi, I.: Primavera gets agile. IEEE Softw. **3**, 7 (2005)

18. Schwaber, K.: Agile Project Management with Scrum, vol. 7. Microsoft Press, Redmond (2004)

19. Technologies, S.: Agile methodologies survey results (2003). http://www.shinetech. com/attachments/104_ShineTechagileSurvey2003-01-17.pdf. Accessed 18 January 2015

20. VersionOne: 8th annual state of Agile survey (2013). http://www.versionone.com/ pdf/2013-state-of-agile-survey.pdf. Accessed 18 January 2015

21. Vijayasarathy, L., Turk, D.: Agile software development: a survey of early adopters. J. Inf. Technol. Manage. **19**(2), 1–8 (2008)

22. West, D.: Agile Systems Integrators: Plausible or Paradoxical? (2010). Accessed 18 January 2015

23. Williams, L., Brown, G., Meltzer, A., Nagappan, N.: Scrum+ engineering practices: experiences of three microsoft teams. In: 2011 International Symposium on Empirical Software Engineering and Measurement (ESEM), pp. 463–471. IEEE (2011)

24. Yin, R.K.: Case Study Research: Design and Methods (Applied Social Research Methods). Sage Publication, California (1989)

A Case Study Investigation of a Lightweight, Systematic Elicitation Approach for Enterprise Architecture Requirements

Nicholas Rosasco[1(✉)] and Josh Dehlinger[2]

[1] Department of Computing and Information Sciences,
Valparaiso University, 219 Gellersen Hall, Valparaiso, IN 46383, USA
nicholas.rosasco@valpo.edu
[2] Department of Computer and Information Sciences,
Towson University, 7800 York Road, Towson, MD 21252, USA
jdehlinger@towson.edu

Abstract. Enterprise architectures (EA) try to develop an alignment between an enterprise's technology infrastructures with its business objectives and are often facilitated by an EA framework (EAF). EAFs provide the processes to create and govern an EA and have been used to understand both strategy and business architecture to synthesize a supporting information system infrastructure. However, existing EAFs do not provide lightweight, systematic process for eliciting the needed inputs to develop an EA. The contribution of this work is a lightweight, systematic approach for eliciting the enterprise vision, mission and objective requirements necessary as input to an EAF. We make two basic claims for this idea. First, the utilization of the Vision-Mission-Objectives-Strategy-Tactics (VMOST) queries provides a lightweight approach for eliciting required EA knowledge from stakeholders. Second, the use of the Grounded Theory Method, a qualitative analysis technique, provides a structured, systematic approach for analyzing and documenting elicited EA requirements. To illustrate these claims, we apply our lightweight, EA elicitation approach to a real world enterprise using the case study approach as a research methodology.

Keywords: Enterprise architecture · Grounded Theory Method · Requirements engineering

1 Introduction

An enterprise architecture (EA) enables an "organizational structure, business processes, information systems and infrastructure" to form a "coherent whole of principles, methods, and models" [11]. The integration, alignment and goal governance for an institution and its information systems (IS) and information technology (IT) is aided in an EA by the use of an EA framework (EAF) [10, 24]. Many EAFs exist, including The Open Group's Architecture Framework (TOGAF) [15] and the European Space Agency Architectural Framework (ESAAF) [7]. EAFs have evolved to assist in aligning the vision, mission and goals of an enterprise resulting in an asset portfolio.

© Springer International Publishing Switzerland 2015
J. Filipe and L. Maciaszek (Eds.): ENASE 2014, CCIS 551, pp. 33–45, 2015.
DOI: 10.1007/978-3-319-27218-4_3

The accuracy of this alignment is the principal factor on the effectiveness of use of an EA, making the correction of any misalignment best done earlier in its creation.

Ownership of an IS portfolio is now the reality for many enterprises that have accumulated a variety of IT systems and solutions to support their operations and structure. Through emphasis on a overall, high-level, abstract conception of both goals and motivations, an EA can provide urgently needed scope and context for decision making, service and platform selection and needs assessment [14]. An enterprise considering the use of an EA is then faced with the question of which of the various EAF approaches, tools and techniques to employ [14, 15].

Literature for EA applications, like the EAFs themselves, is focused on the original community that used them. These were typically large enterprises with large workforces that included large number of IS/IT specialists [7, 15, 24]. The evolution of EAFs reflects this background, as well, presenting a wealth of options and largely non-prescriptive regarding employment and approach. A lightweight, more systematic approach could, potentially, lower the learning curve. This, in turn could put the knowledge and benefits of EAs/EAFs within reach of a larger community of institutions that have become heavy users of IS/IT systems but lack the specialist knowledge. This would decrease their difficulties in navigating the ecology both of EAs and a rapidly evolving range of systems, devices and applications. To present the results of a response to this idea, this paper addresses two research questions:

- Can a general purpose elicitation technique that is lightweight gather data suitable for use in shaping an enterprise vision and mission?
- Can the quantity and quality of data gathered be sufficient to begin the population of an enterprise architecture framework?

This paper presents the conclusions of the experiment conducted to consider and answer these questions and also presents the structure and process devised to handle both the data and experimental conditions. The tools used for the initial elicitation [16, 18] a vehicle for business strategic investigations, the Vision-Mission-Objectives-Strategy-Tactics (VMOST) elicitation approach [19], the Zachman framework [24] as a representative EAF, and as the processing engine for sensemaking [21]) and comprehension of qualitative data, the Grounded Theory Method [20].

To provide procedural structure, this work was conducted using a case study research methodology, as outlined by Yin [22, 23] and Eisenhardt [6]. This allows for demonstration of the ease of use of the selected lightweight elicitation technique and for evaluation of the tool itself. The example this provides can increase the utility of EA tools and methods for institutions like the one under consideration. Should this work result in increased adoption various benefits for engaged enterprises can be expected, including potential maintenance pitfalls will be reduced, the need for costly changes lessened, and potential stakeholder frustration reduced through the adoption of EA. The encouragement of discussion with stakeholders inside and outside of an enterprise will improve overall strategic plans, craft better goals and objectives for the enterprise, and a greater sense of purpose with accompanying improvements in function and morale are like to stem from the adoption.

This work provides several contributions, extending and expanding on the work in [16], which was largely focused on the methodology and tools used to arrive at both the data and evolved theory. This work also provides a full discussion of the results of the analysis performed as well as additional considerations for reuse and possible generalizations of the experimental results. A broader presentation of the overall process and experiment is also included.

The experimental work in the case study demonstrates a possible path for guiding and structuring EA approaches. The use of the GTM shows how qualitative data and techniques can be a systemic approach and mechanism for EA and the needs of software engineering generally. Additionally, the lightweight elicitation technique will demonstrate the collection of data for use as initial EAF input. This work is part of a larger effort to develop systematic requirements engineering approaches, utilizing qualitative methods, to elicit, analyze and operationalize functional and non-functional software requirements within the information systems development process.

The remainder of this paper is organized as follows. Section 2 reviews related work on the GTM, the VMOST strategy approach, and EA. Section 3 details our approach and evaluation. Section 4 presents the general conclusions from the study. Section 5 provides evaluation results, discussion and caveats of our evaluation. Finally, Sect. 6 has the concluding remarks and a discussion of future research directions.

2   Related Work

The process used for this work combines techniques from several areas, including enterprise architecture (EA), EA frameworks (EAF), business strategy studies, the Vision-Mission-Objectives-Strategy-Tactics (VMOST) elicitation approach [1, 2, 19] and components taken from the Grounded Theory Method (GTM) [20].

2.1   Enterprise Architecture Frameworks

Developed in 1987 and then elaborated into an EAF, the Zachman framework provides a way to organize and analyze the views of an enterprise [24]. The Zachman framework provides a taxonomy to document the "building blocks of enterprises" [13] and is based on six interrogatives (i.e., what, how, where, who, when, and why) and six general stakeholder-derived perspectives (i.e., planner, owner, designer, builder, implementer and worker) and is shown in Fig. 1 [24]. The resulting structure provides an overall view of the enterprise that is extremely flexible. Little guidance, however, is provided on how to elicit the necessary enterprise requirements. For the more abstract goal and process areas, this is challenging because the strategic aspects must align with the final plans for the EA to be effective.

The lack of lightweight and systematic procedures to guide enterprise architects in eliciting and analyzing the requirements for an EA is not unique to the Zachman framework. For example, the 780 pages of The Open Group's Architectural Framework (TOGAF) core document poses a similar problem for the user looking for answers about structured procedures for the enterprise architect to elicit and analyze an

	Why	How	What	Who	Where	When
Contextual	Goal List	Process List	Material List	Organizational Unit & Role List	Geographical Locations List	Event List
Conceptual	Goal Relationship	Process Model	Entity Relationship Model	Organizational Unit & Role Rel. Model	Locations Model	Event Model
Logical	Rules Diagram	Process Diagram	Data Model Diagram	Role Relationship Diagram	Locations Diagram	Event Diagram
Physical	Rules Specification	Process Function Specification	Data Entry Specification	Role Specification	Location Specification	Event Specification
Detailed	Rules Details	Process Details	Data Details	Role Details	Location Details	Event Details

Fig. 1. Zachman framework, as a grid [24].

enterprise's mission, goals and objectives [15]. This gap creates a significant barrier to the application of the processes and methods, forestalling the use of these powerful EA concepts outside arenas similar to the original adopting communities. This barrier, in turn firewalls enterprises the insights that can come from viewing a technology infrastructure in the context of items in a portfolio. The evolution of EAFs raise questions of increased specificity and length, increasing the difficulty of understanding and applying these tools.

2.2   Vision-Mission-Objectives-Strategy-Tactics Method

EAs depend on having an enterprise's vision, mission and business strategy in hand as the beginning of integrating, aligning and governing its technology infrastructure with its business architecture using an EAF [14]. The VMOST approach [19] is used by the business community to understand and improve strategic comprehension within commercial enterprises. VMOST is built for the needs of the business community and enables those in management to assess institutional situations so as to rigorously define and explore options in complex situations. While providing a hierarchy of considerations, VMOST is only a scaffold for eliciting and understanding the layout of an enterprise [19].

2.3   The Grounded Theory Method

Elicited requirements typically result in large tracts of qualitative data to be analyzed. GTM is a qualitative analysis technique that facilitates discovery and crafting of theory supported by qualitative data [20]. The method, as originally proposed by Strauss and Corbin [20], includes a three-stage coding process that affords rigorous analysis that can enable full informational comprehension even when faced with a variety of

Table 1. Relating qualitative methods, requirements engineering, enterprise architecture, adapted and extended from [3, 4].

	Qualitative methods	Requirements engineering	Enterprise architecture
Input	Text, such as interviews, field observation notes, documents	Qualitative text such as interviews, use cases, ethnography, specifications, standards, references	Stakeholders, enterprise/institution IT/IS assets, goals
Analysis objective	Synthesis of multiple perspectives into single description	Elicitation of viewpoints into specifications and system models	Understand goals, context, constraints. Apply that information in way that places data in appropriate layers
Output	*Representations* using narrative methods and process diagrams, theory	Representations of specifications in semi-formal models (UML), ER diagrams, SysML, *requirements* docs	*Enterprise architecture plans*: strategic enterprise plan, strategic information systems plan

sources. This manner of data handling is especially adept in circumstances where specialist information sources are involved. By enabling technical data to be processed and considered in a discipline-independent fashion, a fuller and more comprehensive view of the context (i.e., the enterprise) becomes more likely.

GTM has been used in a variety of contexts and aligns with EA effectively; there is has a demonstrated use within the wider arena of software engineering and its processes relate well to their paradigms as shown in Table 1. It has been used to analyze requirements in the development of UML class diagrams, to shape of non-functional requirement goal trees, and help understand software maintenance processes in small organizations [3, 4, 9]. In this work, GTM is utilized in refining the goals, missions and objectives elicited for use in a Zachman EAF (see Fig. 1).

3   Research Methodology

To address the considerations arising from the use of human subjects and an operating enterprise, Eisenhardt and Yin's case study research approach was used [6, 23]. This approach has been influenced by other disciplines, and helps deal with concerns regarding reproducibility and specific versus general cases. This approach generates illustrative examples and feedback, and allows for the method itself to be studied, and is frequently employed in circumstances where variable isolation is difficult or effectively impossible. It also provides overall structure and guidance for design, planning, and method. The combination of this structure with an overlay of the Grounded Theory

(1)	What is the overall, ideal, end-state toward which the organization strives (vision)?
(2)	What is the primary activity that the organization performs to achieve the end-state (mission)?
(3)	How are the responses to Question 1 and 2 (vision and mission, respectively) appropriate and relevant to the environment?
(4)	Are the responses to Questions 1 and 2 (vision and mission, respectively) explicit or implied? How?
(5)	What are the basic activities and their rationale by which the organization competes with industry rivals?
(6)	What goals does the organization set to determine if it is competing successfully?
(7)	What activities does the organization perform to achieve the goals in Question 6?
(8)	How doe the goals in question 6 support the response to question 1 (vision)?
(9)	What are the measurable objectives that indicate achievement of goals identified in Question 6, and what activities does the organization perform to achieve those objectives?
(10)	How do the objectives identified in Question 9 support the goals identified in Question 6?

Fig. 2. VMOST questions, as adapted by Bleistein et al. [1, 2, 19].

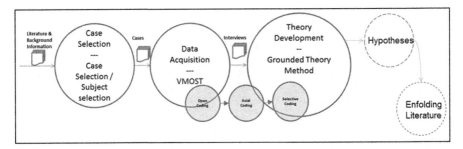

Fig. 3. Elicitation and analysis methodology, set within the case study approach and employing GTM.

Method (GTM) is shown in Fig. 3. This overlay creates a solid structure for managing freeform, unpredictable data while preserving experimental and procedural integrity, and implements a robust solution for both qualitative data and live enterprise circumstances.

3.1 Research Process Design and Case Selections

To conduct the study and gather both observational and response data for the theory development stage, a design phase is necessary. This includes the selection of the actual case to study, in this instance an enterprise, as well as participants and the actual instruments used and processes followed. The entity selected had to meet certain research needs, principally a willingness to participate and a readiness to allow staff time to participate. For this research, a staff member of a regional U.S. public university library suggested an interest in participating during an unrelated discussion. The use of an institution of this sort had numerous advantages, including a large staff and a complex internal committee management system. The environment also included a wide variety of roles, specializations, and functions in a very contained geographical location with a variety of computing assets and systems. By the completion of the study, over 40 % of the professional staff participated, spread across all of the divisions of the internal structure and every layer of the organizational hierarchy.

The Vision-Mission-Objectives-Strategy-Tactics (VMOST) questions, discussed in [19] and adapted by Bleistein et al. [1] and shown in Fig. 2, were used in a one-on-one, closed interview format as the primary elicitation tool for this study. The VMOST questions are general in nature and intended to capture business strategic goals and constructs. The interviews that employed these questions during the fieldwork phase generated seven and half hours of recordings. The responses of the 23 participants formed a broad base of responses both to the original questions as well as reactions to the questions themselves. The full results of the elicitation include more than 100 pages of professionally transcribed text along with the interviewer's notes from each session; these were later reviewed by a second person experienced in the application of qualitative analysis. The VMOST questions also have been used previously in IT/business contexts, providing some prior history in similar context.

3.2 Data Analysis and Hypotheses Shaping

With selection, instrumentation and fieldwork complete, analysis is the next step in Eisenhardt [6] and Yin's case study research approach [22, 23]. To deal with the essentially qualitative nature of the data, a subset of the GTM was employed. This subset takes the coding phases – open, axial, and selection – as defined by Glaser and Strauss [8] for GTM. *Open coding* entailed taking the interviews and identifying key concepts, ideas, and phases. This also, due to the nature of the data, assists in the removing of unintended or conservational artifacts from consideration. In this study, more than 500 open codes were found. These codes were recorded, alongside excerpts from which they originated and with metadata for tracking. Some of the codes reflect reactions to the questions or process, most are derived from responses to the questions. The spreadsheet was used in the next parts of the coding sequence and permitted traceability across the full process of data handling. The *axial coding* stage locates repeated ideas and collects information into overall categories, "sensemaking" the overall picture from the pieces [21]. Looping back is permitted under the GTM process, allowing overlooked information and codes to be captured. From this phrase, collections like stakeholders and assessment emerged as shown in the subset presented in Table 2. This can be seen in the "where they turn" response, which becomes the first open code, 'research center', which is then grouped under 'larger goal' during axial coding. Once the groupings, patterns, and themes emerged from this intense immersion in the result set, *selective coding* was then performed. This required the choosing of one code group as the core, the concept(s) to which all others relate.

With sense made of the data, the case study approach expects hypotheses to be shaped from the overall data. This theory development becomes a set of preliminary conclusions. Chief among these conclusions was that these 10 highly-general, VMOST questions, were remarkably effective at eliciting information for EAF completion, exceeding the initial expectations. Additionally, the timing of the study afforded an opportunity to compare results against a conventionally conducted, concurrent strategic

Table 2. Example data subset, in Grounded Theory Method three-stage coding.

Ex.#	Interview Excerpt (Interview #) Quote	Generated Open code(s) underlined, with note(s)	Axial Code(s)
1	research center for students, faculty (I-1) ...where does the library want to end up? Oh, I think as being a research center for both students and faculty. Interviewee: The place where they turn for their research needs.	1. research center – idea that enterprise is key to investigations 2. Students, Faculty – differentiation between customer types	• Larger goal • Stakeholders
2	expectation that search be suitable easy straightforward as Google (I-5) but they've sort of come up with this expectation that everything that they search for ought to be as suitable or as easy...and straightforward as Google is, which we would like to see as well but it's a whole different model.	1. User expectation – what is desired 2. Scoring – as a target, this should be measured by surveys, etc.	• Assessment/Metrics
3	tailor to what is being taught (I-21) Or it's not just up to us. But we try to tailor our collection to what's being taught at Towson and it does have a curricular slant to it.	1. Curriculum support – course support often identified as key aspect of functions/goals	• Provided service (specifically curricular)

capture effort that had been in preparation during the same period by the enterprise under study. This side-by-side view of the same enterprise provided the basic agreement on strategy and some confirmation of the impressions garnered in the interview. In the large difference of information collected, the same comparison provided an indication of the success of this work's overall data collection process in terms of variety and spread of content.

3.3   The Story and Enfolding Literature

With the data-driven hypotheses created, in this instance that the provided services and related decision making and metrics define the library to stakeholders and to itself, and that various considerations inform and shape this reality, GTM expects the creation of a story to elaborate on the linkages found in the data. With this story, as illustration and as tangible output, artifacts are frequently created to generate conversation and demonstrate the overall understanding. An example artifact is provided in Fig. 4, as an illustration of the complexity of the overall story and comprehension generated. This also shows where the overall understanding created would place the example code previously mentioned. The processed data and codes were also viewed in the context of population of the Zachman framework. Additionally, this artifact can be handed back to the enterprise for consideration and even validation, thereby sparking additional feedback and discussion. The data collected covered represented, to widely varying degrees, components of four of the Zachman columns, which exceeded the expected two.

The Eisenhardt-described research approach for case study execution allows for consideration of "enfolding literature" – data text and artefacts that inform the understanding of the research team [6]. In a commercial, governmental or other structured entity, these will often include various external and internal documents. This

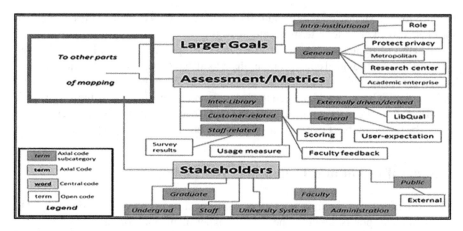

Fig. 4. Sample from a data presentation artifact, after GTM application.

sort of input can include organizational charts, process diagrams and asset inventories, for example, as well as regulatory and oversight data.

The enterprise in this study has a parent enterprise and participates in several larger arrangements and possesses a well-defined internal structure. Consideration of various governing, strategic and planning materials related to these larger and complex entities may yet prove relevant as feedstock for theory and context capture. This investigation and research, as a part of the longer-term project, is still underway. Successful evaluation and identification of these items, if any, may prove useful for other entities, in terms of determining either inputs into an EA process or overall consideration of questions of operational control, scope, stakeholder expectations and general accountability.

4 Primary Results

The data collected was far ranging, rich in both detail and more abstract concepts. The artifacts built from the story realized from this data collection have been found by representatives of the studied enterprise to be interesting, useful and compelling. The coverage and elicitation of the Zachman framework by the data, both in the initial collection and particularly after coding-based qualitative analysis, far exceeded the expectations for the exercise. VMOST derived qualitative data passed through a subset of the GTM's methods has the ability to seed an EAF in an effective way.

The overall chain of techniques, as deployed, does so at relatively low impact in terms of time or cost, and demonstrates that guidance without excessive prescription can open the door to the benefits of EA in a way cost-beneficial for institutions with IS/IT complexity but without the deep expertise bench customarily available to the usual class of institutions that deploy these methods. Lightweight data elicitation, when combined with qualitative methods, shows great promise for leveraging these tools more widely. The conversational process, in particular, additionally fosters a consultative and engaged approach to both strategic capture and IS/IT related data collection, and the engagement thus created is likely a long-term benefit as well.

All of this combines to create a way to accumulate inputs for an EAF. The results, even prior to GTM use, provided considerations that would have sped the population of an EAF through providing indicators for future investigation. When combined with GTM as a handling method for this highly context-aware and contextual data, the coverage – Zachman cells that can have relevant data in them – becomes truly striking when viewed against the relatively brief overall time staff of the enterprise provided [17, 18].

5   Generalization and Limitations Discussion

In this instance, some circumstances merit consideration as potential limiting factors to various success points in both the overall experiment and for the data collection generally. The interview process was made significantly simple to execute by virtue of the 'one building' proximity of the participants. The ease of interviewing might prove difficult to replicate in an entity whose personnel are more spread out.

The enterprise, as an institution, was largely accustomed to self-study, partly inspired by a long-standing professional customs [5, 12, 25]. This enterprise was somewhat coincidentally engaged in such self-study at the time of the experiment, which could both advantage and detriment to the overall experimental results. In this instance, the perception of the interview as an 'alert outsider' was another difficult to isolate consideration. The nature of the bulk of the enterprise staff - largely professionals of a highly-communicative nature who were accustomed to research may also limit the generalizations that can be made.

The receptivity of the participants to involvement may also have in part been influence by the human subjects research reassurances that this was informational and not evaluative may have been key. The nature of this enterprise could also mean that less articulate staff may have, by style of process, been marginalized in terms of contribution.

It is apparent that, whatever the limitations of the experimental parameters deriving from the variability of working under non-laboratory conditions, the coding operations taken from the Grounded Theory Method (GTM) proved apt for the type of data collected. The immersive and abstract expectations of employing this may itself be a limit to reuse, as the focus and engagement with the results required to achieve artifacts that enable discovery and fully present information requires some time and detachment not necessarily available to all personnel. Lastly, identification of common points and discoveries that are reusable may empower greater reuse of these techniques. That VMOST as a lightweight elicitation mechanism worked well is, again with regard to the overall limitations of this work, a reasonable takeaway from this case study.

6   Conclusions

Lightweight guidance and approaches, specifically regarding technique selection, for initial data elicitation and analysis for EA shows promise. The VMOST queries as interview scaffolding proved effective for data collection. That qualitative data, when viewed as a whole and in parts with application of the Grounded Theory Method (GTM), can be used to begin a locally-tailored enterprise architecture (EA) plan that can deliver the benefits of this area of software engineering practice, and create overall objectives and context awareness that can be used to effectively shape requirements and decision making. The case study approach provided useful results for investigation of these approaches and tools, and has detailed the use of EA outside of the customary large institution and specialist regions of application.

The work has shown that the initial expectations – that vision and mission could be understood via simple tools – have far exceeded the initial forecast. The use of the Vision-Mission-Objectives-Strategy-Tactics (VMOST) queries to elicit EA knowledge from stakeholders was found to be a lightweight elicitation approach that yielded the qualitative data needed to feed into the Zachman framework. Paired with the structured qualitative analysis as a part of the Grounded Theory Method to analyze and understand the elicited data, the data collected and analyzed far outstripped the anticipated and modest coverage that was originally expected. The accumulated information, given in response to VMOST derived queries, provides way to satisfy the input needs for enterprise strategic vision, mission, and objectives that are requisites for use of an EAFs. From that demonstration, GTM's coding operations provide a structured and lightweight approach to analyzing and documenting elicited EA information and requirements.

The richness of the resulting artifacts and overall scope of information show real promise and potential, and will be investigated further and with other contexts. Further investigations regarding repeatability and differing scopes, including utilization of different forms of elicitation like surveys to replace interviews for dispersed institutions, are also under consideration. Planned future work will include soliciting additional feedback on those constructed artefacts and assembly of the various stages into a fuller presentation of the process, to better assess their impact will be done. Further investigation of the capabilities and operational considerations for the application of this lightweight methodology are merited, to test the utility of the approach with other enterprises and institutional contexts. The utility of this process and EA generally for prioritization of security needs, meeting the challenges of complex system integration also merit investigation. This approach and technique chain may afford a middle path between "heavy" and "lightweight" techniques for overall enterprise decision making, especially given the modern trend towards mashups and high flexibity environments.

Acknowledgements. Earlier work in the studies for this paper was partially supported by Towson University and this research was conducted under its Institutional Review Board for the Protection of Human Subjects, exemption number 11-0X14. The authors would like to thank the Towson University's Cook Library for their help and the reviewers for their comments and insights.

References

1. Bleistein, S.J., Cox, K., Verner, J.: Strategic alignment in requirements analysis for organizational IT. In: Proceedings of the 2005 ACM Symposium on Applied Computing - SAC 2005, p. 1300 (2005)
2. Bleistein, S., Cox, K., Verner, J.: Validating strategic alignment of organizational IT requirements using goal modeling and problem diagrams. J. Syst. Softw. **79**(3), 362–378 (2006)
3. Chakraborty, S., Dehlinger, J.: Applying the grounded theory method to derive enterprise system requirements. In: 10th ACIS International Conference on Software Engineering, Artificial Intelligences, Networking and Parallel/Distributed Computing, 2009. SNPD 2009, pp. 333–338 (2009)
4. Chakraborty, S., Rosenkranz, C., Dehlinger, J.: A grounded theoretical and linguistic analysis approach for non-functional requirements analysis. In: Proceedings of the International Conference on Information Systems (ICIS) (2012)
5. Dewey, M.: Library notes: improved methods and labor-savers for librarians, readers and writers, vol. 2–3, Library Bureau (1893)
6. Eisenhardt, M.: Building theories from case study research. Acad. Manag. Rev. **14**(4), 532–550 (1989)
7. Gianni, D., Lindman, N., Fuchs, J., Suzic, R.: Introducing the European space agency architectural framework for space-based systems of systems engineering. In: Hammami, O., Krob, D., Voirin, J.-L. (eds.) Complex Systems Design and Management SE - 24, pp. 335–346. Springer, Berlin (2012)
8. Glaser, B., Strauss, A.: Discovery of Grounded Theory - Strategies for Qualitative Research. Sociology Press, Mill Valley (1967)
9. Hasan, R., Chakraborty, S., Dehlinger, J.: Examining software maintenance processes in small organizations: findings from a case study. In: Lee, R. (ed.) Software Engineering Research, Management and Applications 2011. SCI, vol. 377, pp. 129–143. Springer, Heidelberg (2012). SERA (selected papers)
10. Jarvis, R.: Enterprise Architecture: Understanding the Bigger Picture - A Best Practice Guide for Decision Makers in IT. The UK National Computing Centre, Manchester (2003)
11. Lankhorst, M.: Enterprise Architecture at Work (The Enterprise Engineering Series). Springer, Berlin (2012)
12. Leimkuhler, F.F.: Systems analysis in university libraries. In: American Society for Engineering Education (Annual Meeting). College And Research Libraries, Chicago (1965, reprint)
13. Luftman, J.N., Lewis, P.R., Oldach, S.H.: Transforming the enterprise: the alignment of business and information technology strategies. IBM Syst. J. **32**(1), 198–221 (1993)
14. Minoli, D.: Enterprise Architecture A to Z: Frameworks, Business Process Modeling, SOA, and Infrastructure Technology. CRC Press, Boca Raton (2008)
15. The Open Group Architecture Forum (Forde, C.). The Open Group Architecture Framework (TOGAF). 9th edn. Reading, Berkshire, UK (2009)
16. Rosasco, N., Dehlinger, J.: Application of a lightweight enterprise architecture elicitation technique using a case study approach. In: 9th International Conference Evaluation of Novel Approaches to Software Engineering (2014)
17. Rosasco, N., Dehlinger, J.: Eliciting business architecture information in enterprise architecture frameworks using VMOST. In: 2011 1st ACIS/JNU International Conference on Computers, Networks, Systems and Industrial Engineering (CNSI), pp. 474–478 (2011)

18. Rosasco, N., Dehlinger, J.: Business architecture elicitation for enterprise architecture: VMOST versus conventional strategy capture. In: 2011 9th International Conference on Software Engineering Research, Management and Applications (SERA), pp. 153–157 (2011)
19. Sondhi, R.K.: Total Strategy, p. 272. Airworthy Publications International, Kirkby Stephen (1999)
20. Strauss, A., Corbin, J.: Grounded Theory Methodology: An Overview. Sage Publications, Thousand Oaks (1998)
21. Weick, K.E., Sutcliffe, K.M., Obstfeld, D.: Organization science and the process of sensemaking. Organ. Sci. **16**(4), 409–421 (2013)
22. Yin, R.K.: Applications of Case Study Research. Sage Publications, Thousand Oaks (2011)
23. Yin, R.K.: Case Study Research: Design and Methods. Sage Publications, Thousand Oaks (2014)
24. Zachman, J.A.: A framework for information systems architecture. IBM Syst. J. **26**(3), 276–292 (1987)
25. Zwickey, L.: Writing a library's mission and vision statement. In: Future Ready 365/Special Libraries Association, Alexandria (2011)

Using a Domain Specific Language
for Lightweight Model-Driven Development

Christopher Jones[(✉)] and Xiaoping Jia

School of Computing, DePaul University, 243 S. Wabash Ave., Chicago, IL, USA
{cjones,xjia}@cdm.depaul.edu

Abstract. Model-driven development (MDD) emphasizes platform-independent models. Approaches such as the Object Management Group's Model Driven Architecture (MDA) are built on a foundation of standards and specifications, but require significant effort to encode and interpret the models during the transformation to the final application. A second approach to MDD uses domain-specific languages (DSLs) as a means of simplifying the models and transformations for applications within that domain. In this paper we look at AXIOM, a DSL for mobile application development, and how it allows for platform-independent models to be used to generate native code in a lightweight manner.

Keywords: Model-driven development · Domain-specific languages

1 Introduction

Mobile applications are increasingly sophisticated yet must still address platform-specific challenges and constraints such as responsiveness, limited memory and low energy consumption. The most common mobile platforms, Google's Android and Apple's iOS, are similar in capability, but differ in their programming languages and APIs, making it expensive to port a mobile application from one to the other. For developers, it is desirable that their mobile software run on all major mobile platforms without re-engineering. Model-driven development (MDD) aligns well with this desire.

MDD generally refers to any approach that emphasizes software models as the primary artifact from which applications are built. The nature of these models varies widely, from UML in the case of MDA, to domain-specific languages such as Canappi[1]. The goal of MDD is to shift the development focus away from a code-centric application representation [27] and toward a model-centric one instead.

One approach to MDD is MDA [22], which creates applications by transforming platform-independent models (PIMs) into platform-specific models (PSMs) and ultimately into native code. Despite some early successes [24], MDA, with its foundation of UML, OCL, and MOF, has seen only limited industry adoption

---

[1] http://www.canappi.com.

© Springer International Publishing Switzerland 2015
J. Filipe and L. Maciaszek (Eds.): ENASE 2014, CCIS 551, pp. 46–62, 2015.
DOI: 10.1007/978-3-319-27218-4_4

with mixed results [1,9]. Common challenges include: limitations of UML [5,8]; inadequate tool support; and model transformation complexity. It has been argued that differences between modeling and implementation languages make MDD adoption challenging [29]. Another approach to MDD involves domain-specific languages (DSLs), which concisely represent concepts from a particular domain. DSLs trade the flexibility of a general-purpose language for the conciseness provided by a special-purpose language. This leads to the following question: can we use a DSL to model cross-platform applications in a platform-independent way and then transform those models into working implementations that can use each platform's full native capabilities?

In this paper we present a practical and scalable DSL-based MDD approach for developing cross-platform mobile applications: AXIOM (Agile eXecutable and Incremental Object-oriented Modeling). AXIOM's major features include:

(a) A completely generative process that produces native implementations using a single model without any manual coding in the native platform and SDK.
(b) An emphasis on platform-independence that allows full access to all of the features and capabilities for each native platform.
(c) Highly reusable and customizable transformation rules for architecture, design, and styling decisions, as well as reusable templates for code generation that can be easily customized on a per-screen, per-application, and per-platform basis.

The rest of this paper examines AXIOM in more detail. Section 2 examines AXIOM's approach and key architectural elements. Sections 3–5 examine AXIOM's models and explores its transformation process. Section 6 provides the results of our evaluation of AXIOM in both small- and mid-scale tests. Sections 7–9 offer some thoughts about how AXIOM compares to other MDD approaches.

2   The AXIOM Approach

AXIOM [10–12,16] retains the key elements of MDD such as model-centricity and model transformations to generate executable code. Whereas approaches that rely on UML often use MOF [23] meta-models to drive model transformation, AXIOM instead provides a DSL written in the dynamic language, Groovy.

As shown in Fig. 1, the AXIOM approach is divided into three stages: *Construction*, *Transformation*, and *Translation*. Each stage emphasizes different models and activities that are unified by a single representation: the Abstract Model Tree.

2.1   Abstract Model Trees

Abstract Model Trees (AMTs) capture the logical structure and other essential elements of the AXIOM models. For example, each logical UI view and control is

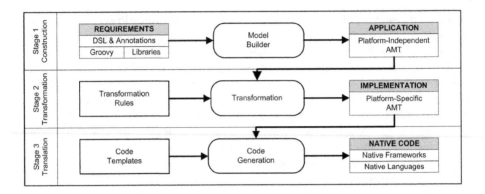

Fig. 1. The AXIOM approach.

represented as a node in the AMT. A key feature of AXIOM is that the models are represented as trees rather than graphs, as in MOF. This enables simpler transformation and code generation processes, as well as simpler transformation rule definitions. AMTs provide a versatile means of supporting different kinds of transformations.

Definition 1. *An abstract model tree, AMT, is formally defined as a 3-tuple:*

$$AMT = (N, E, A)$$

where N is the set of nodes within the model, E is the set of edges connecting those nodes to form a tree, and A is a set of mappings from the nodes in N to a set of attributes in the form of key-value pairs.

Each node in an AMT contains a set of attributes defined as key-value pairs making the AMT similar to an attribute syntax tree used in an attribute grammar [18]. However, AMTs differ from attribute syntax trees in two important respects. First, AMTs allow cross-node relationships and references to be represented as attributes of the nodes. Second, AMTs not only support the simple data types of traditional attribute grammars, but also support complex types such as collections and closures.

3   Construction

During the Construction stage the business requirements, application logic, and user interface are captured in a platform-independent Requirements model using AXIOM's DSL. The DSL aims to maximize the ease of modeling by allowing the Requirements model to be represented in a simple, abbreviated form whenever possible.

Applications are defined as a set of related views. Transitions are defined as attributes on UI controls that trigger the transition and may have optional guard conditions and actions. Views contain logical UI controls such as `Label`, `Button`, `ListView`, `Item`, and `Panel`. Views support both platform-independent and platform-specific widgets. One interesting feature of AXIOM is the ability to define dynamic views, that is, views that are created programmatically at run time.

Because AXIOM is based on a dynamic language it has access to a rich set of libraries and frameworks that traditional MDD notations like UML do not provide.

4   Transformation

Once the Requirements model has been defined, it is transformed into an Application model using an intelligent model builder. This model is further refined during a canonicalization step that simplifies the model as much as possible making it suitable for subsequent transformation and translation. The model builder uses a preprocessed representation of the iOS and Android APIs to expose a platform-independent version of many of the common widgets between the two platforms. This allows the Requirements model to specify a platform-specific widget if desired even though this will constrain the platform of the finished application.

4.1   Transformation Rules

AXIOM's transformation rules were designed with platform-specificity in mind. We followed a bottom-up approach to the abstraction of the different platform APIs, preserving the original APIs so that they may be used when appropriate, while abstracting common features into the core DSL to simplify the development of cross-platform mobile applications. Transformation rules can be applied across an entire application or changed screen-by-screen. This allows them to be reused across different applications and to be customized for different screens within the same application.

Definition 2. *A transformation rule has one of the following forms:*

$$LHS \rightarrow LHS' \qquad (1)$$
$$LHS \rightarrow N_1, ..., N_k \qquad (2)$$
$$LHS \rightarrow \epsilon \qquad (3)$$

where LHS represents a node to which the transformation rules will be applied. The LHS can be matched based on node types and attribute values. Rule (1) allows a node's attributes to be modified. Rule (2) allows a node to be replaced by a sequence of nodes $N_1, ..., N_k$. Rule (3) allows a node to be removed.

The Transformation stage thus results in a series of successive models:

$$M_0, M_1, ..., M_I$$

For $k = 1, 2, ..., I$, $Transform(M_{k-1}, R_k) = M_k$, where R_k is the rule set used at the k-th phase of the transformation. M_0 is the initial Application model, $M_{1..I-1}$ are intermediate, partially-transformed models, and M_I is the final Implementation model. The model transformation process, $Transform(M, R)$, is given by:

$Transform(M, R)$

1   Traverse the source AMT, M, depth-first
2   **while** there are more nodes
3   **if** the node matches the LHS of any rule in R
4   **if** a single match is found
5   apply the matching rule
6   **else**
7   apply the highest-precedence rule

AXIOM first calls $Transform$ against the AMT with a set of platform-independent rules. It then executes $Transform$ again, applying the rules for the target platform. This multi-pass transformation process uses two kinds of transformation rules: structural and styling. Each pass of the transformation process may apply zero or more transformation rules. While it is possible that an ill-defined rule could result in non-termination because of infinite recursion, thus far the rules defined for the evaluation prototype (see Sect. 6) have been simple enough to avoid deep nesting or recursion.

4.2   Structural Transformations

Structural transformations define the macro-organization of the application as the result of a series of architecture and design decisions. These transformations address both platform-independent and platform-specific issues. Structural transformations change the AMT by adding and removing nodes and node attributes, splitting one node into multiple nodes, and merging multiple nodes into a single node.

Definition 3. *A structural transformation on an abstract model tree, AMT, results in a new abstract model tree, AMT', such that:*

$$AMT' = (N', E', A') \tag{4}$$

where N', E' and A' result from the application of the transformation rules from R on the original AMT's N, E and A respectively.

Structural transformations are rule-based and generally reusable. They may alter both the structure of the AMT as well as the attributes of its nodes yielding a new AMT that is functionally isomorphic to the Application model. Common examples of structural transformations include target platform and language, the use of architecture and design patterns, and code distribution. These choices will yield very different implementations when the resulting Implementation model is translated into native code.

4.3   Styling Transformations

In contrast to structural transformations, styling transformations preserve the underlying structure of the AMT but alter its nodes to address intra-class, micro-organizational decisions.

Definition 4. *A styling transformation on an abstract model tree, AMT, results in a new abstract model tree, AMT', such that:*

$$AMT' = (N, E, A') \tag{5}$$

where N and E are the same sets that were defined for the original AMT, and A' results from the application of transformation rules from R on A.

Styling transformations modify node attributes but not the set of nodes or their edges. Examples of styling transformations include implementation idioms, visual layout, and theme. Styling transformations are usually application-neutral and are highly reusable. One common use for this kind of transformation is the handling of platform-specific widgets to address the following three cases:

Case 1. The same widget exists in both platforms. Examples include text fields, labels, and buttons.

Case 2. The same widget does not exist on both platforms, but can be simulated. For example, radio button groups exist natively on Android, but must be simulated or replaced on iOS.

Case 3. The widget does not exist in both platforms and cannot be effectively simulated. Examples include Android's ImageButton and iOS's PageView. The widget can be encoded within the DSL but the application cannot be made cross-platform without changing the transformation rules and code generation templates to use, for example, a new widget library.

Styling transformations can modify the approach to widget generation and embed those decisions within the Implementation model. Deferring these lower-level decisions until model transformation enables us to make selections that are appropriate for the desired characteristics of the target runtime environment. For example, while it may be a functional requirement that a list of items be sortable within the UI, we can further refine the approach to emphasize the characteristics of one sort algorithm over another depending on the target runtime environment and its particular constraints.

5   Translation

The Translation stage is used to convert AXIOM's Implementation model into native code for the target mobile platforms. The Implementation model is a design of the application with the modules, classes, and their relations determined. It defines three key aspects of the application's organization:

Modules. The macro-organizational aspects of the application.

Resources. The files that comprise the completed application. This includes not only source files but any descriptors that are required by the target platform.

Fragments. The fragments of content that are used to construct the final resources.

Modules are composed of resources, which are in turn composed of fragments. The Implementation model does not directly contain these elements but contains the information needed to generate them in the form of injection descriptors.

5.1   Injection Descriptors

Each element in the Implementation model is associated with one or more *injection descriptors*, $D = \{d_1, d_2, ..., d_k\}$. It is the combination of the Implementation model's organization, combined with the injection descriptors that enables AXIOM to successfully generate native code for the target platform.

Definition 5. *An injection descriptor, d_i, is a tuple:*

$$d_i = (\text{target, template-ref, binding}) \tag{6}$$

where target *refers to an Implementation model element,* template-ref *is a reference to the code template to be used to generate the code for this element, and* binding *is a map of key-value pairs that are used within the code templates during code generation.*

5.2   Native Code Generation

The Implementation model, M_I, contains nodes and attributes that will be mapped to specific implementation artifacts such as project, class, and resource files. During the Translation stage AXIOM's code generation process, $Generate(M)$, uses the injection descriptors on the Implementation model's AMT, M_I, combined with a set of code templates to generate complete native code:

Generate(M)

1   Traverse the AMT, M, depth-first
2   **for** each node $n \in N$ in the AMT of M
3   **for** each injection descriptor d_i of n
4   Get the code template, $d_i[template\text{-}ref]$
5   **for** each parameter, p, in the template
6   Substitute $p = d_i[binding][p]$
7   Inject the code to $d_i[target]$ at the point specified by the template.
8   **for** each item in the native implementation
9   Assemble the code fragments into a linear source code file

As shown by the *Generate* algorithm, AXIOM is template-based [4]. Its code templates capture knowledge and information about the target platform's native language and SDK. Each code template contains a *parametric code fragment* and an *injection point*, the location where the code fragment can be inserted. This combination drives the code generation process.

Listing 1 shows a partial code template that generates the Java source for the views in the Requirements model. This template's placeholders, such as ___PACKAGE___, correspond to keys within the injection descriptor being applied to the node in the AMT. Javadoc-like placeholders such as /**IMPORT INJECTION POINT**/ indicate additional injection points with their own code templates. Each injection point has its own injection descriptors and is processed during the execution of the *Generate* algorithm.

```
package ___PACKAGE___;
/**IMPORT INJECTION POINT**/
public class ___VIEWNAME___
extends ___SUPERCLASS___ {
  /**DECLARATION INJECTION POINT**/
  @Override
  public void onCreate(Bundle state) {
    super.onCreate(state);
    /**ONCREATE INJECTION POINT**/
  }
  /**METHOD INJECTION POINT**/
}
```

Listing 1. Partial template for Java view implementation.

AXIOM has symbol tables containing information about many of the core widgets of both the iOS and Android platforms. When AXIOM generates the native code for a target platform these tables are consulted and any property not located in them is ignored. This allows a model to contain both Android and iOS properties but to only translate the properties for the target platform. This keeps with AXIOM's goal of enabling the models to be as platform-specific or platform-neutral as desired.

Each platform has its own default configuration that is used during the code generation process. These defaults include aspects of UI design including font size, style and color. These platform defaults act like a CSS style when they are applied during code generation. These templates can be modified to meet new and changing needs, making them application-independent and reusable.

6   Evaluation

A proof-of-concept prototype tool has been developed to demonstrate the feasibility of AXIOM. The prototype tool transforms AXIOM models into native implementations for the Android and iOS platforms. The design of the generated code follows the common MVC architecture. While only a subset of the native iOS and Android APIs are currently supported, the prototype tool adequately demonstrates the feasibility and the potential benefits of the AXIOM approach.

6.1 Approach

Using the prototype tool, we conducted two kinds of analyses. The first evaluated the initial AXIOM Requirements model against the code generated from that model. The second compared the code generated from the Requirements model to hand-written code provided by experienced software developers.

Small-Scale Analysis. In this analysis we assessed more than 100 small-scale tests, each of which models a working mobile application that can be successfully built and deployed on iOS and Android devices and which demonstrate functionality common to many mobile applications including screen navigation and assorted widgets – some cross-platform, others not.

The sample applications were developed by Masters students from DePaul's Software Engineering program. These students were all experienced software developers, although there were significant differences in their mobile application development expertise. None of them had used AXIOM before and were provided training on the DSL.

Mid-Scale Analysis. For this analysis, five mid-sized applications were developed featuring a variety of navigation and user interactions. Table 1 describes the applications and some aspects of their structure and complexity.

The native-code versions of these applications were developed by Masters students from DePaul's Software Engineering program. The AXIOM models were developed by the authors. To ensure consistency, each application had a pre-defined set of requirements that needed to be met by both the AXIOM and hand-written implementations.

6.2 Metrics

Both analyses emphasized metrics for *representational power* and *information density*.

Table 1. Description of mid-scale applications.

App.	Description	Screen count	Transition count
CAR	Shop for cars by makes and models	6	8
CVT	Unit conversions for weight, volume, etc	8	7
EUC	Data about EU member countries	3	2
MAT	A memory game where players must match pictures	1	1
POS	A simple restaurant point-of-sale system	8	9

Representational Power. Representational power measures how much code in one language is required to produce the same application in another language. This provides a rough indication of the relative effort expended by a developer to produce an application using different languages.

Our evaluation compared the source lines of code (SLOC) of the AXIOM Requirements models to the generated SLOC for both iOS and Android. For the comparative evaluation of the SLOC, we used CLOC[2] with Groovy as the source language for AXIOM. The Android and iOS platforms were accounted for using Java and Objective-C respectively. The SLOC counts do not include "non-essential" code such as comments or block delimiters such as braces.

While SLOC is not ideal in terms of representing application complexity because of the potential size differences introduced by developer ability, in this case we felt the metric to be appropriate. First, the applications were straight-forward enough that developer ability was likely not a significant factor. Second, we had a limited number of developers perform the actual coding, which helped to control for the inevitable variation in ability. Third, had we chosen to analyze story or function points, we would likely have seen significant clustering of the data owing to the comparative simplicity of the applications. By focusing on SLOC we were able to see relative differences in the sizes of the different representations of the applications.

Our analysis of SLOC assumes that developer productivity measured in *source lines-of-code per person-hour* (SLOC/PH) is roughly constant regardless of languages used. Research by Jiang [15] suggests that while language generation can significantly affect developer productivity, differences between languages in the same generation are less pronounced. Since we focus on platforms using Objective-C and Java, both of which are 3GL, we believe our assumption to be reasonable.

Like Jiang, Kennedy [17] identifies language as a significant component of productivity. Kennedy's relative power metric, ρ_L, based on SLOC, measures the relative expressiveness of one language to another.

Definition 6. *Kennedy's Relative Power Metric is given by:*

$$\rho_{L/L_0} = I(M_{L_0})/I(M_L) \tag{7}$$

where $I(M_{L_0})$ is the SLOC required to implement model M in native code and $I(M_L)$ is the SLOC required to implement M in AXIOM.

Information Density. Information density is a measure of a language's conciseness. Languages with high information densities have more compact representations. To evaluate comparative information densities, we created ZIP files using *gzip*, which is based on the DEFLATE algorithm, excluding all files that were not generated by AXIOM. We then compared the compression ratios, CR_L, derived using:

---

[2] http://cloc.sourceforge.net.

$$CR_L = \frac{\text{Uncompressed } I(M_L)}{\text{Compressed } I(M_L)} \qquad (8)$$

where L is the language in question. While compression ratios will vary from model to model, a large number of samples can serve to provide a typical value for CR_L. We then used the compression ratios to derive the *language density*.

Definition 7. *Language Density, δ, is defined as:*

$$\delta_{L/L_0} = CR_{L_0}/CR_L \qquad (9)$$

Language density is similar to Kennedy's relative power metric, but it relates one language to another based on their respective compression ratios. This is different than measuring how many lines of code are required in different languages for similar representations since one language might use a verbose syntax and the other a very concise one even though their SLOC measurements are the same.

6.3   Results

Table 2 summarizes the results of our analysis of representational power and information density based on the median SLOC from the small- and mid-scale tests. To simplify the analysis, we treat all generated code for each platform as a single "language" even though the generated code may comprise several different languages. For example the Android "language" includes XML and Java whereas the iOS "language" includes XML and Objective-C.

Each of our metrics requires one or two languages depending on whether or not it is nominal or ratio. Nominal metrics, such as compression ratio, refer to language L_0 which can be any of iOS, Android or AXIOM. Ratio metrics, such as relative power or language density, compare two languages, L_0 and L. L_0 is the base language and is either Android or iOS. L is the target language, which is always AXIOM for our purposes.

Table 2. Comparison of median small-scale and mid-scale test case metrics.

Metric	Small-scale comparison of AXIOM to an L_0 of			Mid-scale comparison of AXIOM to an L_0 of		
	iOS	Android	AXIOM	iOS	Android	AXIOM
Representational power						
Source LOC	171.50	106.00	15.00	293.00	311.00	64.00
Relative power	11.43	7.07	1.00	4.58	4.86	1.00
Information density						
Compression ratio	12.01	16.71	1.88	10.30	16.27	4.43
Language density	6.39	8.89	1.00	2.33	3.67	1.00

Table 3. Comparison of mid-scale test case metrics.

Metric	Comparison of AXIOM to a Generated L_0 of			Comparison of AXIOM to a Hand-Written L_0 of		
	iOS	Android	AXIOM	iOS	Android	AXIOM
Representational power Source LOC						
CAR	435	488	—	594	889	62
CVT	1,384	1,125	—	431	538	365
EUC	726	506	—	559	913	46
MAT	293	311	—	193	245	64
POS	1,953	1,849	—	677	957	165
Relative power						
CAR	11.45	12.84	—	9.58	14.34	1.00
CVT	3.79	3.08	—	1.18	1.47	1.00
EUC	15.78	11.00	—	12.15	19.85	1.00
MAT	4.58	4.86	—	3.02	3.83	1.00
POS	11.84	10.89	—	4.10	5.80	1.00
Information density Compression ratio						
CAR	9.18	10.82	—	9.53	10.59	4.82
CVT	6.87	7.54	—	9.95	12.87	7.33
EUC	9.69	9.03	—	10.72	11.47	4.94
MAT	10.30	16.27	—	10.96	15.83	4.43
POS	7.35	8.97	—	10.17	10.71	5.93
Language density						
CAR	1.90	2.24	—	1.98	2.20	1.00
CVT	0.94	1.03	—	1.36	1.76	1.00
EUC	1.96	1.83	—	2.17	2.32	1.00
MAT	2.33	3.67	—	2.47	3.57	1.00
POS	1.24	1.51	—	1.72	1.81	1.00

The reduction in the size of the AXIOM Requirements models compared to the size of the generated code represents a significant reduction in development time and hence an increase in developer productivity. Since the median relative power of AXIOM is between 4.58 and 11.43 that of iOS and between 4.86 and 7.07 that of Android, we conclude that AXIOM is more representationally powerful than either iOS or Android. Similarly, the median compression ratio for AXIOM's models, 1.88 for the small-scale tests and 4.43 for the mid-scale tests, is significantly smaller than either iOS or Android, suggesting that AXIOM's DSL is more compact. The median iOS and Android language densities suggest that both languages may involve greater complexity and wordiness to represent the same model than AXIOM although the values seem to gradually converge as the applications get larger. We believe that at that scale, the percentage of the model that is concerned with the mobile-ness of the application is outweighed by the percentage of the application that is concerned with the business logic.

Table 3 shows a more detailed analysis of the individual applications that comprised the mid-scale tests. The preliminary results show that the AXIOM-generated code is often comparable to, if not smaller than, hand-written Android and iOS code. In the cases of the CVT and POS applications, there was significantly less hand-written code than generated code. These differences in SLOC result in similar differences in the languages' representational powers and information densities for those tests. In the case of the CVT application, AXIOM produced several views whereas the hand-written version used only one. Similarly, for the POS application there were 9 hand-written Java files for the Android platform, but 13 for the AXIOM-generated code. Further refinement of the prototype could make the translation more effective by reducing instances of duplicated code and incorporating more concise syntactic structures, thereby bringing the amount of generated code closer to that of the hand-written code.

The compression ratios and language densities suggest that as the size of the application increases, AXIOM becomes more and more comparable to the native languages in terms of its ability to succinctly represent the models. This is not surprising given that the AXIOM syntax uses Groovy as its core syntax.

7 Discussion

The use of a language to represent functionality and requirements is hardly new. However, approaches such as xUML that rely on fUML and ALF [25], use a general-purpose language. While this provides significant flexibility, it remains a least-common denominator approach; the language makes no assumptions about what it will model. AXIOM fixes the target domain to mobile applications and provides a DSL to simplify models in that domain. Because the AXIOM DSL is written in a JVM-based language, it has access to any library that is available to the JVM.

The deviation of the final code from the source model because of the hand-written developer-contributed code makes partially-generative approaches unattractive. AXIOM is completely generative, so developers need not edit the generated code to incorporate additional logic because all such logic is specified in the Requirements model. Since AXIOM models are just source code, they can be managed using existing development tools such as IDEs and source code management systems and do not require specialized software to support concurrent model development.

AXIOM's transformation rules and templates can be used across multiple applications. From a practical perspective, this means that it will likely take longer to develop the rules and templates for new technologies than it might to simply use their APIs directly, but once they have been created, they are usable by any other application that requires them. For one-offs or proofs-of-concept this up-front cost may be significant enough that other, more common approaches, such as incremental prototypes built with hand-written code, may prove to be more economical.

Because AXIOM's transformation process divides the transformations into two discrete types, structural and styling, and because those transformations can be applied at either the application or view scope, it is possible for us to overcome the "least common denominator" problem that arises with some cross-platform development efforts. AXIOM was designed with platform-specificity in mind, even as it attempts to provide platform-independent abstractions that can help simplify the modeling process. Thus, AXIOM is not constrained to work with only the small subset of features that are common across all platforms. Because the Application model defers low-level implementation decisions until structural and styling transformations have produced the Implementation model, it is possible, through the use of the transformation rules and appropriate code templates, to generate virtually any kind of code output.

AXIOM can scale to mobile applications that are similar in size and complexity to those that are developed manually. This is because the process of model transformation and code generation is one of composition from smaller, simpler elements and can thus work at different scales with equal facility.

AXIOM can improve developer productivity because it emphasizes up-front modeling and because the transformation rules and templates can be changed and reused. For these productivity gains to be realized the templates and transformation rules must be designed and implemented up front. These rules and templates need not provided by the development team. For example, the third-party provider of a persistence framework could provide the templates and transformation rules that they believe best reflect the use of their framework. If application-specific changes are required, they can be made as the application is modeled and without being required to start *ex nihilo*.

Our preliminary results with respect to AXIOM's representational power and conciseness are promising. While tests have been conducted on a comparatively small sample of mobile applications, those applications reflect common requirements such as cross-screen navigation and the use of a variety of user interface widgets. Some of the capabilities are easy to model in a platform-independent way, while others are not. Our results may be due in part to natural variability in developer skill, although AXIOM embeds much of that domain knowledge in its DSL, reducing its overall impact. There are doubtless more efficient implementations than those submitted during our tests.

Thus far we have not found any inherent limitations in AXIOM's approach, although we have found several in our prototype and in the current DSL. For example, the DSL does not currently have a formalized entity model, relying instead on available Groovy types such as maps. This limits the automatic discovery and layout of data fields since there is not enough type information available to enable AXIOM to accurately determine which graphical widget is appropriate for each data element. Similarly, as we have seen, the prototype does not always generate the most optimal code. Finally, the prototype currently uses only a subset of the iOS and Android APIs although AXIOM's DSL can be extended by importing additional libraries.

8   Related Work

Executable UML (xUML) uses UML models as the primary mechanism by which applications are built [21], but the process of writing a model compiler requires significant effort. There are publicly available xUML compilers such as xUml-Compiler [2], but each compiler targets specific technologies for code generation. fUML [26] improves on this approach by incorporating ALF [25], a platform-independent imperative language, but fUML suffers from many of the same limitations as UML.

Mayerhofer [20] describes xMOF as a means of specifying the behavioral semantics of models so that they can be incorporated into MOF-based transformation processes. AXIOM avoids MOF in favor of developer-driven semantics in the code templates and transformation rules.

Research on the encoding and accessing of the native platform APIs within models has been done by Cuadrado [3] in describing a process whereby a meta-model is used to generate an intermediate language that produces Java byte-code that references the API. AXIOM relies instead on pre-defined mappings of objects and their properties.

Mobl [6] is a DSL targeting mobile applications. It does not address the model-driven aspects of MDD. Thus while its DSL code may be transformed into executable code, the models are not major artifacts of the software development process.

Vaupel [28] defines an MDD tool for mobile development consisting of complementary meta-models, each with its own notation. Provider models define an implementation of those meta-models. AXIOM uses only a single language and does not suffer from potential inconsistencies between the provider models and the meta-models.

md^2 [7] is similar to AXIOM in principle, but differs in its orientation. AXIOM takes a developer-centric, bottom-up approach to its DSL design, while md^2 was developed top-down and with a business-centric focus. Both approaches generate native code though with differences in the role of the developer in advising the transformation process. Unlike AXIOM, md^2 suffers from certain limitations such as the inability to easily provide scrollable lists of data, a common user experience in data-driven mobile applications.

AXIOM is partly based on the ZOOM [13,14,19] project.

9   Conclusion

AXIOM is a practical, model-driven approach for developing cross-platform mobile applications. AXIOM uses a DSL to represent an entirely platform-independent Requirements model that gradually acquires platform-specific elements through a series of successive structural and stylistic transformation rules.

This resulting model is translated into native code for the target platform using reusable code templates.

AXIOM separates the complexity of the transformation process from the definition of the rules and templates that drive that process. This allows new rules and templates to be defined without complex transformation frameworks or model compilers. The rules and templates have full access to all native APIs for the target platform. This allows them to be modified to accommodate changing technologies, best practices, and organizational standards as needed.

Our initial test results are promising. In small-scale and mid-scale tests we have seen significant improvements in representational power and information density when compared to hand-writing native iOS and Android code. This reflects the AXIOM DSL's concise and mobile-centric syntax.

AXIOM has the potential to scale to large mobile applications, which, when combined with its completely generative nature, enables cost-effective cross-platform mobile development. The transformation process itself is fixed, but its rules and code templates can be changed at will, making AXIOM an extremely flexible approach to MDD.

References

1. Aranda, J., Damian, D., Borici, A.: Transition to model-driven engineering. In: France, R.B., Kazmeier, J., Breu, R., Atkinson, C. (eds.) MODELS 2012. LNCS, vol. 7590, pp. 692–708. Springer, Heidelberg (2012)
2. xUML Compiler: xUML Compiler- Java Model compiler Based on "Executable UML" profile (2009). http://code.google.com/p/xuml-compiler/
3. Sánchez Cuadrado, J., Guerra, E., de Lara, J.: *The program is the model*: enabling transformations@run.time. In: Czarnecki, K., Hedin, G. (eds.) SLE 2012. LNCS, vol. 7745, pp. 104–123. Springer, Heidelberg (2013)
4. Czarnecki, K., Helsen, S.: Classification of model transformation approaches. In: 2nd OOPSLA 2003 Workshop on Generative Techniques in the Context of MDA, Anaheim, CA, USA, pp. 1–17 (2003)
5. France, R.B., Ghosh, S., Dinh-Trong, T., Solberg, A.: Model-driven development using UML 2.0: promises and pitfalls. Computer **39**(2), 59–66 (2006)
6. Hammel, Z., Visser, E., et al.: Mobl: the new language of the mobile web (2010). http://www.mobl-lang.org
7. Heitkötter, H., Majchrzak, T.A., Kuchen, H.: Cross-platform model-driven development of mobile applications with MD2. In: Proceedings of the 28th Annual ACM Symposium on Applied Computing, SAC 2013, pp. 526–533. ACM, New York (2013). http://doi.acm.org/10.1145/2480362.2480464
8. Henderson-Sellers, B.: UML - the good, the bad or the ugly? perspectives from a panel of experts. Softw. Syst. Model. **4**(1), 4–13 (2005)
9. Hutchinson, J., Rouncefield, M., Whittle, J.: Model-driven engineering practices in industry. In: Proceedings of the 33rd International Conference on Software Engineering, ICSE 2011, pp. 633–642. ACM, New York (2011)
10. Jia, X., Jones, C.: Dynamic languages as modeling notations in model driven engineering. In: ICSOFT 2011, Seville, Spain, pp. 220–225, July 2011
11. Jia, X., Jones, C.: AXIOM: a model-driven approach to cross-platform application development. In: ICSOFT 2012, Rome, Italy, pp. 24–33, July 2012

12. Jia, X., Jones, C.: Cross-platform application development using AXIOM as an agile model-driven approach. In: Cordeiro, J., Hammoudi, S., van Sinderen, M. (eds.) ICSOFT 2012. CCIS, vol. 411, pp. 36–51. Springer, Heidelberg (2013)

13. Jia, X., Liu, H., et al.: A model transformation framework for model driven engineering. In: MSVVEIS-2008, Barcelona, Spain, June 2008

14. Jia, X., et al.: Executable visual software modeling: the ZOOM approach. Softw. Qual. J. **15**(1), 27–51 (2007)

15. Jiang, Z., Naudé, P., Comstock, C.: An investigation on the variation of software development productivity. Int. J. Comput. Inf. Sci. Eng. **1**, 461–470 (2007)

16. Jones, C., Jia, X.: The AXIOM model framework: transforming requirements to native code for cross-platform mobile applications. In: ENASE 2014, Lisbon, Portugal, pp. 26–37, April 2014

17. Kennedy, K., Koelbel, C., et al.: Defining and measuring the productivity of programming languages. Int. J. High Perform. Comput. Appl. **18**(4), 441–448 (2004)

18. Knuth, D.E.: Semantics of context-free languages. Math. Syst. Theory **2**(2), 127–145 (1968)

19. Liu, H., Jia, X.: Model transformation using a simplified metamodel. J. Softw. Eng. Appl. **3**, 653–660 (2010)

20. Mayerhofer, T., Langer, P., Wimmer, M., Kappel, G.: xMOF: executable DSMLs based on fUML. In: Erwig, M., Paige, R.F., Van Wyk, E. (eds.) SLE 2013. LNCS, vol. 8225, pp. 56–75. Springer, Heidelberg (2013)

21. Mellor, S.J., Balcer, M.J.: Executable UML: A Foundation for Model-Driven Architectures. Addison-Wesley Publishing Co., Inc., Boston (2002)

22. Object Management Group: MDA guide, June 2003. http://www.omg.org/mda

23. Object Management Group: OMG's MetaObject Facility, January 2006. http://www.omg.org/spec/MOF/2.0/PDF/

24. Object Management Group: Success stories. http://www.omg.org/mda/products_success.htm (2011)

25. Object Management Group: Concrete syntax for a UML action language: Action language for foundational UML (ALF), version 1.0.1. Specification, October 2013. http://www.omg.org/spec/ALF/1.0.1/PDF

26. Object Management Group: Semantics of a foundational subset for executable UML models (FUML), version 1.1. Specification, August 2013. http://www.omg.org/spec/FUML/1.1/PDF

27. Selic, B.: The pragmatics of model-driven development. IEEE Softw. **20**(5), 19–25 (2003)

28. Vaupel, S., Taentzer, G., Harries, J.P., Stroh, R., Gerlach, R., Guckert, M.: Model-driven development of mobile applications allowing role-driven variants. In: Dingel, J., Schulte, W., Ramos, I., Abrahão, S., Insfran, E. (eds.) MODELS 2014. LNCS, vol. 8767, pp. 1–17. Springer, Heidelberg (2014)

29. Volter, M.: From programming to modeling - and back again. IEEE Softw. **28**(6), 20–25 (2011)

A Study of the Relationship Between Class Testability and Runtime Properties

Amjed Tahir[1]([⊠]), Stephen MacDonell[1,2], and Jim Buchan[2]

[1] Department of Information Science, University of Otago,
Dunedin, New Zealand
amjed.tahir@otago.ac.nz
[2] SERL, School of Computer and Mathematical Sciences,
Auckland University of Technology, Auckland, New Zealand
{smacdone,jbuchan}@aut.ac.nz

Abstract. Software testing is known to be expensive, time consuming and challenging. Although previous research has investigated relationships between several software properties and software testability the focus has been on static software properties. In this work we present the results of an empirical investigation into the possible relationship between runtime properties (dynamic coupling and key classes) and class testability. We measure both properties using dynamic metrics and argue that data gathered using dynamic metrics are both broader and more precise than data gathered using static metrics. Based on statistical analysis, we find that dynamic coupling and key classes are significantly correlated with class testability. We therefore suggest that these properties could be used as useful indicators of class testability.

Keywords: Testability · Unit testing · Dynamic metrics · Dynamic coupling · Program comprehension

1 Introduction

Software testing activities typically require significant time and effort in both planning and execution. Testing is thus acknowledged to be expensive [1] as it can consume up to 50 % of the total cost and effort in a software development project [2]. Although software systems have been growing larger and more complex [3], testing resources, by comparison, have remained limited and constrained [4]. Software components with low-level testability may be less trustworthy, even after successful testing [1]. Understanding and reducing testing effort have therefore been enduring fundamental goals for both academic and industrial research.

The notion that a software product has properties that are related to the effort needed to validate that product is commonly referred to as the 'testability' of that product [5]. Binder [6] coined the phrase "Design for Testability" to describe software construction that considers testability from the early stages of development. The core expectation is that software components with a high degree of testability are easier to test and consequently will be more effectively tested, raising the software quality compared to software that has lower testability. Improving software testability should

© Springer International Publishing Switzerland 2015
J. Filipe and L. Maciaszek (Eds.): ENASE 2014, CCIS 551, pp. 63–78, 2015.
DOI: 10.1007/978-3-319-27218-4_5

help to reduce testing cost, effort, and demand for resources. If components are difficult to test, then the size of the test cases designed to test those components, and the required testing effort, will necessarily be larger [7]. Components with poor testability are also more expensive to repair when problems are detected late in the development process. In contrast, components and software with good testability can dramatically increase the quality of the software as well as reduce the cost of testing [8].

While clearly a desirable trait, testability has been recognized as being an elusive concept, and its measurement and evaluation are acknowledged as being challenging endeavors [4]. Researchers have therefore identified numerous factors that (may) have an impact on the testability of software. For instance, software testability is claimed to be affected by the extent of the required validation, the process and tools used, and the representation of the requirements, among other factors [9]. Given their diversity it is challenging to form a complete and consistent view on all the potential factors that may affect testability as well as the degree to which these factors are present and influential under different testing contexts. Several are considered here to illustrate the breadth of factors that potentially influence testability.

A substantial body of work has addressed a diversity of design and code charac-teristics that can affect the testability of a software product. For example, the relation-ships been internal class properties in Object Oriented (OO) systems and characteristics of the corresponding unit tests have been investigated in several previous studies (e.g., [9, 10]). In these studies, several OO design metrics (drawn mainly from the C&K suite [11]) have been used to investigate the relationship between class/system structure and test complexity. Some strong and significant relationships between several complexity- and size-related metrics of production code and internal test code properties have been found [9] in such research.

In their research, Bruntink and van Deursen [9] used only static software measures, and this is the case for all previous work in this area. Others, such as Basili et al. [12], take the view that traditional static software metrics may be necessary but not sufficient for characterizing, assessing and predicting the quality profile of OO systems. In this paper we build on that view and propose the use of dynamic metrics to represent further quality characteristics. Dynamic metrics are the sub-class of software measures that capture the dynamic behavior of a software system and have been shown to be related to software quality attributes [13, 14]. Consideration of this group of metrics provides a more complete insight into the multiple dimensions of software quality when compared to static metrics alone [15]. Dynamic metrics are usually computed based on data collected during program execution (i.e. at runtime). Therefore they can directly reflect the quality attributes of that program, product or system in operation. This paper extends the investigation of software characteristics as factors in code testability by characterizing the code using dynamic metrics. A fuller discussion of dynamic metrics and their relative advantages over static metrics is presented in [16].

The work presented here extends our previous work [17] by adding one more system to the original three systems analyzed [17]. We also improve our analysis and discussion by using a different statistical test of correlation and by providing additional graphical representations of the data.

The rest of the paper is structured as follows. Section 2 provides the research context for this paper by reviewing related work, and confirms the potential of relating dynamic code metrics to testability. Section 3 argues for the suitability of the *dynamic coupling* and *key classes* concepts as appropriate dynamic metrics to characterize the code in relation to testability. These metrics are then used in the design of a set of experiments to test our hypotheses on specific case systems, as described in Sects. 4 and 5. The results of these experiments are then presented in Sect. 6 and their implications are discussed in Sect. 7. Threats to the study's validity are noted in Sect. 8. Finally, the main conclusions from the study and some thoughts on related future work are presented in Sect. 9.

2   Related Work

Several previous works have investigated the relationships between properties of software production code components and properties of their associated test code, with an emphasis on unit tests. The focus of that work has varied from designing measures for testability and testing effort to assessing the strength of the relationships between them. Given constraints on space, we consider a few typical studies here. Our intent is to be illustrative as opposed to exhaustive, and these studies are representative of the larger body of work in this research domain.

Bruntink and van Deursen [9] investigated the relationship between several OO metrics and class testability for the purpose of planning and estimating later testing activities. The authors found a strong correlation between class-level metrics, such as Number of Methods (NOM), and test level metrics, including the number of test cases and the lines of code per test class. Five different software systems, including one open source system, were traversed during their experiments. However, no evidence of relationships was found between inheritance-related metrics, e.g., Coupling Between Objects (CBO), and the proposed testability metrics. This is likely to be because the test metrics were considered at the class level. These inheritance-related metrics are expected to have a strong correlation with testability *at the integration and/or system level*, as polymorphism and dynamic binding increase the complexity of a system and the number of required test cases, and contribute to a consequent decrease in testability [4]. This suggestion can only be confirmed through evaluation at the object level using dynamic metrics. In a similar study, Badri et al. [10] investigated the relationship between cohesion and testability using the C&K static Lack of Cohesion metric. They found a significant positive correlation between static cohesion and software testability, where testability was measured using the metrics suggested by [9]. More recently, Zhou et al. [18] found that most structural code metrics that are obtained from static analysis are statistically correlated with class testability, with class size being the strongest indicator of class testability.

In other work related to testability, Arisholm et al. [19] found significant relationships between dynamic coupling measures, especially Dynamic Export Coupling, and change-proneness. Export Coupling appears to be a significant indicator of change-proneness and likely complements existing coupling measures based on static analysis (i.e., when used with size and static coupling measures).

3 Testability Concepts

In this work we investigate two runtime properties that we contend are related to class testability, and in the following we describe these and justify their suitability.

3.1 Dynamic Coupling

In this study dynamic coupling has been selected as one of the system characteristics to measure and investigate regarding its relationship to testability. Coupling has been shown in prior work to have a direct impact on the quality of software, and is also related to the software quality characteristics of complexity and maintainability [20, 21]. It has been shown that, all other things being equal, the greater the coupling level, the greater the complexity and the harder it is to maintain a system [22, 23]. This suggests that it is reasonable to expect that coupling will be related to testability. Dynamic rather than static coupling has been selected for our investigation to address some shortcomings of the traditional static measures of coupling. For many years coupling has been measured statically, based on the limited structural properties of software [24]. This misses the coupling at runtime between different components at different levels (classes, objects, packages, and so on), which should capture a more complete picture and so relate better to testability. This notion of measuring dynamic coupling is quite common in the emergent software engineering research literature. In our recent systematic mapping study of dynamic metrics, dynamic coupling was found to be the most widely investigated system characteristic used as a basis for dynamic analysis [16].

For the purposes of this work the approach taken by [19] is followed, and dynamic coupling metrics that capture coupling at the object level are used. Two objects are coupled if at least one of them acts upon the other [11]. The measure of coupling used here is based on runtime method invocations/calls: two classes, class A and class B, are said to be coupled if a method from class A (*caller*) invokes a method from class B (*callee*), or vice versa. Details of the specific metrics used to measure this form of coupling are provided in Sect. 4.2.

3.2 Key Classes

The notion of a Key Class is introduced in this study as a new production code property to be measured and its relationship to class testability investigated. OO systems are formed around groups of classes some of which are linked together. As software systems grow in size, so the number of classes used increases in these systems. To analyze and understand a program or a system, how it works and the potential for decay, it is important to know where to start and which aspects should be given priority. From a maintenance perspective, understanding the roles of classes and their relative importance to a system is essential. In this respect there are classes that could have more influence and play more prominent roles than others. This group of classes is referred to here as 'Key Classes'. We define a Key Class as a class that is executed frequently in the typical use profile of a system. Identifying these classes should inform the more effective planning of testing activities. One of the potential usages of these classes is in prioritizing testing activities – testers could usefully prioritize their work by focusing on testing these Key Classes first, alongside consideration of other factors such as risk and criticality information.

The concept of Key Classes is seen elsewhere in the literature but has an important distinction in meaning and usage in this research. For example, in [24], classification as a Key Class is based on the level of coupling of a class. Therefore, Key Classes are those classes that are tightly coupled. In contrast, our definition is based on the *usage* of these classes: Key Classes are those classes that have high execution frequency at runtime. A metric used to measure Key Classes is explained in Sect. 4.2.

4   Study Design

In this section we explain our research questions and the hypotheses that the work is aimed at testing. We also define the various metrics used in operational terms and our analysis procedures.

One of the key challenges faced when evaluating software products is the choice of appropriate measurements. Metric selection in this research has been determined in a goal-oriented manner using the GQM framework [25] and its extension, the GQM/MEDEA framework [26]. Our *goal* is to better understand what affects software testability, and our *objective* is to assess the presence and strength of the relationship between dynamic coupling and key classes on the one hand and code testability on the other. The specific *purpose* is to measure and ultimately predict class testability in OO systems. Our *viewpoint* is as software engineers, and more specifically, testers, maintainers and quality engineers. The targeted *environment* is Java-based open source systems.

4.1   Research Questions and Hypotheses

We investigate two factors that we contend are, in principle, related to system testability: dynamic coupling and key classes. For this purpose, we have two research questions to answer:

RQ1:   Is *dynamic coupling* of a class significantly correlated with the class testability of its corresponding test class/unit?

RQ2:   Are *key classes* significantly correlated with the class testability of their corresponding test classes/units?

The following two research hypotheses are investigated to answer the research questions:

H0:   Dynamic coupling has a significant correlation with class testability.

H1:   Key classes have a significant correlation with class testability.

The corresponding null hypotheses are:

H2: Dynamic coupling has no significant correlation with class testability measures.
H3: Key Classes have no significant correlation with class testability.

4.2   Measurements

In Sect. 3 we described the *dynamic coupling* and *key classes* concepts. In this section we define specific dynamic metrics that can be used to measure these concepts. We also explain the metrics used to measure class testability.

Dynamic Coupling Metrics. As stated in Sect. 3.1, dynamic coupling is intended to be measured in two forms - when a class is accessed by another class at runtime, and when a class accesses other classes at runtime (i.e., to account for both *callers* and *callees*). To measure these levels of coupling we select the previously defined *Import Coupling (IC)* and *Export Coupling (EC)* metrics [19]. IC measures the number of method invocations **received** by a class (*callee*) from other classes (*callers*) in the system. EC measures the number of method invocations **sent** from a class (*caller*) to other classes (*callees*) in the system. Note that both metrics are collected based on method invocations/calls. More detailed explanations of these metrics are provided in [19].

Key Classes Metrics. The concept of Key Classes is explained in Sect. 3.2. The goal here is to examine if those Key Classes (i.e., those classes with higher frequency of execution) have a significant relationship with class testability (as defined in the next subsection). We define the *Execution Frequency (EF)* dynamic metric to identify those Key Classes. EF for class C counts the number of executions of methods within class C. Consider a class C, with methods $m1, m2,..... mn$. Let $EF(mi)$ be the number of executions of method m of class C, then:

$$EF(C) = \sum_{i=1}^{n} EF(mi) \tag{1}$$

where n is the number of executed methods within class C.

Class Testability Measures. The testability of a class is considered here in relation to unit tests. In this work, we utilize two static metrics to measure unit test characteristics: Test Lines of Code (TLOC) and the Number of Test Cases (NTC). These metrics are motivated by the test suite metrics suggested by [9]. TLOC, derived from the classic Lines of Code (LOC) metric, is a size measure that counts the total number of physical lines of code within a test class or classes. NTC is a test design metric that counts the total number of test cases in a test class. Our hypotheses thus reflect an expectation that the dynamic coupling and key classes of production code classes are related to the size and scope of their associated test classes.

Our data collection methods are explained in more detail in the following section.

5 Data Collection

The collection of dynamic metrics data can be accomplished in various ways. The most common (and most accurate) way is to collect the data by obtaining trace information using dynamic analysis techniques during software execution. Such an approach is taken in this study and is implemented by collecting metrics using the *AspectJ* framework, a well-established Java implementation of Aspect Oriented Programming (AOP). Previous works (including [23, 27, 28]) have shown that AOP is an efficient and practical approach for the objective collection of dynamic metrics data, as it can enable full runtime automatic source-code instrumentation to be performed.

Testability metrics data, including LOC, TLOC, and Number of Classes (NOC), are collected using the *CodePro Analytix*[1] tool and the values were later checked and verified using the *Eclipse Metrics Plugin*[2]. Values for the NTC metric are collected from the *JUnit* framework and these values were verified manually by the first author.

We used the two different traceability techniques suggested by [29] to identify unit test classes and link them to their corresponding production classes. First, we used the *Naming Convention* technique to link test classes to production classes following their names. It has been widely suggested (for instance, in the JUnit documentation) that a test class should be named after the corresponding class(es) that it tests, by adding "Test" to the original class name. Second, we used a *Static Call Graph* technique, which inspects method invocations in the test case. The latter process was carried out manually by the first author. The effectiveness of the Naming Convention technique is reliant on developers' efforts in conforming to a coding standard, whereas the Static Call Graph approach reveals direct references to production classes in the test classes.

It is important to note here that we only consider core system code: only production classes that are developed as a part of the system are assessed. Additional classes (including those in jar files) are excluded from the measurement process. These files are generally not part of the core system under development and any dependencies could negatively influence the results of the measurement process.

5.1 Case Studies

To consider the potential relationships between class testability and the chosen dynamic metrics we selected four different open source systems to be used in our experiments. Selection of these systems was conducted with the goal of examining applications of reasonable size, with some degree of complexity, and easily accessible source code. The main criteria for selecting the applications are: (1) each application should be fully open source, i.e., source code for both production code and test code is publicly available; (2) each application must be written in Java, as we are using the JUnit and AspectJ frameworks, which are both written for Java; (3) each application

---

[1] https://developers.google.com/java-devtools/codepro/doc/

[2] http://metrics2.sourceforge.net/

should come with test suites; and (4) each application should comprise at least 25 test classes.

The systems selected for our experiments are: *FindBugs, JabRef, Dependency Finder and MOEA*. Table 1 reports particular characteristics and size information of both the production and test code of the four systems.

Table 1. Characteristics of the selected systems.

System	Version	KLOC	Size	NOC	# Unit Tests	Test KLOC
FindBugs	2.0.3	117	Large	1245	46	2.683
JabRef	2.9.2	90.4	Medium	616	55	5.392
Dependency finder	1.2.1 beta4	58	Medium	450	258	32.095
MOEA	1.17	42	Medium	407	280	16.694

The size classification used in Table 1 is adapted from the work of [30], where application size is categorized into bands based on the number of kilo LOC (KLOC): small (fewer than 1 KLOC), medium (1–10 KLOC), large (10–100 KLOC) and extra-large (more than 100 KLOC).

5.2 Execution Scenarios

In order to arrive at dynamic metrics values that are associated with typical, genuine use of a system the selected execution scenarios must be representative of such use. Our goal is to mimic 'actual' system behavior, as this will enhance the utility of our results. The scenarios are therefore designed to use key system features, based on the available documentation and user manuals for the selected systems, as well as our prior knowledge of these systems. Further information on the selected execution scenario for each system now follows. Note that all four systems have GUI access, and the developed scenarios assume use via the GUI.

FindBugs: The tool is run to detect bugs in a large scale OSS (i.e., JFreeChart) by analyzing the source code and the associated jar files. The web plugin has been installed during the execution and data were uploaded to the FindBugs webserver. Results were stored using all three file formats supported.

JabRef: the tool is used to generate and store a list of references from an original research report. We included all reference types supported by the tool (e.g., journal articles, conference proceedings, reports, standards). Reports were then extracted using all available formats (including XML, SQL and CSV). References were managed using all the provided features. All additional plugins provided at the tool's website were added and used during this execution.

Dependency Finder: this scenario involves using the tool to analyze the source code of four medium-large sized systems one after another, namely, FindBugs, JMeter, Ant and Colossus. We computed dependencies (dependency graphs) and OO metrics at all layers (i.e., packages, classes, features). Analysis reports on all four systems were extracted and saved individually.

MOEA: *MOEA* has a GUI diagnostic tool that provides access to a set of 6 algorithms, 57 test problems and search operators. We used this diagnostic tool to apply those different algorithms on the predefined problems. We applied each of these algorithms at least once on each problem. We displayed metrics and performance indicators for all results provided by those different problems and algorithms. Statistical results of these multiple runs were displayed at the end of the analysis.

6 Results

As we are interested in the potential associations between variables, a statistical test of correlation is used in the evaluation of our hypotheses. After collecting our metrics data we first apply the Shapiro-Wilk (S-W) test to check the normality of each data distribution. This is necessary as selection of the relevant correlation test should be informed by the nature of the distributions, being normal or non-normal. The null hypothesis for the S-W test is that data is normally distributed.

After applying the S-W test the evidence led us to reject the null hypothesis regarding their distribution, and so we accepted that the data were not normally distributed (boxplots of the data are shown in Figs. 1 and 2). We therefore decided to use *Spearman's rho (r)* rank correlation coefficient test. *Spearman's r* is a non-parametric statistical test that measures the association between two measured quantities when ordered and ranked. In our work *Spearman's r* is calculated to assess the degree of association between each dynamic metric of the production code (i.e., IC, EC and EF) and the class testability metrics, defined in Sect. 4.2.

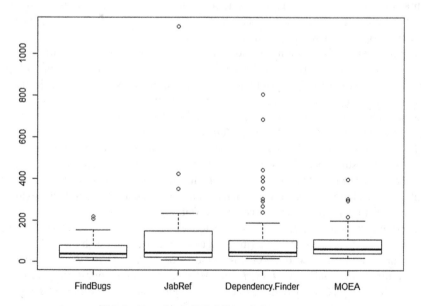

Fig. 1. Boxplots of TLOC in all four systems.

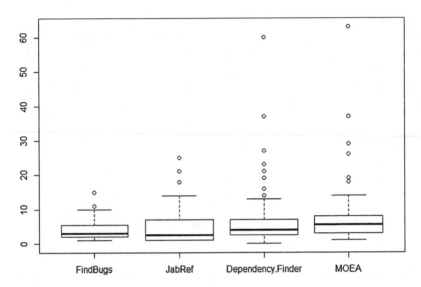

Fig. 2. Boxplots of NTC in all four systems.

We used the classification of Cohen [31] to interpret the degree of association between variables. The value of r indicates the association between two ranked variables, and it ranges from -1 (perfect negative correlation) to $+1$ (perfect positive correlation). We interpret that variables are independent when $r = 0$, that there is a low direct association when $r < 0.3$, a medium direct association when $0.3 \leq r < 0.5$, and a high direct association when $0.5 \leq r$. This interpretation also applies to negative correlations, but the association is inverse rather than direct [32]. The p-value (p) represents the statistical significance of the relationship. We consider an association to be statistically significant where $p \leq 0.05$.

The number of observations considered in each test varies in accordance with the systems' execution scenarios described in Sect. 5.2. Observation points, in fact, represent the number of tested classes that were traversed in the execution (i.e., classes that have corresponding tests and that were captured during the execution by any of the dynamic metrics used). The number of observations for *FindBugs* is 23, *JabRef* is 26, 80 for *Dependency Finder* and 76 for *MOEA*.

Table 2 shows the *Spearman's r* results for the two dynamic coupling metrics against the test suite metrics. Corresponding results for the EF metric against the test suite metrics are presented in Table 3. For all analyses we interpret that there is a significant correlation between two variables if there is statistically significant evidence of such a relationship in at least **three** of the **four** systems examined.

For dynamic coupling, a mix of results is found from the collected metrics (Table 2). EC is observed to have a significant (medium to high) correlation with the TLOC metric in all four systems. The correlation was found to be *high* in *Dependency Finder* and *medium* direct in *FindBugs*, *JabRef* and *MOEA*. A similar significant correlation between EC and NTC is evident in three of the four systems: *FindBugs* (*high* association), *JabRef* and *Dependency Finder* systems (both are *medium* associations).

Table 2. *Spearman r* correlation between dynamic coupling metrics and class testability metrics.

Systems	Metrics	TLOC		NTC	
		r	p	r	p
FindBugs	EC	.43	.04	.58	.00
	IC	−.07	.77	−.09	.69
JabRef	EC	.35	.04	.33	.05
	IC	.28	.09	.23	.13
Dependency Finder	EC	.52	.00	.41	.00
	IC	.52	.00	.33	.00
MOEA	EC	.30	.01	.12	.16
	IC	−.08	.24	−.24	.02

In terms of relationships with the IC metric (Table 2), the correlation between IC and TLOC is evident only in one system (*high* association in *Dependency Finder*). For the relationship between IC and NTC, a direct *medium* correlation was found only in one system i.e., *Dependency Finder*. A low inverse association between IC and NTC is evident for the *MOEA* system.

Table 3. *Spearman r* correlation between EF metrics and class testability metrics.

Systems	Metrics	TLOC		NTC	
		r	p	r	p
FindBugs	EF	.42	.05	.37	.09
JabRef	EF	.44	.01	.38	.03
Dependency Finder	EF	.33	.00	.22	.03
MOEA	EF	.03	.41	−.10	.19

As shown in Table 3, positive significant associations were found between EF and the class testability metrics in three of the four systems (the exception being *MOEA*). A significant *medium* correlation between EF and TLOC was found in *FindBugs*, *JabRef* and *Dependency Finder*. Also, a *medium* correlation between EF and NTC was found in *JabRef*, where a *low* correlation is found in *Dependency Finder*.

7   Discussion

Based on our analysis H_0 is accepted and H_2 is rejected; that is, there is evidence of a significant association between dynamic coupling (either EC or IC) and the two class-testability metrics for all four systems. As EF is also found be significantly associated with the testability metrics for three of the four systems considered, H_1 is also accepted and H_3 is rejected on the balance of evidence. The relationships between coupling and class-testability metrics are shown in Figs. 3 and 4. Due to space con-straints we show only *Scatter Plot* graphs from systems that have the *highest* correlations (i.e., *r* values) between metrics. Figure 3 shows the relationship between EC and NTC in *FindBugs* and Fig. 4 shows the relationship between EC and TLOC in *Dependency Finder*.

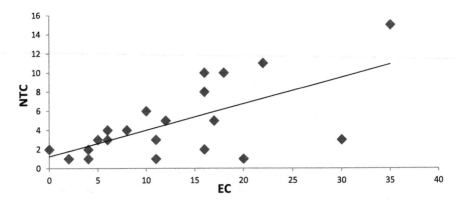

Fig. 3. Scatter plot of the relationship between EC and NTC metrics in *FindBugs*.

An additional test of relevance in this study is to consider whether the dynamic metrics used are themselves related, since this may indicate that only a subset of these metrics needs to be collected. Therefore, a further correlation analysis was performed to investigate this. The results indicate that the two dynamic coupling metrics are correlated with EF (Table 4) to varying degrees for the four systems investigated. High direct and medium direct associations between EC and the EF metric are evident in three systems (the only exception is *FindBugs*). IC is correlated with EF in only two systems (high correlation in *Dependency Finder* and low in *MOEA*).

It is evident that dynamic coupling measures are associated with class-testability metrics. EC is found to be more significantly correlation with both testability metrics. IC association with class testability metrics is not consistence across systems. These results can be interpreted as indicating that dynamic coupling, in some form, has a significant correlation with class testability. A similar inference is drawn regarding key classes; this property is also significantly associated with class testability or unit test size. Additionally, the two dynamic testability concepts studied here, i.e., dynamic coupling and key classes, are found to be themselves significantly correlated. Such results can be helpful for testers and maintainers as they provide empirical evidence regarding the relationship between two important dynamic properties and class

Table 4. *Spearman r* results for the correlation between coupling and EF.

Systems	IC		EC	
	r	*p*	*r*	*p*
EF	*FindBugs*	.32	.14	.31	.15
	JabRef	.27	.09	.81	.00
	Dependency Finder	.56	.00	.51	.00
	MOEA	.29	.01	.40	.00

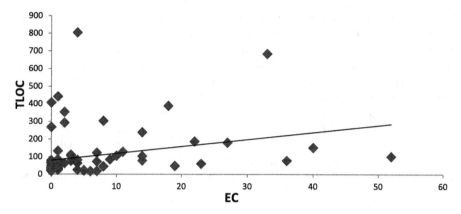

Fig. 4. Scatter plot of the relationship between EC and TLOC metrics in *Dependency Finder*.

testability. We recommend that similar dynamic information should be taken into consideration when developing unit tests or maintaining existing test suites.

In revisiting the list of the investigated research questions, dynamic coupling is found to have a significant (although not very strong) direct association with testability (RQ1). A more significant correlation was found between key classes (i.e., frequently executed classes) and class testability metrics. By answering RQ1 and RQ2, this suggests that dynamic coupling and key classes can act, to some extent, as complementary indicators of class testability (i.e., unit test size). It is contended here that a tightly coupled or frequently executed class would need a large corresponding test class (i.e., higher numbers of TLOC and NTC). This expectation has been found to be evidenced in at least three of the four systems examined.

8 Threats to Validity

We acknowledge the following threats that could affect the validity of our results.

One of the possible threats to the validity of this study is the limited number of systems used in the analysis. The results discussed here are derived from the analysis of four open source systems. The consideration of a larger number of systems, perhaps also including closed-source systems, could enable further evaluation of the associations revealed in this study and so lead to more generalizable conclusions.

Unit test selections can be another validity threat. We only considered production classes that have corresponding test classes, which may lead to a selection bias. Classes that are extremely difficult to test, or are considered too simple, might have no associated test classes. Such production classes are not considered in our analyses. Due to their availability, we only included classes that had associated JUnit test classes, and ignored all others.

The selection of the execution scenarios is another possible threat to the validity of our results. We designed execution scenarios that mimic as closely as possible 'actual' system behavior, based on the available system documentation and, in particular, indications of each system's key features. We acknowledge, however, that the selected scenarios might not be fully representative of the typical uses of the systems. Analyzing data that is collected based on different scenarios might give different results. This is a very common threat in most dynamic analysis research. However, we tried to mitigate this threat by carefully checking user manuals and other documentation of each of the examined systems and deriving the chosen scenarios from these sources. Most listed features were visited (at least once) during the execution. More scenarios will be considered in the future in order to extend our analyses.

Finally, we acknowledge that only available test information from the selected systems was used. We did not collect or have access to any information regarding the testing strategy of the four systems. Test strategy and criteria information could be very useful if combined with the test metrics, given that test criteria can inform testing decisions, and the number of test cases designed is highly influenced by the implemented test strategy.

9   Conclusions and Future Work

In this work we set out to investigate the presence and significance of any associations between two runtime code properties, namely Dynamic Coupling and Key Classes, and the testability of classes in four open source OO systems. Testability was measured based on the systems' production classes and their associated unit tests. Two different metrics were used to measure class testability, namely TLOC and NTC. As we were interested in the relationships between system characteristics at runtime, dynamic coupling and key classes were measured using dynamic software metrics collected via AOP. Results were then analyzed statistically using the *Spearman's r* correlation coefficient test to study the associations.

The resulting evidence indicates that there is a significant association between dynamic coupling and internal class testability. We found that dynamic coupling metrics and especially the Export Coupling metric have a significant direct association with TLOC. A less significant association was found between dynamic Import Coupling and NTC. Similarly, Key Classes are also shown to be significantly associated with our test suite metrics in at least three of the four systems examined.

The findings of this work contribute to our understanding of the nature of the relationships between characteristics of production and test code. The use of dynamic measures can provide a level of insight that is not available using static metrics alone. These relationships can act as an indicator for internal class level testability, and should be of help in informing maintenance and reengineering tasks.

Several future directions are suggested by the outcomes of this research. This work can be extended by examining a wider range of systems (such as closed-source systems) to enable further evaluation of the findings. Another research direction would be to investigate whether *dynamic coupling* and *key classes* information can be used together to predict the size and structure of test classes. Predicting class-level testability should improve the early estimation and assessment of the effort needed in testing activities. This work could also be extended to an investigation of the association between other source code factors and testability using runtime information. It would also be potentially beneficial to incorporate the current information about class testability with other testing information such as test coverage and test strategy.

References

1. Bertolino, A., Strigini, L.: On the use of testability measures for dependability assessment. IEEE Trans. Softw. Eng. **22**(2), 97–108 (1996)
2. Myers, G.J., Sandler, C., Badgett, T.: The Art of Software Testing, p. 240. Wiley Publishing, New York (2011)
3. Sommerville, I., et al.: Large-scale complex IT systems. Commun. ACM **55**(7), 71–77 (2012)
4. Mouchawrab, S., Briand, L.C., Labiche, Y.: A measurement framework for object-oriented software testability. Inf. Softw. Technol. **47**(15), 979–997 (2005)
5. ISO, Software engineering - Product quality-Part 1. In: Quality model 2001, International Organization for Standardization Geneva
6. Binder, R.V.: Design for testability in object-oriented systems. Commun. ACM **37**(9), 87–101 (1994)
7. Traon, Y.L., Robach, C.: From hardware to software testability. In: International Test Conference on Driving Down the Cost of Test, pp. 710–719. IEEE Computer Society (1995)
8. Gao, J.Z., Jacob, H.-S., Wu, Y.: Testing and Quality Assurance for Component-Based Software. Artech House Publishers, Norwood (2003)
9. Bruntink, M., van Deursen, A.: An empirical study into class testability. J. Syst. Softw. **79**(9), 1219–1232 (2006)
10. Badri, L., Badri, M., Toure, F.: An empirical analysis of lack of cohesion metrics for predicting testability of classes. Int. J. Softw. Eng. Appl. **5**(2), 69–86 (2011)
11. Chidamber, S.R., Kemerer, C.F.: A metrics suite for object oriented design. IEEE Trans. Softw. Eng. **20**(6), 476–493 (1994)
12. Basili, V.R., Briand, L.C., Melo, W.L.: A validation of object-oriented design metrics as quality indicators. IEEE Trans. Softw. Eng. **22**(10), 751–761 (1996)
13. Cai, Y.: Assessing the effectiveness of software modularization techniques through the dynamics of software evolution. In: 3rd Workshop on Assessment of COntemporary Modularization Techniques, Orlando (2008)
14. Scotto, M., et al.: A non-invasive approach to product metrics collection. J. Syst. Architect. **52**(11), 668–675 (2006)
15. Dufour, B., et al.: Dynamic metrics for java. In: 18th Annual ACM SIGPLAN Conference on Object-Oriented Programing, Systems, Languages, and Applications, pp. 149–168. ACM, Anaheim (2003)
16. Tahir, A., MacDonell, S.G.: A systematic mapping study on dynamic metrics and software quality. In: International Conference on Software Maintenance. IEEE Computer Society (2012)
17. Tahir, A., MacDonell, S.G., Buchan, J.: Understanding class-level testability through dynamic analysis. In: 9th International Conference on Evaluation of Novel Approaches to Software Engineering (ENASE), pp. 38–47, Lisbon (2014)
18. Zhou, Y., et al.: An in-depth investigation into the relationships between structural metrics and unit testability in object-oriented systems. Sci. China Inf. Sci. **55**(12), 2800–2815 (2012)
19. Arisholm, E., Briand, L.C., Foyen, A.: Dynamic coupling measurement for object-oriented software. IEEE Trans. Softw. Eng. **30**(8), 491–506 (2004)
20. Offutt, J., Abdurazik, A., Schach, S.: Quantitatively measuring object-oriented couplings. Softw. Qual. J. **16**(4), 489–512 (2008)
21. Al Dallal, J.: Object-oriented class maintainability prediction using internal quality attributes. Inf. Softw. Technol. **55**(11), 2028–2048 (2013)

22. Chaumun, M.A., et al.: Design properties and object-oriented software changeability. In: European Conference on Software Maintenance and Reengineering, p. 45. IEEE Computer Society (2000)

23. Tahir, A., Ahmad, R., Kasirun, Z.M.: Maintainability dynamic metrics data collection based on aspect-oriented technology. Malays. J. Comput. Sci. **23**(3), 177–194 (2010)

24. Zaidman, A., Demeyer, S.: Automatic identification of key classes in a software system using webmining techniques. J. Softw. Maintenance Evol. **20**(6), 387–417 (2008)

25. Basili, V.R., Weiss, D.M.: A methodology for collecting valid software engineering data. IEEE Trans. Softw. Eng. **10**(6), 728–738 (1984)

26. Briand, L.C., Morasca, S., Basili, V.R.: An operational process for goal-driven definition of measures. IEEE Trans. Softw. Eng. **28**(12), 1106–1125 (2002)

27. Cazzola, W., Marchetto, A.: AOP-HiddenMetrics: separation, extensibility and adaptability in SW measurement. J. Object Technol. **7**(2), 53–68 (2008)

28. Adams, B., et al.: Using aspect orientation in legacy environments for reverse engineering using dynamic analysis–an industrial experience report. J. Syst. Softw. **82**(4), 668–684 (2009)

29. Rompaey, B.V., Demeyer S.: Establishing traceability links between unit test cases and units under test. In: European Conference on Software Maintenance and Reengineering, pp. 209–218. IEEE Computer Society, Kaiserslautern (2009)

30. Zhao, L., Elbaum, S.: A survey on quality related activities in open source. SIGSOFT Softw. Eng. Notes **25**(3), 54–57 (2000)

31. Cohen, J.: Statistical Power Analysis for the Behavioral Sciences, 2nd edn. Lawrence Erlbaum Associates, London (1988)

32. Daniel, W.W.: Applied Nonparametric Statistics. KENT Publishing Company, Boston (2000)

Online Testing: A Passive Approach for Protocols

Xiaoping Che[1]([✉]), Jorge Lopez[2], and Stephane Maag[2]

[1] Beijing Jiaotong University, Beijing, China
`xpche@bjtu.edu.cn`
[2] Institut Mines-Telecom/Telecom SudParis, CNRS UMR 5157, Evry, France
`{Jorge.eleazar.lopez_coronado,stephane.maag}@telecom-sudparis.eu`

Abstract. Online testing approaches are becoming crucial in today's complex systems. By that way, testing a protocol at run-time has to be performed during a normal use of the system without disturbing the process. The traces are observed and analyzed on-the-fly to provide test verdicts and no trace sets should be studied as a posteriori to the testing process. In this process, it is a challenging work to keep the same preciseness in conformance testing and the same efficiency in performance testing. In this paper, aiming to find a solution, we present a novel online passive testing approach based on Horn-Logic. In order to evaluate and assess our approach, we also developed a prototype and experimented it with a set of Session Initiation Protocol properties in a real IP Multimedia Subsystem environment. Finally, the preliminary results and discussions are provided.

Keywords: Online testing · Passive testing · Formal methods

1 Introduction

Testing is a crucial activity in the evaluation process of a system or an implementation under test (IUT). Among the well known and commonly applied approaches, the *passive* testing techniques (also called *monitoring* or *run-time verification*) are today gaining efficiency and reliability [1]. These techniques are divided in two main groups: *online* and *offline* testing approaches. Offline testing aims at collecting set of protocol traces while running (through interfaces, ports or points of observations (P.O)) and then checking some properties through these traces afterwards. Several model based offline testing techniques have been studied by the community in order to passively test systems or protocol implementations [2,12,14,16]. Nevertheless, though offline testing still raises many interesting issues [10], online testing approaches bring out these same issues plus the challenges that are inherent to online testing. Among these inherent constraints, we shall cite the *non-collection* of traces. Indeed, in passive online testing, the traces are observed (through an eventual sniffer), analyzed on-the-fly to provide test verdicts and no trace sets are studied a posteriori to the testing

© Springer International Publishing Switzerland 2015
J. Filipe and L. Maciaszek (Eds.): ENASE 2014, CCIS 551, pp. 79–92, 2015.
DOI: 10.1007/978-3-319-27218-4_6

process. In our work, we focus on the online testing of an IUT using passive testing technique.

Testing an implementation of a protocol is often associated to the checking of its conformance and performance. Conformance testing is a functional test which verifies whether the behaviors of the protocol satisfy defined requirements. Performance testing is a qualitative and quantitative test which checks whether the performance requirements of the protocol have been satisfied under certain conditions. They are mainly applied to validate or verify the scalability and reliability of the system. Many benefits can be brought to the testing process if conformance and performance testing inherit from the same approach and can be applied online.

Our main objective is then to propose a novel passive online testing approach based on formal conformance and performance testing techniques [3,4]. Although some crucial works have been done in run-time conformance testing area [1], they study run-time verification of properties expressed either in linear-time temporal logic (LTL) or timed linear-time temporal logic (TLTL). Different from their work focusing on testing functional properties based on formal models, our work concentrates on formally testing functional and non-functional properties without formal models, through real protocols in an online manner.

In this work, we firstly extend one of our previous proposed methodologies to present a passive testing approach for checking the conformance and performance requirements of communicating protocols. Furthermore, we design an online testing framework to test these requirements in real-time, with new verdicts definitions of 'Pass', 'Fail', 'Time-Fail' and 'Inconclusive'. Finally, since several protocol conformance and performance requirements need to be tested in order to verify the efficiency of our online approach, we perform our approach in a real IP Multimedia Subsystem (IMS) communicating environment for assessing its preciseness and efficiency.

Our paper's primary contributions are:

- A formal approach is proposed for formally expressing the conformance and performance requirements, and data portions are taken into account.
- An online testing framework is designed for testing conformance and performance requirements in real-time, and new definition of testing verdicts are introduced.

The reminder of the paper is organized as follows. In Sect. 2, a short review of the related works are provided. In Sect. 3, a brief description of the syntax and semantics used to describe the tested properties is presented. In Sect. 4, we illustrate our online testing framework and relevant algorithms. Our approach has been implemented and experimented in Sect. 5. It has been performed through a real IMS framework to test Session Initiation Protocol (SIP) properties. The real-time communications of the IMS allow to evaluate our approach efficiently. Finally, we conclude and provide interesting perspectives in Sect. 6.

2 Related Works

While a huge number of papers are dedicated to online testing. In this section we present the prior works in these fields.

Model Based Online Testing. Model based testing is a crucial technique in the testing research domain. In [11], the authors present T-UPPAAL– a tool for online black-box testing of real-time embedded systems from non-deterministic timed automata specifications. They describe a sound and complete randomized online testing algorithm and implement it by using symbolic state representation and manipulation techniques. They propose the notion of relativized timed input/output conformance as the formal implementation relation. Likewise, some other researchers describe a practical online testing algorithm that is implemented in the model-based testing tool called Spec Explorer [16], which is being used daily by several Microsoft product groups. They formalize the model programs as interface automata, and use the interface automata for conformance testing. The conformance relation between a model and an implementation under test is formalized in terms of refinement between interface automata. Besides, in [14], the authors describe how timed automata can be used as a formalism to support efficient online monitoring of timeliness, reliability and throughput constraints expressed in web service SLAs. And they present an implementation to derive on-line monitors for web services automatically form SLAs using an Eclipse plugin and Apache AXIS handlers. The readers would notice that all these works are based on modeling the system by automata or timed automata, due to the convenience that the constructed models can be handled by existing verification tools. However, when the system can not be accessed or modeled, our work will be a complementary to these techniques since we do not need to formalize the system by any automata.

Online Conformance Testing. In the online testing area, there are lots of work focus on conformance testing. In [2], the authors present a framework that automatically generates and executes tests "online" for conformance testing of a composite of Web services described in BPEL. The proposed framework considers unit testing and it is based on a timed modeling of BPEL specification, and an online testing algorithm that generates, executes and assigns verdicts to every generated state in the test case. Nevertheless, in [13], the authors defined a formal model based on Symbolic Transition Graph with Assignment (STGA) for both peers and choreography with supporting complex data types. The local and global conformance properties are formalized by the Chor language in their works. The local properties are used to test behaviors of one isolated peer with respect to its specification model, while the global properties test the collaboration of a set of peers with respect to its choreography model. Inspired from all these works, our work does not require to model the IUT and tackles not only conformance requirements, but also the performance requirements.

Moreover, another similar work is provided by the authors of [8]. They presented an algorithm for the runtime monitoring of data-aware workflow constraints.

Sample properties taken from runtime monitoring scenarios in existing literature were expressed using LTL-FO^+, an extension of Linear Temporal Logic that includes first-order quantification over message contents. Similarly to our work, data are a more central part of the definition of formulas, and formulas are defined with quantifiers specific to the labels. Although the syntax of the logic they used is flexible, it can quickly lose clarity as the number of variables required increases. Our work improves on this by allowing to group constraints with clause definitions.

Online Performance Testing. Many studies have investigated the performance of online systems. A method for analyzing the functional behavior and the performance of programs in distributed systems is presented in [9]. In the paper, the authors discuss event-driven monitoring and event-based modeling. However, no evaluation of the methodology has been performed. In [5], the authors present a distributed performance-testing framework, which aimed at simplifying and automating service performance testing. They applied Diperf to two GT3.2 job submission services, and several metrics are tested, such as *Service response time, Service throughput, Offered load, Service utilization* and *Service fairness.*

Besides, in [17], the authors propose two online algorithms to detect 802.11 traffic from packet-header data collected passively at a monitoring point. The algorithms have a number of applications in real-time wireless LAN management, they differ in that one requires training sets while the other does not. Moreover, in [18], the authors present a monitoring algorithm SMon, which continuously reduces network diameter in real time in a distributed manner. Nevertheless, most of these approaches are based on monitoring techniques, they do not provide a formalism to test a specific performance requirement. Our approach allows to formally specified protocol performance requirements in order to check whether the real-time performance of the protocol remains as expected in its standard.

Although lots of works have been done in the online testing area. Inspired from and based on their works, our work is different from focusing on using model-driven techniques, evaluating the performance of the system. We concentrate on how to formally and passively test the conformance and performance requirements written in the standard. And also we are trying to converge the online conformance and performance testing by using the same formal approach.

3   Formal Approach

We will provide in this section basic definitions, syntax and semantics of our formalism which are necessary for the understanding of our approach.

3.1   Basics

A communication protocol message is a collection of data fields of multiple domains. Data domains are defined either as *atomic* or *compound* [3]. An *atomic* domain is defined as a set of numeric or string values. A *compound* domain is defined as follows.

Definition 1. A *compound* value v of length $n > 0$, is defined by the set of pairs $\{(l_i, v_i) \mid l_i \in L \wedge v_i \in D_i \cup \{\varepsilon\}, i = 1...n\}$, where $L = \{l_1, ..., l_n\}$ is a predefined set of labels and D_i are sets of values, meaningful from the application viewpoint, and called data domains. Let D be a Cartesian product of data domains, $D = D_1 \times D_2 \times ... \times D_n$. A *compound* domain is the set of pairs (L, d), where d belongs to D.

Once given a network protocol P, a *compound* domain M_p can generally be defined by the set of labels and data domains derived from the message format defined in the protocol specification/requirements. A *message* m of a protocol P is any element $m \in M_p$.

For each $m \in M_p$, we add a real number $t_m \in \mathbb{R}^+$ which represents the time when the message m is received or sent by the monitored entity.

Example 1. A possible message for the SIP protocol, specified using the previous definition could be

$$m = \{(method, \text{'\textbf{INVITE}'}), (time, \text{'210.400123000'}),$$
$$(status, \varepsilon), (from, \text{'alice@a.org'}), (to, \text{'bob@b.org'}),$$
$$(cseq, \{(num, 7), (method, \text{'\textbf{INVITE}'})\})\}$$

representing an INVITE request from *alice@a.org* to *bob@b.org*. The value of *time* '210.400123000' ($t_0 + 210.400123000$) is a relative value since the P.O started its timer (initial value t_0) when capturing traces.

A *trace* is a sequence of messages of the same domain containing the interactions of a monitored entity in a network, through an interface (the P.O), with one or more peers during an arbitrary period of time. The P.O also provides the relative time set $T \subset \mathbb{R}^+$ for all messages m in each *trace*.

3.2 Syntax and Semantics of Our Formalism

In our previous work, a syntax based on Horn clauses is defined to express properties that are checked on extracted traces. We briefly describe it in the following. Formulas in this logic can be defined with the introduction of terms and atoms, as it follows.

Definition 2. A *term* is defined in BNF as $term ::= c \mid x \mid x.l.l...l$ where c is a constant in some domain, x is a variable, l represents a label, and $x.l.l...l$ is called a *selector variable*.

Definition 3. A *substitution* is a finite set of bindings $\theta = \{x_1/term_1, ..., x_k/term_k\}$ where each $term_i$ is a *term* and x_i is a variable such that $x_i \neq term_i$ and $x_i \neq x_j$ if $i \neq j$.

Definition 4. An *atom* is defined as

$$A ::= \overbrace{p(term, ..., term)}^{k}$$
$$| \ term = term$$
$$| \ term \neq term$$
$$| \ term < term$$
$$| \ term + term = term$$

where $p(term, ..., term)$ is a predicate of label p and arity k. The *timed atom* is a particular atom defined as $\overbrace{p(term_t, ..., term_t)}^{k}$, where $term_t \in T$.

The relations between *terms* and *atoms* are stated by the definition of clauses. A *clause* is an expression of the form

$$A_0 \leftarrow A_1 \wedge ... \wedge A_n$$

where A_0 is the head of the clause and $A_1 \wedge ... \wedge A_n$ its body, A_i being *atoms*.

A *formula* is defined by the following BNF:

$$\phi ::= A_1 \wedge ... \wedge A_n \ | \ \phi \rightarrow \phi \ | \ \forall_x \phi \ | \ \forall_{y>x} \phi$$
$$| \ \forall_{y<x} \phi \ | \ \exists_x \phi \ | \ \exists_{y>x} \phi \ | \ \exists_{y<x} \phi$$

where $A_1, ..., A_n (n \geq 1)$ are *atoms*, x, y represent for different messages of a trace and $\{<, >\}$ indicate the order relation of messages.

In our approach, while the variables x and y are used to formally specify the messages of a trace, the quantifiers commonly define "it exists" ($\exists$) and "for all" ($\forall$). Therefore, the formula $\forall_x \phi$ means "for all messages x in the trace, ϕ holds".

The semantics used in our work is related to the traditional Apt–Van Emdem–Kowalsky semantics for logic programs [6], from which an extended version has been provided in order to deal with messages and trace temporal quantifiers. Based on the above described operators and quantifiers, we provide an interpretation of the formulas to evaluate them to $\top$ ('*Pass*'), $\bot$ ('*Fail*') or '?' ('*Inconclusive*') [3].

Then the truth values $\{\top, \bot, ?\}$ are provided to the interpretation of the obtained formulas on real protocol execution traces. However, different from offline testing, definite verdicts should be immediately returned in online testing. Which indicates that only $\top$ ('*Pass*') and $\bot$ ('*Fail*') should be emitted in the final report, and the indefinite verdict '?' ('*Inconclusive*') will be used as temporary unknown status, but finally must be transformed to one of the definite verdicts.

4   Online Testing Framework

In this section, we will introduce our novel online testing framework and provide the relevant algorithm for testers.

4.1   Framework

For the aim of testing conformance and performance requirements in an online way, we design and use a passive online testing architecture. As Fig. 1 depicts, the testing process consists of five following parts.

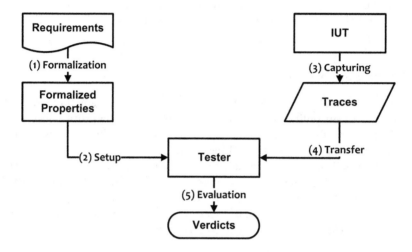

Fig. 1. Core functions of our testing framework.

1. **Formalization:** Initially, the informal protocol requirements are formalized to formulas by using Horn-logic based syntax and semantics mentioned in Sect. 3. Due to the space limitation, we will not go into details. The interested readers may have a look at the papers [3,10].
2. **Setup:** When all the requirements are formalized to formulas, they will be sent to the Tester with the definition of verdicts.
   - Pass: The message or trace satisfies the requirement.
   - Fail: The message or trace does not satisfy the requirement.
   - Time-Fail: Since we are testing on-line, a timeout is used to stop searching target message in order to provide the real-time status. The timeout value should be the maximum response time written in the protocol. If we can not observe the target message within the timeout time, then a Time-Fail verdict will be assigned to this property. It has to be noticed that this kind of verdict is only provided when no time constraint is required in the requirement. If any time constraint is required, the violation of requirements will be concluded as Fail, not as a Time-Fail verdict.
   - Inconclusive: Uncertain status of the properties. It only exists at the beginning of the test or at the end of the test.
3. **Capturing:** The monitor consecutively captures the traces of protocols to be tested from the IUT. When the messages have been captured, each message will be tagged with a time-stamp in order to test the properties with time requirements.

4. **Transfer:** The tagged messages are transferred to the Tester when the Tester is capable for testing. Since we optimize our algorithm in order to have the best effort, the tester is always capable for testing when dealing with less than 20 million packages per minute.

5. **Evaluation:** The Tester checks whether or not the incoming traces satisfy the formalized requirements and provide the final verdicts. Based on different results and the definition of verdicts, we conclude the verdicts as: Pass, Fail or Time-Fail.

4.2 Testing Algorithm

The online testing algorithm is described in Algorithm 1. Algorithm 1 describes the behaviors of an online tester. Firstly, the tester will capture packets from the predefined interface by using libpcap[1], and it will tag time stamps to all the captured packets at the same time (Line 1–3).

Secondly, it will load all the properties (formalized requirements) have to be tested, and match each packet with the properties in chronological order. In this step, only the packets needed for the current property will be saved and tackled. The other irrelevant packets will be discarded in order to accelerate the testing process (Line 4–15). This process will keep running until all the properties have been checked.

When finishing the checking process, it will report the testing result and empty the buffer immediately in order to make good use of the limited memory (Line 16–29).

5 Experiments

After introducing our novel framework, we will describe the testing environment and interpret the experiments results in this section.

5.1 Environment

The IP Multimedia Subsystem is a standardized framework for delivering IP multimedia services to users in mobility. It aims at facilitating the access to voice or multimedia services in an access independent way, in order to develop the fixed-mobile convergence. The core of the IMS network consists on the Call Session Control Functions (CSCF) that redirect requests depending on the type of service, the Home Subscriber Server (HSS), a database for the provisioning of users, and the Application Server (AS) where the different services run and inter-operate. Most communication with the core network and between the services is done using the Session Initiation Protocol [15].

The Session Initiation Protocol is an application-layer protocol that relies on request and response messages for communication, and it is an essential part

---

[1] http://www.tcpdump.org/.

Algorithm 1. Algorithm of online tester.

Input: open_live_capture_on_interface(INTERFACE_NAME) //Using libpcap
Output: property verdicts report

```
1  thread_init(report_live_status) //thread to report the live
2  for each packet on live_capture do
3  |    last_observed_packet_time ← get_time(packet);
4  |    for each prototype on prototype_packets do
5  |    |    property ← get_prototype_property(prototype);
6  |    |    if match_properties_of(prototype, packet) then
7  |    |    |    prototype_list ← get_prototype_list(prototype);
8  |    |    |    for each prototype_dependency on dependencies(prototype) do
9  |    |    |    |    matched_dependency ← FALSE;
10 |    |    |    |    for each stored_packet on
   |    |    |    |    get_dependency_prototype_list(prototype_dependency) do
11 |    |    |    |    |    if match_properties_dependency(prototype_dependency,
   |    |    |    |    |    packet, stored_packet) then
12 |    |    |    |    |    |    associate(packet, stored_packet, property),
   |    |    |    |    |    |    matched_dependency ← TRUE;
13 |    |    |    |    |    |    goto next_dependency;
14 |    |    |    |    |    end
15 |    |    |    |    end
16 |    |    |    |    if !matched_dependency then
17 |    |    |    |    |    goto next_prototype
18 |    |    |    |    end
19 |    |    |    end
20 |    |    |    if prototype_determines_property(prototype) then
21 |    |    |    |    associations_list ← get_associations(packet)
   |    |    |    |    report_property_pass(property, packet, associations_list)
   |    |    |    |    delete_from_prototype_lists(associations_list)
22 |    |    |    end
23 |    |    |    else
24 |    |    |    |    push(prototype_list, packet)
25 |    |    |    end
26 |    |    end
27 |    |    next_prototype;
28 |    end
29 end
```

---

for communication within the IMS framework. Messages contain a header which provides session, service and routing information, as well as an body part to complement or extend the header information. Several RFCs have been defined to extend the protocol to allow messaging, event publishing and notification. These extensions are used by services of the IMS such as the Presence service and the Push to-talk Over Cellular (PoC) service.

For our experiments, communication traces were obtained through ZOIPER[2]. ZOIPER softphone is a VoIP soft client, meant to work with any IP-based

---

[2] http://www.zopier.com/softphone/.

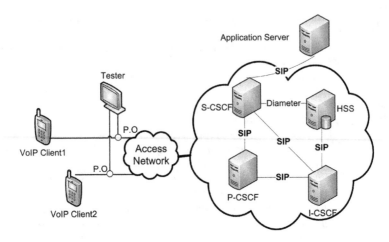

Fig. 2. Environment for experiments.

communications systems and infrastructure. It provides secure high-quality voice calls and conference, fax sending and receiving functionality, and enhanced IP-calling features wrapped in a compact interface and small download size.

As Fig. 2 shows, a simple environment is constructed for our experiments. We run two ZOIPER VoIP clients on the virtual machines using VirtualBox for Mac version 4.2.16. The virtual machines have 4 GB of RAM, one processor Intel i5 @2.3 GHz and the software being used is Zoiper 3.0.19649. On the other side, the server is provided by Fonality[3], which is running Asterisk PBX 1.6.0.28-samy-r115. The P.Os are placed on the client side. Tests are performed using a prototype implementation of the formal approach above mentioned, using the algorithm introduced in the previous section.

5.2 Tests Results

In our approach, the conformance and performance requirement properties are formalized to formulas. These formulas will be tested through the testers in real-time. Simultaneously, not only '*Pass*', '*Fail*', '*Time-Fail*' and '*Inconclusive*' verdicts are returned, but also N_p, N_f, N_{tf} and N_{in} will be given to the tester, which represent the accumulated number of '*Pass*', '*Fail*', '*Time-Fail*' and '*Inconclusive*' verdicts respectively. We may write:

$$N_p(\phi) = \sum [eval(\phi, \theta, \rho) = `\top']$$

$$N_f(\phi) = \sum [eval(\phi, \theta, \rho) = `\perp']$$

$$N_{tf}(\phi) = \sum [\begin{matrix} eval(\phi, \theta, \rho) = `\perp' \\ term_t \notin \phi, timeout \in \theta \end{matrix}]$$

$$N_{in}(\phi) = \sum [eval(\phi, \theta, \rho) = `?']$$

---

[3] http://www.fonality.com.

Table 1. Online testing result for Client1 and Client2.

P.O	ϕ_1				ϕ_2				ψ_1			
	Pass	Fail	Time-Fail	Incon	Pass	Fail	Time-Fail	Incon	Pass	Fail	Time-Fail	Incon
Client1	50	0	0	0	43	0	7	0	645	240	0	0
Client2	36	0	0	0	34	0	2	0	473	6	0	0

Properties: In order to formally design the properties to be passively tested online, we got inspired from the TTCN-3 test suite [7] and the RFC 3261 of SIP [15]. Several properties relevant to session establishment are designed.

Conformance requirements ϕ_1, ϕ_2 ("Every **INVITE** request must be responded", "Every successful **INVITE** request must be responded with a success response") and a performance requirement ψ_1 ("The response time for each request should not exceed $T_1 = 8s$") are tested. They can be formalized as the following formulas:

$$\phi_1 = \begin{cases} \forall_x (request(x) \wedge x.method = \text{`INVITE'} \\ \rightarrow \exists_{y>x} (nonProvisional(y) \wedge responds(y,x))) \end{cases}$$

$$\phi_2 = \begin{cases} \forall_x (request(x) \wedge x.method = \text{`INVITE'} \\ \rightarrow \exists_{y>x} (success(y) \wedge responds(y,x))) \end{cases}$$

$$\psi_1 = \begin{cases} \forall_x (request(x) \wedge x.method! = \text{`ACK'} \\ \rightarrow \exists_{y>x} (nonProvisional(y) \wedge responds(y,x) \\ \wedge withintime(y,x,T_1))) \end{cases}$$

The two hours online testing results are illustrated in Table 1. A number of '*Fail*' and '*Time-Fail*' verdicts can be observed when testing ϕ_2 and ψ_1. Let's have a look at the '*Time-Fail*' verdicts in ϕ_2. They indicate that during the testing, the tester can not detect some successful responses to '**INVITE**' requests within the maximum response time. However, there is no time constraint required in ϕ_2, we have to conclude these verdicts as '*Time-Fail*'. Which means probably the server refused some '**INVITE**' requests, the responses are lost during the transmission or the responses will arrive later than the timeout time. Combining the results of ϕ_1, we can know that it was due to the first reason.

Similarly, we can observe some '*Fail*' verdicts when testing ψ_1, they are caused by the same reason that the tester can not find the target message within the required time. On the contrary, there is a specific time constraint required in ψ_1, which is 8 seconds. It shows some responses exceeded the required time 8s, they exactly violated the requirement and we have to conclude them as '*Fail*'.

These testing results successfully show that our approach can detect both the usual and unusual faults. Moreover, by using the verdicts obtained from these properties. We can also test the performance issues of session establishment in real-time, which can be defined as:

- Session Attempt Number: $N_p(\phi_1)$
- Session Attempt Rate: $N_p(\phi_1)/t_{slot}$

- Session Attempt Successful Rate: $N_p(\phi_2)/N_p(\phi_1)$
- Session establishment Number: $N_p(\phi_2)$
- Session establishment Rate: $N_p(\phi_2)/t_{slot}$
- Session Packets Delay: $N_p(\psi_1)$.

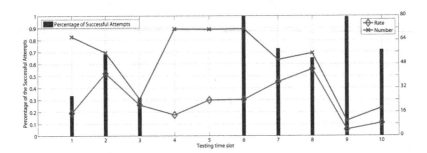

Fig. 3. Session Attempt Number, Rate and Successful Rate.

Figure 3 illustrates the testing results of Session Attempt Number, Rate and Successful Rate in each hour. We can observe that in the 4th and 5th hour, the successful attempt rates are zero while the attempts numbers/rates are not, which denotes that in those two periods, all the session attempts ('**INVITE**' requests) were refused. And it returned to normal in the 6th hour. In this way, we can have a clear view of the protocol performance during online testing. It has to be noticed that when the tester receive an incoming trace, it will apply the formalized requirements on the trace and get the verdicts in a short time. During our experiments, all the testing results for requirements without time constraints are obtained in 1s, which proves the efficiency of our approach.

6   Perspectives and Conclusion

This paper introduces a novel online approach to test conformance and performance of network protocol implementation. Our approach allows to define relations between messages and message data, and then to use such relations in order to define the conformance and performance properties that are evaluated on real protocol traces. The evaluation of the property returns a *Pass, Fail, Time-Fail* or *Inconclusive* result, derived from the given trace.

The approach also includes an online testing framework. To verify and test the approach, we design several SIP properties to be evaluated by our approach. Our methodology has been implemented into an environment which provides the real-time IMS communications, and the results from testing several properties online have been obtained successfully.

Furthermore, our approach can not only test requirements and return relevant verdicts, but also it can reflect current protocol performance status based on these verdicts. We extended several performance measuring indicators for SIP. As Fig. 3 shows, these indicators are used for testing the performance of session establishment in SIP. The real time updated results displayed in the screen can precisely reflect the performance of the protocol in different time periods.

Consequently, extending more testers in a distributed environment based on the work [4] and building an online testing system for all the network protocols would be the work we will focus on in the future. In that case, the efficiency and processing capacity of the system would be the crucial point to handle, leading to an optimization of our algorithms to severe situations.

References

1. Bauer, A., Leucker, M., Schallhart, C.: Runtime verification for LTL and TLTL. ACM Trans. Softw. Eng. Methodol. **20**(4), 14 (2011)
2. Cao, T.-D., Félix, P., Castanet, R., Berrada, I.: Online testing framework for web services. In: Third International Conference on Software Testing, Verification and Validation, pp. 363–372 (2010)
3. Che, X., Lalanne, F., Maag, S.: A logic-based passive testing approach for the validation of communicating protocols. In: Proceedings of the 7th International Conference on Evaluation of Novel Approaches to Software Engineering, Wroclaw, Poland, pp. 53–64 (2012)
4. Che, X., Maag, S.: A formal passive performance testing approach for distributed communication systems. In: ENASE 2013 - Proceedings of the 8th International Conference on Evaluation of Novel Approaches to Software Engineering, Angers, France, 4–6 July, 2013, pp. 74–84 (2013)
5. Dumitrescu, C., Raicu, I., Ripeanu, M., Foster, I.: DiPerF: an automated distributed performance testing framework. In: 5th International Workshop in Grid Computing, pp. 289–296. IEEE Computer Society (2004)
6. Emden, M.V., Kowalski, R.: The semantics of predicate logic as a programming language. J. ACM **23**(4), 733–742 (1976)
7. ETSI: Methods for testing and specification (MTS); conformance test specification for SIP (2004)
8. Hallé, S., Villemaire, R.: Runtime enforcement of web service message contracts with data. IEEE Trans. Serv. Comput. **5**(2), 192–206 (2012)
9. Hofmann, R., Klar, R., Mohr, B., Quick, A., Siegle, M.: Distributed performance monitoring: methods, tools and applications. IEEE Trans. Parallel Distrib. Syst. **5**, 585–597 (1994)
10. Lalanne, F., Maag, S.: A formal data-centric approach for passive testing of communication protocols. IEEE/ACM Trans. Netw. **21**, 788–801 (2013)
11. Larsen, K.G., Mikucionis, M., Nielsen, B.: Online testing of real-time systems using UPPAAL. In: Grabowski, J., Nielsen, B. (eds.) FATES 2004. LNCS, vol. 3395, pp. 79–94. Springer, Heidelberg (2005)
12. Lee, D., Miller, R.: Network protocol system monitoring-a formal approach with passive testing. IEEE/ACM Trans. Netw. **14**(2), 424–437 (2006)
13. Nguyen, H.N., Poizat, P., Zaïdi, F.: Online verification of value-passing choreographies through property-oriented passive testing. In: 14th International IEEE Symposium on High-Assurance Systems Engineering, pp. 106–113 (2012)

14. Raimondi, F., Skene, J., Emmerich, W.: Efficient online monitoring of web-service slas. In: Proceedings of the 16th ACM SIGSOFT International Symposium on Foundations of Software Engineering, pp. 170–180 (2008)
15. Rosenberg, J., Schulzrinne, H., Camarillo, G., Johnston, A., Peterson, J.: SIP: Session initiation protocol (2002)
16. Veanes, M., Campbell, C., Schulte, W., Tillmann, N.: Online testing with model programs. In: Proceedings of the 10th European Software Engineering Conference Held Jointly with 13th ACM SIGSOFT International Symposium on Foundations of Software Engineering, pp. 273–282 (2005)
17. Wei, W., Suh, K., Wang, B., Gu, Y., Kurose, J.F., Towsley, D.F., Jaiswal, S.: Passive online detection of 802.11 traffic using sequential hypothesis testing with TCP ACK-pairs. IEEE Trans. Mob. Comput. **8**(3), 398–412 (2009)
18. Yuen, C.-H., Chan, S.-H.: Scalable real-time monitoring for distributed applications. IEEE Trans. Parallel Distrib. Syst. **23**(12), 2330–2337 (2012)

Experiences of Use of a Multi-domain Tool for Collaborative Software Engineering Tasks

Jesús Gallardo[1(✉)], Ana Isabel Molina[2], Crescencio Bravo[2], and Fernando Gallego[2]

[1] Escuela Universitaria Politécnica de Teruel, Universidad de Zaragoza,
Ciudad Escolar, s/n, Teruel, Spain
jesus.gallardo@unizar.es
[2] Escuela Superior de Informática, Universidad de Castilla-La Mancha,
Paseo Universidad, 4, Ciudad Real, Spain
{anaisabel.molina,crescencio.bravo}@uclm.es,
fgallego82@gmail.com

Abstract. Many processes in Software Engineering, and specifically in the Unified Software Development Process, require the participation of several actors who may play different roles. Collaborative software (groupware) can solve the problems that arise when trying to deal with such processes. Within this scope, we have developed a domain independent synchronous collaborative tool that can be specialized to work with several types of diagrammatical domains. Among those domains, the diagrams used in the Unified Process can be found. In this paper we describe how we have instantiated this model-based tool to work with some diagrams in the Unified Process. Also, in the paper we explain how we have carried out some studies with this tool to obtain conclusions regarding several issues, including the analysis of the communication and coordination among users, and the relationship between them and the quality of the work.

Keywords: Use cases · Groupware · Collaborative modeling · Empirical study

1 Introduction

Currently, many fields in industry, research and education are taking advantage of the advances in collaborative software applications and systems. These applications have been classified in the so-called field of groupware [1]. Groupware is defined as those computer-based systems that give support to a group of people who work together on a shared task, and that provide an interface to a shared environment [2]. By means of computer networks and groupware systems, shared workspaces are created and group tasks of several kinds can be carried out.

Software Engineering is one of the fields that can take advantage of the boom in the groupware area. Specifically, many processes within the Unified Software Development Process require the participation of several actors with different or equal roles. Thus, such actors may create or modify the diagrams integrated in the Unified Modeling Language (UML) in a collaborative way. This leads us to the fact that a

© Springer International Publishing Switzerland 2015
J. Filipe and L. Maciaszek (Eds.): ENASE 2014, CCIS 551, pp. 93–108, 2015.
DOI: 10.1007/978-3-319-27218-4_7

groupware tool can assist in the development of such work and allow higher quality diagrams to be developed. Another way in which groupware contributes to Software Engineering is distributed collaborative programming, in which several programmers work on the same source code when solving problems [3].

In this work, we focus on the use of synchronous collaborative tools. By means of these tools, several users who are physically separated are able to work on the same diagram at the same time. This is also known as real time collaboration in the literature. As explained in Sect. 2, the synchronous collaborative building of several UML diagrams using groupware tools is an area in which there is a lack of relevant works. In synchronous collaborative settings, participants are usually grouped in work sessions in which they work together on a given goal. In order to help the collaborative work be done, these tools should integrate several widgets or components for the support of communication and coordination among the members of the collaborative work session.

In processes such as software development, developers usually have to face the use of tools that handle several types of artifacts, particularly diagrams that make models visible. Thus, developers may have problems when adapting themselves to the use of different tools with different user interfaces and ways of operation. A possible solution to this is the use of a *multi-domain* system. This type of system includes a configuration process in which an administrator carries out a setup process from which a tool for working with a specific domain is generated. Therefore, all tools generated within this process own the same user interface and are used in the same way, so that users only have to learn once how they are used. This can imply an important saving of time and higher work productivity. In this paper, we are going to deal with some multi-domain tools we have developed and instantiated for several domains in the field of Software Engineering.

The tool we have chosen to give support to our study is SPACE-DESIGN [4]. SPACE-DESIGN is a domain-independent synchronous groupware tool that can be specialized to a wide set of application domains by means of a simple process of configuration. In this case, we have configured the tool to support the development of use case diagrams and some other UML diagrams. In order to analyze how a group of users' use such tools and whether they accept that as a feasible option, several empirical studies have been carried out. In this paper we will describe in detail one of them. In it, we have analyzed the development of a collaborative work task in the domain of use case diagrams. Thus, our goals have been, on the one hand, to prove that the development of use case diagrams in a synchronous collaborative way by using a groupware tool is feasible, and, on the other hand, to analyze how the different possibilities of communication and coordination users were provided with have an effect on the process and also on the results of the work.

The remaining part of this work is organized as follows: in Sect. 2, we deal with some systems and approaches related to the work described in this paper. Then, the SPACE-DESIGN collaborative tool and its evolution are described. In Sect. 4, we explain the empirical study we have carried out in detail and we discuss the results obtained. Lastly, we present some conclusions and future work.

2 Related Work

In this section, we tackle systems and technologies related to the work approached. Firstly, in Subsect. 2.1 we discuss those tools that support synchronous collaborative modeling in any domain. Afterwards, in Subsect. 2.2 we mention some tools that are used for the development of use case diagrams.

2.1 Tools for Synchronous Collaborative Modeling

A few tools that support the synchronous collaborative modeling of diagrams and artifacts in several application domains exist. Some of them are specific of a given domain and some others are generic or domain independent, with this meaning that they can be adapted to work on different domains by means of a configuration process.

Some examples of domain independent collaborative modeling tools are Cool Modes and Synergo. Cool Modes [5] is a cooperative modeling system that contains a workspace including a set of plug-ins. These plug-ins are actually palettes that contain the objects that can be placed over the shared workspace and the links to create relationships between the objects. In Cool Modes it is not possible for users to reconfigure or extend the functionality of the tool by adding new palettes that support new application domains. Synergo [6] is also a tool for the design on a shared whiteboard. Synergo contains a predefined set of objects that can be placed on that whiteboard. This set cannot be extended. Another feature included in Synergo is a powerful communication system in the form of a chat for the discussion among the members of the work session. This chat includes the possibility of sending predefined messages that can direct the communication. Such messages usually deal with making proposals and accepting or denying them. Thus, Synergo introduces the concept of structured chat, about which we will talk later.

SPACE-DESIGN [4] is a synchronous collaborative modeling tool. It is reconfigurable and extensible. In order to configure it for a specific application domain, XML-based files are used. This tool includes some widgets for awareness and coordination support, which are implemented as reusable components. One of those widgets is a structured chat, as explained in Sect. 3. The presence of the chat is one of the main reasons for the selection of this tool for the empirical study. The usefulness of chats and similar communication mechanisms has been proved in diverse collaborative tasks [7], and specifically in requirements elicitation in software engineering [8]. In fact, we have used SPACE-DESIGN in our research group for other works in which we have needed a synchronous collaborative tool [9]. Of course, we have specialized SPACE-DESIGN in order to make it work over the use case diagrams domain. Other systems, such as the aforementioned Cool Modes and Synergo, could not have been configured in such a way. Further explanations about SPACE-DESIGN can be found in Sect. 3.

Now, we go back to the concept of structured chat. The usual way to support communication in synchronous collaborative tools is to include a chat that allows users to communicate to each other. The use of a chat is especially important in tasks such as creating artifacts or diagrams on a synchronous way, as it allows communication during the work sessions. A special kind of chat is the structured chat, in which users can use specific sentence openers that are used to have a more directed conversation. Usually, sentence openers are related to the specific domain of the tool.

Synergo and SPACE-DESIGN are examples of tools that include a structured chat. Another one is COLER [10]. This system is a web based collaborative environment for the learning of Entity-Relationship diagrams. Some other interesting tools that use structured communication are C-CHENE [11], which deals with the building of energy chains, and EPSILON [12], for object-oriented design with OMT diagrams.

2.2 Collaborative Tools for the Development of UML Diagrams

There exist several tools for the development of UML diagrams, both collaborative and non-collaborative ones. In the scope of our higher education institution, Rational Rose and Visual Paradigm are the ones that have been used in the recent times, both of them being non-collaborative tools. Next, we are going to talk about some collaborative tools that have been developed in the scientific and commercial spheres.

An interesting approach to UML diagram collaborative edition is CUML [13]. In this approach, each user works on a copy of the model that is synchronized with a central server. A group of users can work together or different users can lock different parts of the model for exclusive editing while the changes are visible to all other users. Therefore, both synchronous and asynchronous editing is allowed.

These kinds of tools are often used for learning purposes. For example, COLLECT-UML [14] is a constraint-based intelligent tutoring system that teaches object-oriented analysis and UML-based design. This system teaches users how to design UML class diagrams and provides them with feedback on collaboration.

As the study in this paper is focused on use case diagrams, we are going to review now some tools for the collaborative development of such diagrams. Fuenzalida and Antillanca [15] two tools for the textual edition of use cases. One of these tools is synchronous, whereas the other one is an asynchronous tool. Neither tool handles diagrams, but they allow the textual edition of the use cases and the relationships among them. The comparison between the tools is done by calculating some metrics. Most metrics give best values to the asynchronous tool, but the synchronous modeling seems to have some relevant advantages. For instance, it takes less time to obtain the final model.

Most existing systems that implement some kind of collaboration to edit use cases or to build use case diagrams actually implement asynchronous collaboration. Even this collaboration is sometimes just a mere management of group work or a kind of version control system. Some tools implementing such approaches are CaseComplete [16] or Visual Use Case [17]. Another category is that of those tools that deal with software lifecycle in a wider sense and contain specific components for the management of use cases. This is the case of the Rommana system [18]. This tool includes requirements management, tests management and so on, together with a use cases management unit.

Summarizing, we can conclude that synchronous collaborative use cases modeling is a field that has not been explored enough and that can provide some advantages when carrying out the modeling tasks. In the following section, the SPACE-DESIGN tool is described in detail. SPACE-DESIGN is the tool used to carry out the collaborative use case diagrams modeling in the empirical study described in Sect. 4. As mentioned in Sect. 2.1, this tool has been chosen because it presents some features that make it more suitable than other tools.

3   The SPACE-DESIGN Tool

The SPACE-DESIGN tool (Fig. 1) is a system that is the first version of the instrumental part of a methodological approach for the model-driven development of collaborative modeling systems [19]. In particular, SPACE-DESIGN supports distributed synchronous work, allowing users to build models collaboratively. It is domain-independent since the system processes the domain specification, expressed by means of an XML-based language, and spawns the user interface and the necessary functionality to support that specific type of modeling, including specific interaction and awareness design aspects in the groupware user interface. Thus, it is a multi-domain system of the type we dealt with in the introduction.

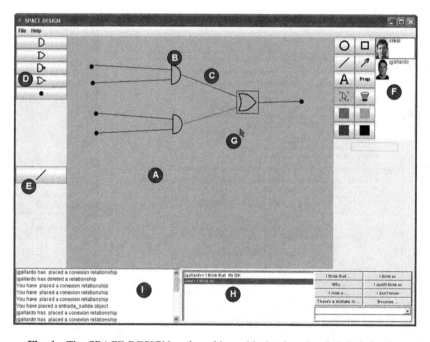

Fig. 1. The SPACE-DESIGN tool working with the domain of digital circuits.

As shown in Fig. 1, SPACE-DESIGN has a shared whiteboard (A) where users can work with the different elements that make up the application domain. These elements can be one of two types: objects (B) and relationships (C). Both types are instantiated from the toolbars that are located on the left-hand side of the user interface (D, E). These toolbars will vary according to the domain in which the system is working, and the objects and relationships will be those that appear in the domain specification.

An important characteristic of SPACE-DESIGN are the elements for awareness [20] and collaboration support that are included by default. These elements are: a session panel that shows the users who is participating in the design session and identifies them by means of a specific color (F), the identification of the elements that users select by means of colors, the tele-pointers that indicate where the other users are pointing to (G), a structured chat feature for communication between the participants (H), and a list of interactions indicating what actions have taken place and who has carried them out (I).

The presence of these awareness and collaboration support elements is one of the features that make SPACE-DESIGN different from other similar systems, such as Synergo or CoolModes. However, the main differences between SPACE-DESIGN and these systems are that, while the former adapts itself in a flexible way to new domains, incorporates awareness mechanisms, and stores the developed models in XML files (Fig. 2), the other systems have difficulty incorporating new domains, have fewer awareness mechanisms and, in the case of CoolModes, store the models in a propri-etary format [21].

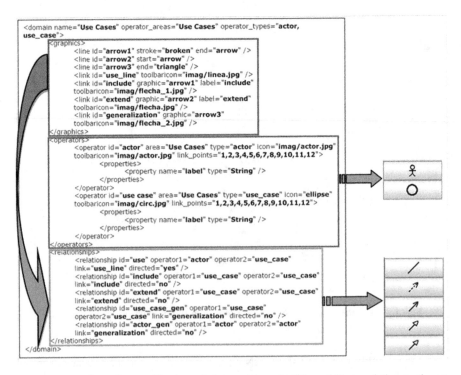

Fig. 2. Excerpt from the specification of the use cases domain and its translation to the user interface.

Concerning the supported domains, the aforementioned systems allow for the modeling of several domains from a series of specifications programmed in the system itself, whereas SPACE-DESIGN defines the domains in a way that is external to the system, by means of specifications that can be built by end users. This means that any domain made up of objects and relationships between them, and actions to manipulate them can be modeled in this way, and as such, SPACE-DESIGN can be used to work with this domain in a collaborative way. Specifically, in this work, starting from the use cases domain specification, SPACE-DESIGN adapts its user interface to give support to use case diagram modeling.

As stated before, communication is a very important issue when performing collaborative tasks, especially in real time working environments; the most usual communication mechanism is the exchange of textual messages. SPACE-DESIGN supports three types of synchronous textual. The first one is *free communication*, which is the kind of communication that happens in traditional chats. That is, communication that is based on the free exchange of textual messages among the members of the work team. No constraints are defined in this sense. A second approach is *communication with references to objects*. In this kind of chat, the conversation is enriched with some references to the domain objects in the collaborative modeling task in which the work is being done. The different domain objects (e.g., actors and use cases in the domain of use case diagrams) that can be placed in the shared context can be selected and included in the conversation. The third and last kind of chat is the *structured chat*. This kind of chat provides users with a set of predefined messages with which the user can show the kind of contribution or message, as well as its intention. Thus, the organization of the talk is favored. The categories of the messages can be defined according to the particular needs of the collaborative task to support and to the specific domain in which work is being done. Moreover, this technique allows reusing structures from previous conversations. In the case of SPACE-DESIGN, messages have been classified regarding their *type* (statement, question or answer) and their *position in the conversation* (some of them are conversation starters, such as "*Why...*" and others are reactive ones, such as "*Because...*"). Table 1 depicts the generic sentence openers in SPACE-DESIGN. In this kind of chat, references to objects are also possible. In fact, SPACE-DESIGN offers the possibility to have a structured chat with references to objects.

The SPACE-DESIGN tool has been instantiated for several application domains that are made up by nodes and connections among them. For example, digital circuits, conceptual maps, Bayesian networks, etc [4]. Some studies have been developed in order to test the suitability and usefulness of our approach [9]. Software Engineering has been one of the fields in which SPACE-DESIGN has been found as an interesting and promising tool. Therefore, the tool has been configured by instantiating the corresponding models so that it allows the work with several diagrams of the Unified Process, such as use cases diagrams, class diagrams, state transition diagrams, package diagrams, etc. In Fig. 3 we show some screenshots of the SPACE-DESIGN tool working with some of these diagrams. The screenshots are of an early version of the tool, so the user interface is slightly different from the one in other screenshots in this paper.

Table 1. Sentence openers in SPACE-DESIGN.

Sentence opener	Type	Position in the conversation
I think that...	Statement	Conversation starter
Why...	Question	Conversation starter
I miss a...	Statement	Conversation starter
There's a mistake in...	Statement	Conversation starter
I think so	Statement	Reactive
I don't think so	Statement	Reactive
I don't know	Answer	Reactive
Because...	Answer	Reactive

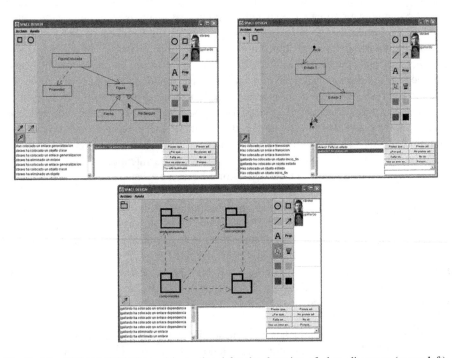

Fig. 3. The SPACE-DESIGN tool instantiated for the domains of class diagrams (upper left), state transition diagrams (upper right) and package diagrams (bottom).

The SPACE-DESIGN tool has been improved from its initial version, which is the one we have shown in previous subsections. The current version of SPACE-DESIGN is called SpacEclipse and it has been fully integrated in the model-driven development method [22]. Specifically, the new version improves certain elements, such as the way in which the domain is specified, the extension of the working process to cover new tasks, and the reusability and extensibility of the generated tool. We have integrated several technologies from the Eclipse Modeling Project[1] and extended them to obtain collaborative functionality. Therefore, Eclipse is used as a container platform for the developed modeling tools. Its use has some additional advantages, for example developers may be familiar with Eclipse-based systems, as it is a common platform in the Software Development field. An example of tool generated using the new version of the method is the one shown in Fig. 4.

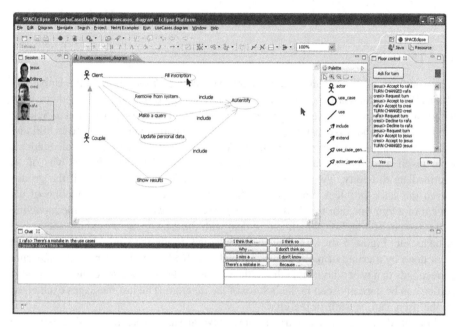

Fig. 4. New version of the collaborative modeling tool working with the use case diagram domain.

4   Empirical Study

In this section, we describe in depth a empirical study carried out to evaluate the SPACE-DESIGN. We have considered it interesting to analyze how users collaborate using the different communication mechanisms, and how such mechanisms have an influence on the work performed and the results obtained. In this sense, we have tested the three kinds of chat in SPACE-DESIGN. We have tried to state whether there is an influence of the kind of chat on the work carried out. In addition, we have an interest in knowing the subjective perception users have regarding the *usefulness* of the mechanisms, as well as their *preference* for one or another kind of communication. Regarding

---

[1] http://eclipse.org/modeling/.

communication issues, we have also asked users for their preference between the three kinds of chats.

Thus, the research questions we contemplate in this scenario are the following:

- Does the choice of a certain communication mechanism have an influence on the fluency of the communication?
- Does the communication mechanism have an influence on coordination?
- What relationship between the communication mechanism and the quality of the use cases models exists?

4.1   The Study

A total number of 28 students of the *Escuela Superior de Informática* in the University of Castilla-La Mancha (Spain) took part in the study voluntarily. All of them were taking a course on Software Engineering in the third year of a Computer Science degree. The collaborative task to be carried out by the participants consisted in building a use case diagram making use of the SPACE-DESIGN collaborative tool. Students were given a textual specification of the problem to be solved, which was of an intermediate difficulty. Two different problems were proposed, so not all the groups solved the same problem. Specifically, the problems were: (P1) the modeling of the system of a tour operator that had to manage trips and travelers, and (P2) the modeling of the system of a harbor, which had to deal with the management of ships, the arrival of boats, etc. Figure 5 shows a screenshot obtained during the study. In the figure, the work done by a group of participants that had to solve P2 can be seen. The screenshot corresponds to a user who is not editing the diagram. The tele-pointer of the user who is editing can be partially seen in the bottom of the diagram. The last messages exchanged by the users can be seen in the chat.

For the design of this empirical study, several steps were followed. Firstly, the students who were to take part in it attended a seminar about the SPACE-DESIGN tool. There, students could try the tool and learn how it works, which features it includes and what it can be used for.

Then, the 28 participants were divided into two groups of 10 members and one group of 8 members. Two groups worked on problem P1, whereas the remaining group worked on problem P2. Participants in each group were then grouped in pairs whose participants were physically separated while carrying out the study. Each group was randomly assigned a different communication mechanism. Thus, 4 pairs (8 participants) used the traditional chat, 5 pairs (10 participants) used the chat with references to objects, and 5 pairs (10 participants) used the structured chat.

During the problem solving, in which the modeling task was carried out, participants were allowed to look up the help manual of the tool, as well as the formulation of the problem to be solved. Each participant was provided with a unique user name and password so that they could use the tool and access the work session they should join. The structure of sessions and groups is depicted in Table 2.

Once the task was completed, the participants in the study went to fill out a test made up of 10 questions with a five-point Likert scale format. This test allowed users to

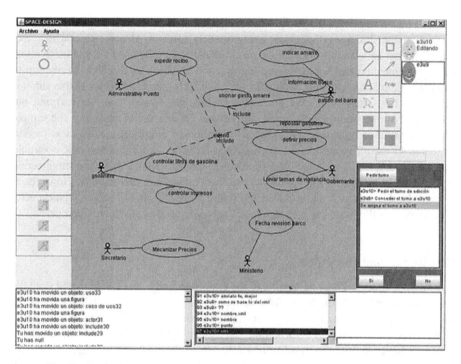

Fig. 5. Screenshot of the use of SPACE-DESIGN during the empirical study.

Table 2. Structure of sessions and groups in the empirical study.

Problem	Chat	Participants	Groups
P1	Chat with reference to objects	10	2
	Traditional chat		1
	Structured chat		2
P2	Chat with reference to objects	8	1
	Traditional chat		2
	Structured chat		1
P1	Chat with reference to objects	10	2
	Traditional chat		1
	Structured chat		2

evaluate the usefulness of the tools, as well as of the different communication mechanisms included in it. The test also included a section for additional remarks, in which participants could express their opinion or make suggestions for the improvement of the tool and the study.

This empirical testing was designed with the aim to lighten some threats to internal and external validity. For example, each group was randomly assigned a different communication mechanism. In addition, the universe of discourse of the problem to be solved was well known by the participants. Regarding fatigue effects, the average time spent in completing the designing tasks was approximately 60 min. Hence, we consider that fatigue did not have an influence on the result obtained. In relation to subject motivation, we have to mention that subjects were highly committed to this research. In relation to external validity, one issue that could affect the validity of the conclusions of this study is the size of the sample data. We are aware of this, so we will consider carrying out replications of this study with a larger sample size. Other issue to analyze is the sample nature. In order to guarantee the external validation of empirical studies, it is recommendable to recruit representative participants. Because of the difficulty of obtaining professional subjects, we used undergraduate students from a software engineering course. This fact threatens the validity of conclusions and external validity. However, if we consider that students can be considered future professionals and had enough capacity to participate in this task, these experimental subjects can be considered appropriate.

4.2   Results and Discussion

Now, we are going to show the results of the empirical study, discuss them and state the conclusions that have been drawn from them. We are going to start by talking about the metrics we have calculated for the groups taking part in the study. Firstly, we are going to consider the *amount of information* exchanged by the groups, which we have measured by means of the *number of messages* exchanged, the *average number of words per message* and the *total number of words exchanged*. In these three metrics, when grouping the values considering the kind of chat, the chat with references to objects obtained better values (Table 3).

Table 3. Statistics on messages and words communicated during the study. Each cell includes the mean value (M) and, in parentheses, the standard deviation (SD).

	Traditional chat	Chat with references to objects	Structured chat
Total number of messages per group	104.25 (45.26)	**151.40 (48.86)**	98.60 (48.94)
Average number of words per message	5.10 (0.91)	**5.98 (1.33)**	5.06 (0.55)
Total number of words	61.25 (33.89)	**106.00 (24.38)**	70.40 (46.26)
Number of interrogative messages	16.50 (13.08)	**24.40 (5.46)**	12.60 (6.88)
Percentage of interrogative messages	14.39 (6.93)	**18.72 (11.24)**	12.73 (5.12)
Number of domain dependent words	51.25 (31.08)	**76.60 (20.68)**	53.60 (38.89)

In addition to this analysis of the amount of information exchanged, we have also analyzed the content of the messages and their nature. From these data, we calculated the *number and percentage of interrogative messages* as well as the *number of domain dependent words exchanged* between the members of the group (see Table 3). We classify domain dependent words as those that refer to use case diagrams ("use", "case", "actor", "extends", etc.) as well as those which are specific to the problem formulation. In this sense, the values were again higher when calculating the totals and averages for the chat with references to objects. Thus, we can state that the communication was more fluent in the groups working with that kind of chat.

Regarding *coordination needs*, we measured the *number of turn changes* accomplished by each group. Groups using the traditional chat obtained higher values ($M = 7.25$; $SD = 2.06$), whereas groups with the chat with references to objects received smaller values ($M = 5.80$; $SD = 1.92$).

Taking into account all the data collected up to this point, we can conclude that the possibility of including references to domain objects seems to cause the users to focus on the conversation and make longer contributions, which are centered on the problem to be solved. In addition, it seems that with this chat it is less necessary to move the conversation between the members of the group. At the very least, we have detected fewer turn changes than in other cases.

Next, we are going to match these results with the *performance* of the groups when solving the modeling problem. The teacher evaluated the models developed during the study by giving each one a grade on the solution given to the problem. The grade was later divided into two separate grades regarding *use cases* and *relationships*. All these grades were calculated with 0 as the lowest and 10 the highest value. In this sense, again those that made use of the chat with references to objects obtained better grades ($M = 6.21$; $SD = 1.35$), whereas those who used the structured chat obtained the worst ones ($M = 4.31$; $SD = 2.21$). To check whether these results were influenced by the previous knowledge of the participants, their teacher was asked about the *previous grades* they had obtained in the course. Taking all of this into account, it was discovered that some groups were made up by students with similar previous grades (*homogeneous groups*), whereas some other groups consisted of two students with significant differences in their previous grades (*heterogeneous groups*). As we did not intentionally arrange the groups in this way, it is difficult to draw definitive conclusions about how this difference affected the other variables being analyzed. Thus, in future studies we will study the influence of the distribution in homogeneous and heterogeneous groups on the performance.

In addition to the descriptive analysis of the data collected, we also carried out a *correlation analysis* between the variables. Next, we are going to discuss the main correlations that appeared. The first correlation we detected was that those groups whose members had higher previous grades used more domain dependent words when using the chat ($r = 0.60$; $p = 0.05$). It can be deduced from this correlation that those groups whose members performed better in the course were more focused on carrying out the activity. In addition, these groups were those that exchanged a higher number of messages ($r = 0.64$; $p = 0.05$). The correlation with the number of interrogative messages was also positive ($r = 0.69$; $p = 0.05$).

On the other hand, a negative correlation ($r = -0.57$; $p = 0.05$) was detected between the number of turn changes and the number of exchanged words. This makes us think of two styles of working between the members of the group: a style in which one of the two members is working most of the time and the collaboration is made by means of the chat, and a second style in which members make less use of the chat and prefer to frequently change turns.

Lastly, it is worth noting a correlation that is not related to communication issues, but is specific to the domain of use case diagrams. Specifically, a positive correlation between the size of the model and the grade given by the teacher to the model regarding the suitability of the use cases chosen was detected ($r = 0.69$; $p = 0.05$). From this correlation, we can infer that, in those cases in which users did not select the proper set of use cases, the usual situation was that they used fewer uses cases than the amount included in the solution of the problem, and not the inverse situation in which they had used too many use cases.

To finish with the analysis of the study, we are going to talk about the results related to the *subjective perception* of the participants concerning the use of the tool and its communication mechanisms. In order to collect the information, participants filled out a test made up of some questions with a Likert scale (1 to 5). Some questions were meant to find out the opinion of the participants about the *usefulness* of SPACE-DESIGN for the collaborative modeling of use case diagrams. Participants gave a mean value of 3.6 ($SD = 0.4$) to that variable. This led us to think that users expressed their interest for the use of a collaborative tool such as SPACE-DESIGN for the collaborative design of use case diagrams. Thus, we could state that users would choose SPACE-DESIGN or a similar tool when willing to carry out such collaborative tasks instead of using single user tools shared by means of any software mechanism. This is a preference we have found in previous works [9].

In addition, the test contained some questions about the *preference* of the participants on the different communication mechanisms. In this sense, most users preferred the traditional chat, being the chat with references to objects the second one most valued and the structured chat the one which was least valued by the participants. However, in the case of these two kinds of chat, the possibility of referring domain objects during the conversations was given high values ($M = 3.4$; $SD = 0.34$).

4.3   Other Evaluation Studies

Some other evaluation studies have been carried out in order to validate our approach. We may highlight the studies we have performed with the new version of our approach fully integrated with Eclipse [22]. This study was made up of some activities that tested the different frameworks in the development method. Regarding the use of the tool itself, the activity consisted of making the participants use a collaborative tool to work with the COMO-UML notation defined in the AMENITIES approach [23].

Participants in this study were randomly organized in pairs and they performed a task with the aforementioned notation. After the activity was completed, participants answered some questions so that their opinions about the tool and the study were reflected. The results of the questionnaires are quite satisfactory as users evaluated most items with high values. A remarkable result is that users gave high values to all awareness support elements, so this seems to be a strong point of the tool. As a weak point, participants did not find the user interface self-explanatory enough. We have already performed a more detailed analysis of the study that can be read in order to know more about it [22].

5 Conclusions and Future Work

In this paper, we have introduced an approach to generate synchronous collaborative tools that can be specialized to work with several modeling domains. In this case, we have instantiated the tool to make it work with UML diagrams, and we have used it to do some studies so that we can draw some conclusions about how users carry out collaborative tasks.

The first conclusion we can draw from all the work done with the different versions of the tool and the method is that users find interesting our approach. Some items that are found especially interesting are the multi-domain approach and the awareness and communication support in the generated tools. In this paper, we have detailed one of the studies carried out. In it, we have drawn some interesting conclusions about the variables being studied. For example, it has been possible to identify a difference between two potential styles of collaborative work: one in which collaboration occurs at a communication level, and another in which there are frequent turn changes.

To conclude, it will be necessary in further studies to improve the weak points that have arisen in the studies that have already been carried out. For example, we will try to modify the communication mechanisms, as the structured chat features have not been widely accepted. We may change sentence openers in order to select a set of them more interesting for users. Also, some other elements in the user interface may be changed so that they become more self explanatory.

Acknowledgements. This research has been partially supported by the Ministerio de Economía y Competitividad (Spain) in the TIN2011-29542-C02-02 project and by the Junta de Comunidades de Castilla-La Mancha (Spain) in the PPII11-0013-1219 and PPEII-2014012-A projects.

References

1. Guareis de Farias, C.R.: Architectural design of groupware systems: a component-based approach. Ph.D. thesis (2002)
2. Ellis, C.A., Gibbs, S.J., Rein, G.: Groupware: some issues and experiences. Commun. ACM **34**(1), 39–58 (1991)
3. Bravo, C., Duque, R., Gallardo, J.: A groupware system to support collaborative programming: design and experiences. J. Syst. Softw. **86**(7), 1759–1771 (2013)
4. Duque, R., Gallardo, J., Bravo, C., Mendes, A.J.: Defining tasks, domains and conversational acts in CSCW systems: the SPACE-DESIGN case study. J. Univ. Comput. Sci. **14**(9), 1463–1479 (2008)
5. Pinkwart, N., Hoope, U., Gassner, K.: Integration of domain-specific elements into visual language based collaborative environments. In: Proceedings of the Seventh International Workshop on Groupware. IEEE Computer Society (2001)
6. Avouris, N., Margaritis, M., Komis, V.: Modelling interaction during small-groups synchronous problem-solving activities: the Synergo approach. In: Proceedings of the 2nd International Workshop on Designing Computational Models of Collaborative Learning Interaction, pp. 13–18 (2004)

7. Lund, K., Baker, M.J., Baron, M.: Modelling dialogue and beliefs as a basis for generating guidance in a CSCL environment. In: Lesgold, A.M., Frasson, C., Gauthier, G. (eds.) ITS 1996. LNCS, vol. 1086, pp. 206–214. Springer, Heidelberg (1996)

8. Calefato, F., Damian, D., Lanubile, F.: Computer-mediated communication to support distributed requirements elicitations and negotiations tasks. Empirical Softw. Eng. **17**(6), 640–674 (2012)

9. Gallardo, J., Molina, A.I., Bravo, C., Redondo, M.A., Collazos, C.: Empirical and heuristic-based evaluation of collaborate modeling systems: an evaluation framework. Group Decis. Negot. **20**(5), 535–562 (2011)

10. Constantino-González, M., Suthers, D.: Coaching web-based collaborative learning based on problem solution differences and participation. In: Moore, J.D., Redfield, C.L., Lewis Johnson, W. (eds.) Proceedings of the International Conference on AI-ED 2001, pp. 176–187 (2001)

11. Baker, M.J., Lund, K.: Flexibly structuring the interaction in a CSCL environment. In: Brna, P., Paiva, A., Self, J. (eds.) Proceedings of the EuroAIED Conference, pp. 401–407 (1996)

12. Soller, A., Lesgold, A.: Knowledge acquisition for adaptive collaborative learning environments. In: Proceedings of the AAAI Fall Symposium: Learning How to Do Things, Cape Cod, MA (2000)

13. Chan, S.C.F., Lee, P.S.H., Ng, V.T.Y., Chan, A.T.S.: Synchronous collaborative development of UML models on the internet. Concurrent Eng. Res. Appl. **9**(2), 111–119 (2011)

14. Baghaei, N., Mitrovic, A., Irwin, W.: Supporting collaborative learning and problem-solving in a constraint-based CSCL environment for UML class diagrams. Int. J. Comput. Supported Collaborative Learn. **2**(2–3), 159–190 (2007)

15. Fuenzalida, C.M., Antillanca, H.B.: Synchronous versus asynchronous interaction between users of two collaborative tools for the production of use cases. CLEI Electron. J. **13**(1) (2010)

16. Serlio Software. www.casecomplete.com. Accessed 24 July 2013

17. TechnoSolutions Corporation. www.visualusecase.com. Accessed 24 July 2013

18. Rommana Software. www.rommanasoftware.com. Accessed 24 July 2013

19. Gallardo, J., Molina, A.I., Bravo, C., Redondo, M.A., Collazos, C.: An ontological conceptualization approach for awareness in domain-independent collaborative modeling systems: application to a model-driven development method. Expert Syst. Appl. **38**(2), 1099–1118 (2011)

20. Dourish, P., Bellotti, V.: Awareness and coordination in shared workspaces. In: Proceedings of the Conference on Computer Supported Cooperative Work CSCW 1992, pp. 107–114 (1992)

21. Gallardo, J., Bravo, C., Redondo, M.Á.: Developing collaborative modeling systems following a model-driven engineering approach. In: Meersman, R., Tari, Z., Herrero, P. (eds.) OTM-WS 2008. LNCS, vol. 5333, pp. 442–451. Springer, Heidelberg (2008)

22. Gallardo, J., Bravo, C., Redondo, M.A.: A model-driven development method for collaborative modeling tools. J. Netw. Comput. Appl. **35**(3), 1086–1105 (2012)

23. Garrido, J.L., Noguera, M., González, M., Hurtado, M.V., Rodríguez, M.L.: Definition and use of computation independent models in an MDA-based groupware development process. Sci. Comput. Program. **66**, 25–43 (2007)

Taking Seriously Software Projects Inception Through Games

Miguel Ehécatl Morales-Trujillo[1]([✉]), Hanna Oktaba[1],
and Juan Carlos González[2]

[1] KUALI-KAANS Research Group,
National Autonomous University of Mexico, Mexico City, Mexico
{migmor, hanna.oktaba}@ciencias.unam.mx
[2] ENTIA, Av. López Mateos 2077-Z16, Col. Jardines de Plaza del Sol,
Guadalajara, Mexico
jgonzalez@entia.com.mx

Abstract. Inherent properties of games, such as rules, goals and interaction, have made them popular to address challenges and sort obstacles in a wide variety of contexts. Within Software Engineering, a challenging activity of the software development process is the Inception phase, in which stakeholders' needs, required functionalities, objectives, risks and constraints of a software product are established. An alternative to optimize stakeholders' participation during the Inception phase and make more efficient its outcomes is to do it through games.

Taking into account the uncommonness of games in Software Engineering development process and the lack of complex methods that include games, this paper presents ActiveAction, a method that combines classical requirements specification techniques with games. ActiveAction resulted in a successful game-based strategy that has improved the Inception phase of the software development projects based on the fact that stakeholders express their ideas freely in an unstressed environment; real-life scenarios are simulated to identify exceptions; requirements and risks are determined in a collaborative manner. It is concluded that the inclusion of games in such a challenging activity as software projects inception, is feasible and reported promising results that benefit both stakeholders and software developer organizations.

Keywords: Games · Inception phase · Requirements specification · Stakeholders' involvement · Software project · Workshop

1 Introduction

A game could be defined informally as an amusement activity with rules, undertaken for entertainment but still pursuing a goal. A game can be seen as an activity in which a player must learn new skills and apply them to overcome challenges, getting rewards or punishments, depending on their success or failure, respectively. The application of games in education, government or military areas has become an important and feasible alternative to face challenges. Since the entertainment is not the main purpose of these games, they are labeled as serious games.

© Springer International Publishing Switzerland 2015
J. Filipe and L. Maciaszek (Eds.): ENASE 2014, CCIS 551, pp. 109–124, 2015.
DOI: 10.1007/978-3-319-27218-4_8

A serious game is a game that does not have entertainment, enjoyment or fun as their primary purpose [1]. Even thought, according to [2] games may be played seriously or casually, it does not mean that serious games are not, or should not be, entertaining.

Nowadays, serious games are becoming more popular and have a broad scope of usage solving business problems and challenges that face the public sector [3]. The ludic and playful aspects inherent to games, serious or not, can be used as a strategy to address different kind of challenges and sorting obstacles. Enclosing to Software Engineering, it can be asserted that developing software and systems is a challenging activity. In 2010, Standish Group, through CHAOS Report [4], revealed that only 32 % of software projects were successful, 44 % challenged and 24 % were cancelled. Comparing these data with that of other industries, Construction for example, 94 percent of the customers were satisfied with the results of their projects, which suggests that construction projects have much lower failure rates than software projects [5].

But, why is developing software different to producing any other product? Why is it so difficult to develop good products in a consistent way from their inception phase and on? The purpose of the Inception phase of a software projects is establish the business case for the system and delimit the project scope [6]. The stakeholders' involvement in this phase is inherent and fundamental.

This necessity for stakeholders' involvement becomes evident if we analyze the CHAOS reports. Since 1994 the top three main success factors in projects are:

- Executive Support.
- User Involvement.
- Clear Business Objectives.

The three of them are evidently related to the stakeholders and the Inception phase of the project.

However, including stakeholders as part of the team, but in the real sense, requires time and money. With that in mind this paper presents ActiveAction, a workshop used as an alternative into the software project's Inception phase. ActiveAction combines classical with game-based techniques to improve stakeholders' involvement in the Inception phase of a project and increase its effectiveness.

The paper is organized as follows: Sect. 2 presents main success factors in IT projects, while Sect. 3 expands on the strategies to conceptualize projects using traditional, agile and game-based techniques. Section 4 then goes on to introduce and analyze the ActiveAction workshop, while Sect. 5 presents results of the usage of this method, its advantages and disadvantages. Conclusions and future work are provided in Sect. 6.

2   Success Factors in Software Projects

Are software projects different to other projects? According to [5] the main difference relies on the characteristics of software and technology. On one hand, software is abstract and complex while the requirements to be developed are incomplete. On the other hand, the vast domain of technology changes rapidly, causing lack of technical experience and immaturity of best practices.

According to Gartner [7] the most common "anti-success" project factors are: poor quality, cancelling after launch, high cost variance, substantially late delivery and functionality issues. Determining if a project is successful or not could be hard, the success can be determined by a combination of factors like scope, time or cost, but another one could be ROI, quality or the healthiness of the workplace [8].

However, failure aspects related to technical issues are not a critical factor [9]. It means that improving technical aspects of projects will not always lead to higher ratios of success. Moreover, studies like [10] found that:

- Business is usually or always out of sync with project requirements.
- Stakeholders need to be more involved and engaged in the requirements process.
- Business objectives are fuzzy.
- Requirements definition processes do not reflect business needs.

As it can be noticed, the "theory" of what to look for is clear, the problem is how to achieve it.

Building robust business-oriented requirements can be half of the solution; according to [11] one group of success factor is to manage strategy and stakeholders. In other words, the focus should be on obtaining clear business objectives, well-defined business cases, major stakeholders' alignment, a stable scope and executive support instead of concentrating on budget and scheduling. Taking these ideas into account, a first approach is to focus on the very beginning of the project, and increase the stakeholders' involvement in order to improve business modeling and specification of requirements.

Nevertheless, the stakeholders' involvement implies investing time, money, experience and patience from both parties: software developer organization and stakeholders.

Furthermore, one of the major problems with most business engineering efforts, is that the Software Engineering and the Business Engineering community do not communicate properly with each other [6]. If this is true, increasing the stakeholders' participation won't be a solution. But, what happened if both communities started to talk in another language? For example using games as a way of communication.

We believe that inclusion of games is a beneficial strategy to conceptualize a project together with the stakeholders and increase the success rate of projects.

3 Software Projects Inception Phase

Conceptualization begins at the early steps of projects, in the words of RUP [6], it occurs during the Inception phase. At the Inception phase the business process is documented in order to assure a common understanding among all stakeholders, the system is described determining the required functionalities, objectives, risks and constraints, to deliver, successfully, a product which meets the stakeholders' needs.

The Inception phase includes two core process workflows: Business Modeling and Requirements. And one core supporting workflow: Project Management.

During the Business Modeling workflow, the business process is documented using use cases in order to assure a common understanding among all stakeholders.

The Requirements workflow is in charge of describing what the system should do and allows the developers and the stakeholders to agree on that description. To achieve this, the required functionalities and constraints should be elicited, organized and documented.

Lastly, Project Management workflow is the art of balancing competing objectives, managing risks, and overcoming constraints to deliver, successfully, a product which meets the stakeholders' needs [6].

The outcomes of the Inception phase, defined by RUP, are:

- A vision document: a general vision of the core project's requirements, key features, and main constraints.
- An initial use-case model.
- An initial project glossary may optionally be partially expressed as a domain model.
- An initial business case, which includes business context, success criteria, and financial forecast.
- An initial risk assessment.
- A project plan showing phases and iterations.
- A business model, if necessary.
- One or several prototypes.

In order to achieve and create these outcomes, during an ordinary Inception phase, development teams deal with plenty of meetings with different stakeholders, final users and management staff getting a broad idea of their sometimes contradictory needs. Business analysts start to mediate inconsistent requests and the work that was intended to take a couple of weeks becomes longer.

A feasible solution, applied during Inception phase, could be to elicit, envision, design and prioritize the business needs until a minimal viable product is clearly seen by key stakeholders involved in the project, collaborating with the development team.

In light of this, three approaches to manage activities during the Inception phase are presented in the next subsections.

3.1 Agile Approach

Small releases and stakeholders', users' and customers' involvement in day-to-day activities are part of the philosophy of agile practices to face the requirements elicitation and prioritizing.

According to agile practices, conceptualization and development of a project occurs almost at the same time. It is achieved thanks to the Product Owner (PO), a role in charge of having a vision of what to build: they create and prioritize a list of desired features, the Product Backlog. PO must have a solid understanding of users, market place, competition, and future trends for the domain or type of system being developed. Also the PO requires working closely with key stakeholders [12].

An important complication of agile approach is that the PO could be more than one person, and most important, not all of them are ready or available to be involved in a day-to-day dynamic.

3.2   Traditional Approach

The traditional approach is a process-centered way of working. First, adequate stake-holders are identified. Later, fixed interviews with clients and stakeholders are held in order to identify their needs. The input of this process is obtained from meetings, focus groups, questionnaires or user observations. The information is transformed by the development team until a business model or requirements specification is created and agreed upon with stakeholders.

This approach is expensive and demands an arduous effort from both parties.

3.3   Game-Based Approach

Inception is a suitable phase to include stakeholders as a real part of the team and not only as a source of needs. They can be involved in depth because of the non-technical nature of the phase activities.

Key concepts of games such as goals, rules, challenge and interaction are also present in several real-world activities, for example a structured software development process [13].

On the other hand, developing software is a challenging activity that is seldom regarded as fun. Just like many other types of activities, it can be organized as a set of hierarchical and partially ordered challenges that must be overcome, often requiring several different skills from developers, and lots of teamwork effort [14].

In fields of industry, such as marketing and sales, games are used to help to understand customers, market, business opportunities and to improve everyday employee-related issues within an organization [15]. The application of these games has a broad spectrum: some examples taken from [16] define their variety. For instance, Empathy Map's objective is to gain insight and understanding for a targeted public image; How-Now-Wow Matrix pursuits the goal of selecting the best ideas as a group; Job or Joy aims at improving working environment of the organization; lastly, there are classical techniques, such as SWOT analysis and Pros/Cons adapted as games.

On the other hand, the application of such games tends to be isolated strategies in order to accomplish specific goals that may not be related to Software Engineering. Besides, they are not organized as a interrelated set of activities that reuses the result of a previous activity as an input for the next, thus making difficult to compose a method to attack more complex problems.

Few reports of games that support approaches to perform Software Engineering activities with objectives not related to education nor training can be found. One of those games is Software Quantum Metaphor, a game that makes an allusion to the chemical units known as quantum. The requirements of the software project are visualized as a bag of balls. Each ball visualizes one requirement or quantum. There are balls of different colors, each color representing a different state of analysis of the requirements [17].

Another game is the Labor Game Method, described in [18]. In this game the requirements are presented through cards on a board. Each card can be changed, or some cards can be added or removed from the board. This game permits to visualize all the requirements of the project, their structure and priorities.

Taking into account the uncommonness of games in Software Engineering development process and the lack of a method that puts together games in order to accomplish complex goals, the next section presents a method that combines a set of classical techniques with games, and is intended to improve the Inception phase of software projects.

4   ActiveAction Workshop

Entia [19] is a Mexican IT organization established in 2003 as a software developer organization conformed at the beginning by 4 employees, now 20. Entia has executed projects to construct custom software related to finance, retail, manufacturing and service sectors. They can be classified into "process systematization" and "business venture". The former consists in developing a software system that automates a specific process in the stakeholder's organization. The latter is aiming at adding a new service or product that will be offered to the stakeholder's clients.

In order to increase the projects' success rate and, consequently, the number of projects, Entia developed Innocamp strategy. Innocamp consisted in an intense workshop where all stakeholders collaboratively design their new custom software development project. This envisioning strategy was created in order to avoid continual coming and going between customers and Entia work team, caused by the lack of definition, clarity and consensus in their needs.

The Innocamp workshop let the organization achieve such benefits as: bringing all of the stakeholders to the organization at the same time and place; stakeholders and work team invested quality time during the workshop; complexity and size of a project was better understood by the stakeholders; and both parties developed synergy and emotional attachment to the project.

Since 2007 Innocamp has evolved into ActiveAction workshop. The evolution started with the inclusion of games as a way of entertaining the stakeholders during the workshop. Over the time the work team noticed that games helped to decrease resistance and increase concentration level of the stakeholders, causing an important impact on the results of each workshop.

ActiveAction is a game-based workshop focused on the software project conceptualization. It consists of the following activities:

- **Pre-Day:** It enables Entia to figure out stakeholders' real motivations that made the new project feasible. It includes negotiations between the customer and the organization, calendar planning for the rest –Days and collecting relevant customer information. The organization chooses adequate participants to take part in the following –Days.
- **Intensive-Day:** It is the actual method that gathers stakeholders and consultants during 8-12 h in the same place. 5 roles are required for the consultant team: Coach, Analyst, Process Engineer, Logistics and Customer Service and Support. The purpose of the Intensive-Day is to extract expectations, objectives, needs, risks, and functional and non-functional requirements from stakeholders using a collaborative and game-based strategy.

- **Post-Day:** The information gathered during Pre- and Intensive-Day is structured in order to create an IT strategy to deal with the project.
- **Action-Day:** on this –Day a meeting takes place in which the context, technological strategy and supplier proposals are discussed with the stakeholders in order to define the path that a project will take.

For the purposes of this paper, the Intensive-Day is presented in detail in the next subsection.

4.1 Intensive-Day Method

To carry out the Intensive-Day practices the following requirements and material are supplied: a room with 4.5 square meters per participant; speakers, a whiteboard, a glass wall or canvas, a projector, a TV, a special table for personal belongings and toys, such as little balls and office supplies like post-its, tacks, pencils and markers. Additionally each consultant needs a computer, Internet connection, source of electrical power and connection to the projector. All participants are seated in circle.

Intensive-Day method is composed by 19 practices that can be classified in two groups:

- **Core** practices produce meaningful outcomes for the Inception phase of the project and have a defined order.
- **Auxiliary** practices are focused on keeping order, reducing stress and maintaining high entertainment level. They have no special order to follow.

Figure 1 presents the Intensive-Day method where the game-based practices are marked with a "balero" icon, which is a traditional Mexican toy. The core practices are colored in light green, while the auxiliary are dark green. Flows between practices indicate the order of their execution.

The Intensive-Day method was expressed as a composition of practices using KUALI-BEH approach [20]. This approach establishes that a practice provides a systematic and repeatable way of work focused on the achievement of an objective. Each practice pursues the objective of producing a result that originates from an input.

Using these three elements, objective, input and result, the Intensive-Day game-based practices are described below.

4.2 Game-Based Practices

This section presents 10 game-involving practices.

Cover Story and Product Box (Core). The objective of the practice called Cover Story and Product Box [21] is to identify and express the stakeholders' objectives. An interesting fact is that the identified objectives should be expressed as if they had already been achieved.

The practice of Cover Story is suitable when the stakeholders' objectives belong to the area of improving their companies' image, functioning or prestige. The practice of Product Box is more appropriate if the stakeholders' objective is to own and sell a particular product.

In the former the stakeholders have to design a cover story for a magazine that would be published in the future and would narrate their success story; while in the latter they design a box that would contain the final product.

The input of these practices is objectives provided by the stakeholders, while the results are the cover story or the product box with comprehensive objectives.

Persons (Core). The objective of Persons is to identify priorities of cost, time and scope and their control strategy.

Three persons from the stakeholders' team portray each one of those variables, highlighting the pros and cons in order to clarify the importance of reducing or increasing their values. The stakeholders listen and watch the game and have to make a decision at the end, putting the three variables in a priority order.

The input of the practice is an example of a variable control matrix while the result is a matrix with the agreed values of cost, time and scope.

Role Play (Core). The Role Play objective is to simulate the organization's everyday process. The simulation consists in role-playing performed by stakeholders.

The role-play scenario is based on a frequent, but complex episode from everyday business-oriented activities in the stakeholders' organization. It also should have exceptions or miscommunication issues and needs to be rebuilt from a happy path.

The input of this practice is the actual process of the organization used as a role play script. The results are: a matrix of involved roles and a successful criteria list of an everyday process. It also provides contextual information of the stakeholders' organization.

Metaphor (Core). The Metaphor practice is based on the well-known game Lego Serious Play, developed by LEGO [22]. It is a structured process, where participants use LEGO bricks to create models that express their thoughts, reflections and ideas [23]. Here the prime objective is to obtain product expectations from every member of the stakeholders' organization.

The input is the matrix of involved roles and a metaphor to motivate generation of ideas that will be expressed as a LEGO figure. Each person of the stakeholders team builds a figure, explains its meaning and all of them are put together to interpret their relationships and interactions working as one team.

The results are: an interpretation of each LEGO figure and a better understanding of relationships among the roles in the matrix and within the process through the set of LEGO figures.

Speedboat (Core). The game practice of Speedboat is adapted from the game designed by Luke Hohmann [21] and its objective is to identify the project's potential risks by and for the whole stakeholders' team.

A speed boat is drawn on the top part of a whiteboard while the participants write any risks that can affect the project on post-its. Then they place them on the white board as if they were anchors. The lower a post-it is placed, the heavier the anchor is, which means a high risk that will impact the project the most. After all the "anchors" are set, a moderator groups similar ones together and the participants discuss the identified risk factors. The probability of occurrence is determined by the number of repeated risks and the impact by the lowest position.

The input of this practice is post-its used by each person, while the result is the list of identified risks associated with their probability of occurrence and impact.

AVAX Storming (Core). Based on the popular brainstorming technique [24], the practice of AVAX Storming is focused on finding the desired functional requirements for the system. All the participants write a one functional requirement on a piece of paper named Added Value Actionable Items (AVAX). Later AVAXes are grouped in order to sketch the system future modules.

This practice helps users to figure out the size of their project because soon the walls start to be filled up and the size of the project starts to grow. It is a visual way to show users that each need has its complexity and weight. If the project has a limited budget, each AVAX has a section where each person chooses if the requirement is "Needed" or "Desired". When all AVAX are posted on the wall, each person explains in detail their AVAX to the rest of the team opening it to discussion.

The result of the practice is a mind map of the identified AVAXes.

Buy a Feature (Core). The objective of the practice called Buy a Feature is to determine the scope of what will be built by the end of a single iteration. Buying a feature with a fixed budget is oriented to identify the top-rated requirements. The stakeholders' team has to buy the most necessary requirements and define the Minimum Viable Product (MVP).

The input of the practice is the list of required functionalities or AVAX, each with a price tag and fake bills for each stakeholder.

The result is the MVP or a list of AVAXes bought by the stakeholders' team. The MVP is also helpful to validate the project's feasibility.

Gunfight (Auxiliary). During ActiveAction there are "rules" to be followed, such as not to use smart phones or not to leave the room except during breaks. If anybody disobeys the rule, the rest of the participants can shoot at them with NERF guns until the "order" is restored, which is actually the objective of the practice.

Time Police (Auxiliary). The stakeholders' team chooses a person who will play the Time police role. He or she has a vuvuzela (horn) that is blown when somebody is talking about a closed topic or is digressing. The objective of the practice is to maintain discussions focused and to watch the time.

Circle of Trust (Auxiliary). The practice of Circle of Trust pursuits the objective that anybody in the room is allowed to express their opinions. To start a circle of trust, the interested person rings a bell and puts forward a topic. Every single person in the room has to express their sincere opinion on the question without being pressured.

4.3   Non-ludic Practices

This section presents the rest of the practices carried out during the Intensive-Day. Making a total of 9, they have no ludic aspects included.

- **Preparation:** planning and organizing the logistics required for the Intensive-Day.
- **Opening and Welcoming:** opening the day and presenting schedule, rules and logistics to the stakeholders.
- **Team Roles:** introducing the teams and explaining the roles to be used.
- **Concepts:** explaining concepts, dynamics and supporting tools to be used during the -Day.
- **Enclosing:** stakeholders define initial objectives, individual expectations and expand on the actual reasons for being there.
- **Packages:** categorizing needs and requirements expressed by the stakeholders. Identified packages are used to initially group desired functionalities obtained during AVAX Storming practice.
- **Non-functional Requirements:** determining the non-functional requirements of the desired system. Consultants use a fixed questionnaire based on the Pre-Day information.
- **Final Agreements:** closing all open topics, dispelling doubts and getting the last comments.
- **Closure and Raising a Toast:** applying a satisfaction survey of the -Day and making a farewell toast.

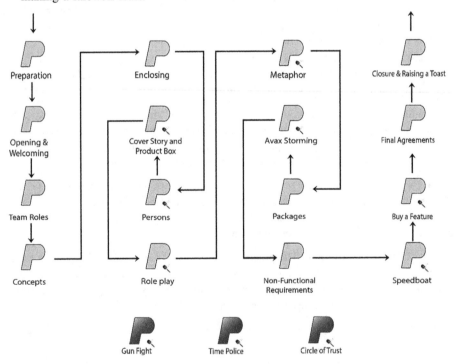

Fig. 1. Intensive-day method diagram.

4.4   Intensive-Day Work Products

During Intensive-Day the Coach guides practices' execution while the Analyst and the Process Engineer are responsible for concentrating the results of each practice in the following work products:

- Contextual information and Everyday Process.
- Stakeholders' expectations.
- Objectives and priorities.
- Functional requirements.
- Strategy and work to be done.
- Non-functional requirements.
- Risks analysis.
- Consequences of undertaking the project for the developing organization.
- Minimum Viable Product.
- Supplier proposals summary.

A summary of the work products is concentrated in a mind map. The left part of the mind map provides a description of each work product, while the right part summarizes the Functional Requirements as AVAXes, see Figs. 2 and 3.

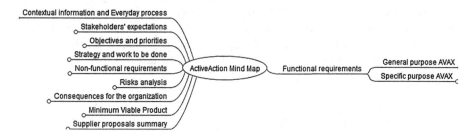

Fig. 2. ActiveAction mind map.

Based on the objective of each practice, the generated work products can be associated to the Inception phase outcomes defined earlier. Table 1 shows the association between outcomes and work products. The Intensive-Day practice that generates the respective work product is shown between parentheses.

In an intent to verify the usefulness of the Intensive-Day products, RUP evaluation criteria were taken into account. According to [6] the following criteria were identified:

- Stakeholder concurrence on scope definition and cost/schedule estimates.
- Requirements understanding as evidenced by the fidelity of the primary use cases.
- Credibility of the cost/schedule estimates, priorities, risks and development process.

The mapping between outcomes shows that the stakeholders agree on the scope definition through *Functional requirements* and *Minimum Viable Product*, also top requirements are prioritized. Besides, an initial cost and schedule estimation can be derived from *Strategy and work to be done*.

Table 1. Mapping of outcomes.

Inception phase outcomes	Intensive-day outcomes
A vision of the project's core requirements, key features, and main constraints	Contextual information (metaphor)
An initial use-case model	Functional requirements (AVAX storming)
An initial project glossary or a domain model	Contextual information (metaphor) Stakeholders' expectations (persons)
An initial business case, which includes business context, success criteria, and financial forecast	Objectives and priorities (cover story or product box) Stakeholders' expectations (Persons)
An initial risk assessment	Risks analysis (speedboat)
A project plan showing phases and iterations	Strategy and work to be done (mind map)
A business model, if necessary	Everyday process (role play)
One or several prototypes	Minimum viable product (buy a feature)

Understanding of requirements is achieved through the AVAXes, which are initially defined by the stakeholders' team. Priorities are obtained using *Objectives and priorities* which are expressed directly by stakeholders. Identified objectives and priorities consequently affect the selection of features of the *Minimum Viable Product*. Later, risks are identified and weighed during *Risk Analysis*. Finally the credibility of the resulting work products predicts to be high due to the fact that they were created with active participation of the stakeholders.

4.5 AVAX Mind Map for Project Tracking

The AVAX mind map, in particular its right part which contains the functional requirements in the form of AVAXes, is used along the project as a tool to track its health and progress.

For this purpose each AVAX has a set of valid states:

- **Identified:** applies to all AVAXes identified during the Intensive-Day.
- **Posterior:** applies to AVAXes that are added by the stakeholder after the Intensive-Day. A "light bulb" icon is used to represent it.
- **Deleted:** applies to an AVAX which is not needed anymore or is outside the priorities of scope, cost or time. A "No trespassing" icon is used to represent it.
- **Delivered:** applies to an AVAX which is passed on to the stakeholders. A "check" icon is used to represent it.
- **Validated:** applies to an AVAX which is approved by the stakeholders and gets a "smiley face" icon.
- **Externally Done:** applies to an AVAX which is provided by an external organization. An "exclamation mark" icon represents this state.

Fig. 3. AVAX detail and status.

Figure 3 shows *Invoices* package (in green) that contains the AVAXes *Create invoice* and *Show Invoices* (in blue) which is decomposed into three branches: *Cancel invoice*, *Send invoice* and *Export invoice* (in red). The branch *Cancel invoice* generates three more branches: *Cancel payment*, *Send cancelation* to seal it and *Send notification* (in black). Their states with their respective icons can be observed in the map.

To maintain trustworthy relationships between stakeholders and development team, the AVAX Mind Map used by the organization for project development and tracking must be exactly the same as the one generated during the Intensive-Day.

5   Results

ActiveAction workshop resulted in a successful game-based strategy that has improved the Inception phase of the software development projects based on the fact that: stakeholders express their ideas freely in an unstressed environment; simulate real-life scenarios to identify exceptions; prioritize risks and identify requirements in a collaborative manner.

ActiveAction has been applied in 19 projects with the following time distribution of the Intensive-Day: 65 % dedicated to game-based core practices, 17 % of resting time and 18 % of non-ludic practices.

5.1   ActiveAction Advantages and Disadvantages

ActiveAction has resulted in a powerful tool for Entia, which started to sell it as a separate service, giving the customer the right to choose Entia or another organization for further construction.

The following are ActiveAction workshop benefits identified by Entia:

- Software products' origin and rationale are known and understood by stakeholders.
- Each and every of the stakeholders' points of view are taken into account.
- The whole team takes the project as something of its own, not something imposed.
- Relatively relaxed in-game environment helps to come to agreements among many people.
- Applying games helps to establish rules, objectives and behaviors in a natural way.
- Customer satisfaction and emotional engagement is easily achieved.
- The Inception phase is completed within three weeks.
- The Entia successful project rate has grown 25 percentage points, from the initial 56 % up to 81 %.

On the other hand, ActiveAction requires a high demand of skills, concentration and knowledge from the Coach, Analyst and Process Engineer roles. 12 h in-a-row, independently of the activity to do, requires a lot of effort and concentration, so finding adequate pace is important. Besides, the organization must distribute carefully their key personnel, consultant team members, between their daily work and the ActiveAction Days, which can compromise other projects of the organization.

The following are drawbacks identified by Entia:

- Difficulty in getting stakeholders together if they are geographically distributed.
- Difficulty involving stakeholders in the –Day's activity due to their passivity.
- Uneasiness to share opinions when the "boss" is present.
- Including stakeholders' clients into the Intensive-Day may not always be possible.

5.2   Validation and Improvement Suggestions

In order to get feedback on limitations and identify opportunities of improvement, three surveys are applied both to stakeholders and consultants. A scale from 1 to 5 is used to rate each item, also a free comment section is also considered.

Two of the surveys are applied at the end of the Intensive-Day with the objective to measure stakeholders and consultants' satisfaction. The third survey is applied to stakeholders at the end of the Action-Day. The grades average from the last 10 ActiveActions is summarized in Table 2.

Table 2. Surveys' results summary.

Intensive-day stakeholders' survey	Average
Overall experience	4.8
Achievement of expectations	4.8
Intensive-day consultants' survey	**Average**
Overall experience	4.4
Stakeholders team involvement	4.7
Consultants team performance	4.7
ActiveAction stakeholders' survey	**Average**
Proposed solution	4.6
Has ActiveAction benefited your organization?	4.7
Would you use ActiveAction again?	4.8

To improve ActiveAction stakeholders have expressed a number of suggestions: to split the Intensive-Day into two sessions; add ambient music; reduce the duration of breaks but increase their number and make a summary at the end of each practice, mainly in Buy a Feature practice.

Consultants have observed that: information about stakeholders is fundamental to prepare Intensive-Day; a list of pre-prepared questions about the stakeholders' business is useful to "re-activate" discussions; more "standing-up" practices should be added; playing with LEGOs is not fun for everybody; AVAXes could be created and reviewed in teams instead of individually; Non-Functional Requirements practice could be omitted if the stakeholders do not have technical background; and lastly, if the product owners are not present Intensive-Day must be postponed.

6 Conclusions and Future Work

Considering the non-technical nature of software project Inception activities, stakeholders can be involved in depth and join software developer organization at this particular moment. In fact, addressing factors like executive support, engagement of key stakeholders and clearly defined needs increases the success rate of a project. However, stakeholders' involvement is a complex action that requires investment of extra effort and time and be intrusive for both parties.

The strategy of using games within software developing projects in order to address and improve collaboration between stakeholders and development teams can be considered as a novel and beneficial approach. Consequently, game-based approach has been adopted as a strategy to improve the Inception phase outcomes.

ActiveAction is a workshop service which objective is to clarify and process stakeholders' needs and priorities. During the Intensive-Day, game-based activities provide a favorable environment in which stakeholders and development teams collaborate and produce results of great importance for the Inception phase of a project.

Two lines are identified as future work: (i) to replicate the workshop in affiliates and (ii) to define a continuous improvement process for ActiveAction. At the moment one affiliate has replicated its first three ActiveActions with promising results. Moreover, documenting the method will reduce the possibility of variation and find ways to improve.

Finally we can conclude that the inclusion of games in such a challenging and over-whelming activity as software projects inception, is feasible and reported promising results which benefit both stakeholders and software developer organizations.

Acknowledgements. The authors thank Miriam Eréndira Jiménez-Hernández and Roberto Azrael Medina-Díaz for on-site observation and initial analysis of the data.

This work has been funded by the GEODAS-BC project (Ministerio de Economía y Competitividad and Fondo Europeo de Desarrollo Regional (FEDER), TIN2012-37493-C03-01); GLOBALIA project (Consejería de Educación, Ciencia y Cultura (Junta de Comunidades de Castilla — La Mancha) and FEDER, PEII11-0291-5274); SDGear project (TSI-100104-2014-4), framed under the ITEA 2 Call 7, and co-funded by "Ministerio de Industria, Energía y Turismo (Plan Nacional de Investigación Científica, Desarrollo e Innovación Tecnológica 2013-2016) and FEDER"; the Graduate Science and Engineering Computing (PCIC-UNAM) and the grant scholarship program of CONACYT.

References

1. Michael, D., Chen, S.: Serious Games: Games That Educate, Train, and Inform, 1st edn. Muska & Lipman/Premier-Trade, Cincinnati (2005)
2. Abt, C.: Serious Games. Viking Press, New York (1970)
3. Serious game initiative. http://www.seriousgames.org/
4. The Standish Group International, Inc., CHAOS Summary for 2010 (2010)
5. Stepanek, G.: Software Project Secrets: Why Software Projects Fail, 1st edn. Apress, New York (2005)
6. Kruchten, P.: Rational Unified Process – An Introduction, 3rd edn. Addison-Wesley, Boston (2003)
7. Gartner survey shows why projects fail. http://thisiswhatgoodlookslike.com/2012/06/10/gartner-survey-shows-why-projects-fail/
8. Ambler, S.: Defining success. Dr. Dobb's J. (2007). http://www.drdobbs.com/architecture-and-design/defining-success/202800777
9. Ibrahim, R., Ayazi, E., Nasrmalek, S., Nakhat, S.: An investigation of critical failure factors in information technology projects. J. Bus. Manage. IOSR **10**(3), 87–92 (2013). ISSN 2319-7668
10. Geneca, LLC: Doomed from the start? Why a majority of business and IT teams anticipate their software development projects will fail. Geneca Industry Survey (2011)
11. Bloch, M., Blumberg, S., Laartz, J.: Delivering Large-Scale IT Projects on Time, on Budget, and on Value. Insights & Publications, McKinsey & Company, New York (2012)
12. Mountain goat. http://www.mountaingoatsoftware.com/scrum/product-owner/
13. Passos, E., Medeiros, D., Neto, P., Clua, E.: Turning real-world software development into a game. In: Proceedings of the Brazilian Symposium on Games and Digital Entertainment, pp. 260–269 (2011). ISBN: 978-0-7695-4648-3
14. Claypool, K., Claypool, M.: Teaching software engineering through game design. In: Proceedings of the Innovation and Technology in Computer Science Education Conference, vol. 37, no. 3, pp. 123–127 (2005). ISBN: 1-59593-024-8
15. Gamestorming. http://www.gogamestorm.com/
16. Innovation games. http://innovationgames.com/
17. Knauss, E., Schneider, K., Stapel K.: A game for taking requirements engineering more seriously. In: Proceedings of the International Workshop on Multimedia and Enjoyable Requirements Engineering, pp. 22–26 (2008). ISBN: 978-0-7695-3626-2
18. Torvinen, V.: The labour game method. In: Proceedings of the International Workshop on Database and Expert Systems Applications, pp. 382–386 (1999). ISBN: 0-7695-0281-4
19. Entia. http://www.entia.com.mx/
20. Morales, M., Oktaba, H.: KUALI-BEH kernel extension. Annex B (informative). In: Essence – Kernel and Language for Software Engineering Methods. Object Management Group (2012)
21. Hohmann, L.: Innovation Games: Creating Breakthrough Products through Collaborative Play, 1st edn. Addison-Wesley Professional, Boston (2006)
22. LEGO: LEGO Serious Play: Open Source. The LEGO Group, Billund (2010)
23. Cantoni, L., Faré, M., Frick, E.: User Requirements with LEGO. University of Lugano. webatelier.net & NewMinE Lab, version 1.0 (2011)
24. Osborn, A.: Applied Imagination: Principles and Procedures of Creative Problem Solving, 3rd edn. Charles Scribner's Sons, New York (1993)

Natural Language Generation Approach for Automated Generation of Test Cases from Logical Specification of Requirements

Richa Sharma[1](✉) and K.K. Biswas[2]

[1] School of Information Technology, IIT, Delhi, India
Sricha@Gmail.Com
[2] Department of Computer Science, IIT, Delhi, India
Kkb@Cse.Iitd.Ernet.in

Abstract. The quality of the delivered software relies on rigorous testing performed and testing is as good as the test-cases. However, designing good test-cases is a challenging task. The challenges are multi-fold and designing test-cases is often delayed towards the end of implementation phase during software development. In this paper, we propose an approach to automatically generate the test-cases from logical form of the requirements specifications during early phases of software development. Our approach is based on courteous logic representation of requirements. The knowledge stored in the courteous logic representation of requirements is used to automatically generate trivial as well as functional test-cases. We present an evaluation of the effectiveness of our generated test-cases through the case-studies conducted. We further report our observations for the empirical study conducted with subjects from different backgrounds.

Keywords: Test cases · Logical specification · Courteous logic · Natural language generation

1 Introduction

Software testing is an important and integral activity of the software development. The testing process entails designing effective test-cases; generating test-data; executing test-cases for the test-data and comparing the results of execution against actual results mentioned in test cases [1]. Amongst these activities, designing effective test-cases, that can uncover crucial functional faults, remains a key-challenge. Test cases can be derived from requirements specifications, design artifacts or the source code [1]. Requirements Specifications provide useful pointers for designing functional test cases and conducting functional testing; the design artifacts influence architectural testing and, the source code provides technical know-how for test case design as well as for the requisite test data formats. The research effort towards automation of testing has resulted in some very useful tools like JUnit, Visual test, SQA test, Testmate [2] etc. However, designing functional test cases based on requirements is still a hard problem. Several authors have proposed approaches for designing functional test cases from UML diagrams like [4–8]; from use-case specifications [9, 10] and also, from

© Springer International Publishing Switzerland 2015
J. Filipe and L. Maciaszek (Eds.): ENASE 2014, CCIS 551, pp. 125–139, 2015.
DOI: 10.1007/978-3-319-27218-4_9

user-stories used in Agile development [11]. These suggested approaches assist test engineers by providing them with automatically generated test-cases. These test cases can be further refined by manual intervention, if required, thereby reducing the effort and time spent on writing the test-cases. However, the challenge involved with these approaches arises from the fact that the use-cases and user-stories are expressed in Natural Language (NL) and, the UML diagrams also depend on requirements specifications expressed using NL. The inherent ambiguities and inconsistencies, present in NL specifications of requirements, often lead to misinterpretations and difference of understanding between the client and the development team.

In this paper, we propose an approach to generate test cases automatically from logical specification of requirements to circumvent these challenges. Logical specifications are formal in nature and, have the advantage of automated analysis and validation [3]. Our test cases generation approach is based on courteous logic based representation of the software requirements; the adequacy of these representations of the software requirements for inconsistency resolution has been shown in [12]. We use these representations of requirements for automated generation of test cases. Since formal representations are not the preferred form of representation in industry, therefore, we have also proposed semi-automated approach towards the generation of courteous logic form of representation of requirements from their corresponding NL representations in our work [13]. This increases applicability of courteous logic based requirements representations in industry. This work is an extension of our preliminary investigation of using Natural Language Generation (NLG) approach for generating test cases from courteous logic based representation of requirements [15]. We have extended our earlier work [15] of generating trivial test cases to functional test cases. In this work, we have further validated the effectiveness of our approach through an empirical study conducted with 9 subjects – 5 of these subjects are graduate students having taken course on Software Engineering and, the 4 subjects are software professional having experience from 2 to 4 year in industry.

Our approach involving test case generation from courteous logic representation of requirements borrows heavily from semantic head-driven approach for NL Generation [14]. NL generation has its own challenges for generating meaningful NL text. However our main focus is not NL generation, we have adopted and modified Shieber et al.'s approach in our work to formulate functional test cases.

The rest of the paper is organized as follows: Sect. 2 presents an overview of the courteous logic form of requirements specifications along with the related work done. Section 3 presents our approach of automated test-case generation followed by the case studies and the empirical study conducted in Sect. 4. In Sect. 5, we present discussion and conclusion.

2 Related Work

2.1 Courteous Logic Representation of Requirements

Courteous Logic, as proposed by Grosof, is a non-monotonic logic form [18]. Courteous Logical representation is an expressive subclass of ordinary logical representation with which we are familiar and, it has got procedural attachments for prioritized conflict handling. First Order Logic (FOL) has not become widely popular for two main reasons: it is pure belief language and, secondly it is logically mono-tonic; it can not specify prioritized conflict handling which are logically non-monotonic.

Our motivation behind using Courteous Logic representation of requirements is that real-world knowledge and system requirements for any system in real-world correspond to common-sense form of reasoning. This common-sense reasoning is non-monotonic in nature and, therefore there is a need for non-monotonic logic for representing real-world requirements. Of various available forms of non-monotonic logic like default logic [16, 17], we preferred courteous logic for its simplicity, ease of use and English-like constructs. Our Courteous Logic representations for requirements are based on IBM's CommonRules, available under free trial license from IBM alpha works [19]. In these representations, prioritization is handled by assigning optional labels to the rules (or predicates) and, specifying priority relationship between the rules using in-built "overrides" predicate. The scope of'what is conflict' is specified by pair-wise mutual exclusion statements called "mutex's". For example: a mutex may specify that the grades of student can have only one value at one point of time. There is an implicit mutex between a rule (or predicate p) and its classical negation.

An illustration of requirements representation in Courteous Logic:
Let us consider a scenario of book issue in a library. The requirements are often expressed with inconsistent and, possibly repetitive statements as we observed:

- If a person is a library member, then he can borrow the book.
- If a book is available, then library member can borrow the book.

These two statements of specifying the above-mentioned scenario are contradictory to each-other – the second statement adds one more condition for borrowing the book in addition to a person's being library member, namely: 'availability of the book'. We have considered such a simple scenario to illustrate how minor mistakes in expressing the requirements can result in faulty software. One may consider that everyone knows about the library rules; however, it is not always possible that requirements analysts as well as test engineers are familiar with the domain knowledge under study. In the absence of formal specifications, requirements cannot be validated in the early phases of software development, nor an appropriate set of test cases be generated. Ambiguity and inconsistency in requirements may percolate to the test cases as well. We have looked for solution to such a scenario in our earlier work. The above-mentioned requirements statements, when translated to courteous logic representations appear as:

```
<rule1> if   librarymember(?X) and  book(?Y)
          then  borrow(?X, ?Y).
<rule2> if   librarymember(?X) and  book(?Y) and
             status(?Y, available)
          then  borrow(?X, ?Y).
```

These two rules correspond to the two requirements statements stated above. Both of these rules are labeled as <rule1> and <rule2> respectively. Without any additional information, rule 1 may allow a book to be issued even if it is not available. This is contrary to real-world supposition that only an available book can be issued to a library member. The result of inference engine indicates that these requirements are inconsistent in nature and the requirements are corrected in consultation with domain experts. The suggested correction to these requirements can be added as another rule to above courteous logic representation of requirements as:

```
overrides(rule1, rule2).
```

Having obtained formal and consistent set of requirements specifications, we can design better test-cases; the process of which, we have automated in this work.

2.2   Test-Case Generation

Automated functional test generation has been an intriguing problem in research arena. Significant amount of effort towards test case generation has been reported in survey reports too like [20, 21]. Kaur and Vig [20] have attempted to find the most widely used UML diagrams for automated test case generation and the corresponding advantages. In addition to this, they have explored the type of testing addressed in various works and what are the challenges involved. Their findings indicate that activity diagrams, state diagrams and a combination of use-case diagram and activity diagram have been mostly used for generating test cases. They observe that functional testing has been the extensively studied; however, the challenges involved are incomplete or incorrect requirements specifications and UML diagrams. The survey conducted by Gutierrez et al. [21] also suggests that UML models and use-case specifications have been mostly used for automatically generating the test cases.

Survey reports summarize that UML diagrams and requirements specifications in the form of use-cases (an NL representation) have been explored most for automated test case generation. Activity Diagrams have been used for the purpose in the works of [4–6]. The fact that activity diagrams represent the behavior of the real-world system for a given scenario can be attributed to the use of activity diagrams for test case generation. State charts form the basis of generation of test cases in the works of [7, 8]. Use-cases also describe the expected behavior of the system. Therefore, use cases have also been used for test case generation as reported in the works of [9, 10]. The user-stories used in agile development have also been considered for automatically generating test cases [11]. However as reported in the survey of Kaur and Vig [20], the challenge involved with these approaches is that of the representation of requirements. NL requirements representation results in ambiguity, incompleteness and inconsistency of requirements and consequently, generation of incorrect test cases.

However, there are few instances where test cases have been generated from either formal representation of requirements or using approaches or formal intermediate requirements representation like [22, 23]. Pretschner [22] propose test case generation from constraint logical representation of the behavior of reactive (embedded) systems. Mandrioli et al. [23] suggest an interactive tool for semi-automated generation of functional test cases for real-time systems using the formal specification language, TRIO. We also support formalism in requirements representation and our focus is on business applications for which we have found courteous logic a suitable choice. In our work, we have made use of courteous logic based representation of requirements for automatically generating test cases as discussed in the following section.

3   Our Approach

Our approach borrows from semantic-head- generation algorithm for unification-based formalisms as proposed by Sheiber et al. [14]. However, our goal is different from NLG that has its own challenges. NLG requires "glue-word" in addition to the grammar rules followed for generating NL expressions from the source input [24]. Our interest lies only in generating the test-cases from courteous logic representations of requirements. Our courteous logic representations have been generated semi-automatically (only override predicates have been added manually), therefore the variable names and the

---

Algorithm: Test-case Generation from Courteous Logic Representation of Requirements

Input: Set of requirements represented in the form of courteous logic
Output: Set of test-cases for the input requirements

Processing Steps:
1.   For each rule in the input file (collection of rule-base), extract the label (optional) and the pivot predicate (identified as predicate after 'then') and store them for future reference.

2.   Start generating test-cases for the rule-body:
3.   If there is a single predicate in rule-body,

   (i)   Then, for each variable (recognised by a prefix character '?'), add test cases for Nullness check and validity check. Express actual result as "Error Message displayed" for null and invalid values.

   (ii)   Else, store each of the predicates joined by conjunctions separately. Process each of these predicates as described in the step (i)

4.   Perform this step for each of the predicates in the rule-body for entering valid values of the variables. The result of execution of these predicates is that the rule head gets fired, i.e. the predicate in rule-head is executed. Express this actual result as:

   (i)   If the rule-head starts with "value" followed by another string S, then extract the first parameter, (P1) of the rule-head then actual result is: "value of S is P1".

   (ii)   Else express the actual result as "<rule-head> is executed.

5.   Generate all the possible combinations of the labels. If the pivots in combination have no priority relationship, then each of these holds good else if the labels en-countered in combination have higher precedence relationship expressed in any of the 'override' predicates, then

   (i)   Search for the stored pivots in the labelled rule and ensure that conditions for both pivots corresponding to the labels in 'override' hold good.

   (ii)   Add test-case stating: "Enter valid values for variables such that both the <pivots> hold good".

   (iii) Actual result in this case is expressed in similar manner as in step 5

Note: The pivots expressed in angular brackets <> will be replaced by their actual values for the rule under process. The logic in step 5 – (i) follows from the way we have gener-ated the courteous logic representation of NL requirements.

Fig. 1. Algorithm for Test-Case Generation.

predicate names are more meaningful and self-understood. This makes the generated test cases more *readable* and *comprehensible*. We have conducted an empirical study in order to validate the comprehensibility and readability of the test case generated using our approach. The algorithm for generating test-cases is shown in Fig. 1.

We first identify the pivot element for the input rule like Shieber et al.'s approach but we are not interested in considering it as semantic head unlike their approach. In our case, the pivot element is the predicate or the rule-head of the given rule. For example: for the library rules discussed in Sect. 2.1, the pivot element is 'borrow'. Next we consider the body of the rule, which can simply be another predicate or clause (like rule-head) or conjunction of two or more predicates. We process each of these predicates one by one as described in the algorithm above. Test cases are first laid out for null checks, invalid as well as valid values of the variables in each of the predicate of the requirements expression. We, then, generate functional test cases by combining the predicates in the rule-body and also by considering the rules that are relevant to a given scenario. The step of functional test case generation needs to take into account conflicting, prioritizing as well as exceptional scenarios too. For this purpose, our algorithm takes into account the labels for each of the rules and generates all the possible combinations of those labels. It is possible that all the generated combinations are not semantically correct. Nevertheless, such combinations indicate pointers to the possibilities that need to be taken care of.

NL generation is performed only for expressing the actual output. Since the actual outputs of test-cases are in terms of the pivot elements, which have been earlier generated from NL document only, we need not have to refer to any 'glue-words' in between. This reduces the complexity considerably in our approach.

4 Case-Study

We conducted our case-study for test case generation on requirements from various business domains like banking, academics and corporate action. In this Section, we will consider same examples as illustrated in our earlier work [12] so that establishing the relationship between the requirements studied and the generated test-cases will be easy. In this current work, we have modified the previous algorithm for generating the courteous logic representations to generate predicates and variable with complete words instead of mnemonics. This modification has been done to reduce number of look-ups in mnemonics database for test case generation. Therefore, the representations of requirements illustrated in following sub-sections will slightly differ in having complete words instead of mnemonics.

4.1 Test-Cases Generated Using Our Proposed Algorithm

Example 1 - Representing and Prioritizing Conflicting Views (Academic Grade Processing). This example is about the specifications of students' grade approval process where the students' grades are approved by the course-coordinator, the department head and the dean. The expected behavior of the system refers to the fact that at any point in time, approval from department head holds higher priority over course-coordinator; and approval from dean higher priority over department head and in turn, the course coordinator. In order to capture this observable behavior, we have earlier suggested the use of courteous logic representations as shown below:

```
<new>
   if assignGrades           (
   ?RegistrationNumber, ?Year, ?Semester, ?Group, ?Subject,
   ?GradePoint          )
   then value_Status(
   new, ?RegistrationNumber, ?Year, ?Semester, ?Group, ?Subject);

<cdn>
    if approvedby           (
   ?RegistrationNumber, ?Year, ?Semester, ?Group, ?Subject,
   ?GradePoint, ?Status,   coordinator )
   then value_Status(
   coordinatorApproved, ?RegistrationNumber,   ?Year, ?Semester,
   ?Group, ?Subject );

<hod>
   if approvedby     (
   ?RegistrationNumber, ?Year, ?Semester, ?Group, ?Subject,
   ?GradePoint, coordApproved,   hod   )
   then value_Status(
   hodApproved, ?RegistrationNumber, ?Year,   ?Semester, ?Group,
   ?Subject   );

<dean>
   if  approvedby  (
   ?RegistrationNumber, ?Year, ?Semester, ?Group, ?Subject,
   ?GradePoint,     hodApproved, dean)
   then value_Status        (
   deanApproved, ?RegistrationNumber, ?Year,   ?Semester, ?Group,
   ?Subject   );
   overrides(cdn, new);
   overrides(hod, new);
   overrides(dean, new);
   overrides(hod, cdn);
   overrides(dean, cdn);
   overrides(dean, hod);
   MUTEX

      value_Status( ?Status1,        ?RegistrationNumber, ?Year,
      ?Semester, ?Group, ?Subject   )

      AND

      value_Status( ?Status2, ?RegistrationNumber, ?Year, ?
      Semester, ?Group, ?Subject   )
   GIVEN notEquals( ?Status1, ?Status2 );
```

The test cases generated corresponding to above requirements for nullness, validity checks and for functional test-cases have been presented in Table 1 below:

Table 1. Test Cases – Example 1.

Sl. No.	Test case	Action performed	Actual result
1.	Null Checks for 'assignGrades'	Enter null value of RegistrationNumber	Error Message displayed
2.		Enter null value of Year	Error Message displayed
3.		Enter null value of Semester	Error Message displayed
4.		Enter null value of GradePoint	Error Message displayed
5.	Validity Checks for 'assignGrades'	Enter invalid value of RegistrationNumber	Error Message displayed
6.		Enter invalid value of Year	Error Message displayed
7.		Enter invalid value of GradePoint	Error Message displayed
8.	Execute assignGrades	Enter valid values for variables: RegistrationNumber, Year, Semester, Group, Subject, GradePoint	Value of Status is new
9.	Execute approvedby (under label – cdn)	Enter valid values for variables such that both the 'assignGrades' and 'approvedby' hold good	Value of Status is coordinatorApproved
10.	If cases: cdn and hod have executed	Enter valid values for variables such that the rules under label: cdn and hod hold good	Priority Relationship exists and hod has higher priority over cdn. Value of Status is hodApproved
11.	*If cases: new and dean have executed*	*Enter valid values for variables such that the rules under label: new and dean hold good*	*Priority Relationship exists and dean has higher priority over cdn. Value of Status is deanApproved*
12.	If cases: new, cdn and hod have executed	Enter valid values for variables such that the rules under label: new, cdn, and hod hold good	Priority Relationship exists and hod has higher priority over cdn and cdn has higher priority over new. Value of Status is hodApproved
13.	*If cases: new, cdn and dean have executed*	*Enter valid values for variables such that the rules under label: new, cdn and dean hold good*	*Priority Relationship exists and dean has higher priority over cdn and cdn has higher priority over new. Value of Status is deanApproved*
14.	If cases: new, cdn, hod and dean have executed	Enter valid values for variables such that the rules under label: new, cdn, hod and dean hold good.	Priortiy Relationship exists and dean has higher priority over hod and hod has higher priority over cdn and cdn has higher priority over new. Value of Status is hodApproved.

In the above table, the test cases 1 to 4 are examples of *null checks*; the cases - 5 to 7 are examples of *validity test cases* whereas, 8th and 9th test-cases represent *trivial functional test cases*. The points 10 to 14 illustrate few of the possible functional test-cases for the given scenario of grade assignment and approval. The 10th test case corresponds to combination of two labels; similarly, 12th and 14th test cases respectively represent the combinations of three and four labels respectively. However, each of such combination may not be semantically or logically correct. For example: 11th and 13th test cases (indicated in italics) violate the given workflow scenario of grade approval. The current version of our algorithm of test case generation does not take into account any workflow or sequencing information between different rules. Therefore, the *'action performed'* as well as the *'actual result'* in Table 1 are incorrectly stated for these hypothetical scenarios – 11 and 13. Nevertheless, these test cases serve as examples of negative testing.

Example 2 – Representing Default and Exceptional Scenario Processing (Saving and Current Account Processing). Consider the account processing scenario of a bank customer. Let us consider that a bank customer can have a current account and a saving account. The customer can choose one of these accounts as default account for any transaction that he wants to carry out. The customer is also free to select the other account for some of his transactions. The NL expression for such default operation and the associated exception can be easily understood by the involved stakeholders as well as developers. But what is often overlooked by developers is the implicit interpretation here – the account chosen for default processing should remain unaffected in case selection is made for the non-default account and often, this is uncovered till testing phase. Such overlooked implicit interpretation results in implicit internal inconsistency. Such a defect can be easily detected during RE phase if we have an executable model for representation of requirements that can sufficiently express the domain knowledge. We have translated the requirements for this scenario in courteous logic from NL as:

```
<def-deposit>
    if deposit(?TransactionId, ?Client, ?Amount) and
    holds(?Client, ?AccountId)  and default(?AccountId)
    then add_Amount(?Client, ?AccountId, ?Amount);
<sel-deposit>
    if deposit(?TransactionId, ?Client, ?Amount) and
    holds(?Client, ?AccountId) and
    option(?Client, ?TransactionId, select, ?AccountId)
    then add_Amount(?Client, ?AccountId, ?Amount);
<def-withdraw>
    if withdraw(?TransactionId, ?Client, ?Amount) and
    holds(?Client, ?AccountId) and default(?AccountId)
    then subtract_Amount(?Client, ?AccountId, ?Amount);
<sel-withdraw>
    if withdraw(?TransactionId, ?Client, ?Amount) and
    holds(?Client, ?AccountId) and
    option(?Client, ?TransactionId, select, ?AccountId)
    then subtract_Amount(?Client, ?AccountId, ?Amount);
    overrides(sel-deposit, def-deposit);
    overrides(sel-withdraw, def-withdraw);
    MUTEX
    add_Amount(?Client,    ?Account1, ?Amount)         AND
    add_Amount(?Client,    ?Account2, ?Amount)
    GIVEN notEquals(?Account1,?Account2)
    MUTEX
    subtract_Amount(?Client, ?Account1, ?Amount) AND
    subtract_Amount(?Client, ?Account2, ?Amount)
    GIVEN notEquals(?Account1,?Account2)
```

We applied the algorithm described in Fig. 1 to the deposit and the withdraw transactions separately as each of these transactions represent different scenarios. The test cases generated corresponding to above requirements for nullness, validity checks and for functional test-cases are presented in Table 2 below:

Table 2. Test Cases – Example 2.

Sl. No.	Test case	Action performed	Actual result
1.	Null Checks for 'deposit'	Enter null value of Transaction Id	Error Message displayed
2.		Enter null value of Client	Error Message displayed
3.		Enter null value of Amount	Error Message displayed
4.	Validity Checks for 'deposit'	Enter invalid value of Transaction Id	Error Message displayed
5.		Enter invalid value of Client	Error Message displayed
6.		Enter invalid value of Amount	Error Message displayed
7.	Execute deposit	Enter valid values for variables: Transaction Id, Client and Amount	addAmount is executed
8.	Execute option	Enter valid values for variables: Client, Transaction Id and Account Id	option is executed
9.	If cases: def-deposit and sel-deposit have executed	Enter valid values for variables such that the rules under label: def-deposit and sel-deposit hold good.	Priority Relationship exists and sel-deposit has higher priority over def-deposit. addAmount is executed.
10.	If cases: def-withdraw and sel-withdraw have executed	Enter valid values for variables such that the rules under label: def-withdraw and sel-withdraw hold good.	Priority Relationship exists and sel-withdraw has higher priority over def-withdraw. subtractAmount is executed.

Here, the first three test cases (1 to 3) indicate examples of *null checks* and the cases 5 to 7 examples of *validity test cases*. The next two cases, namely 7th and 8th test-cases are examples of *trivial functional test cases*. These cases correspond to the 'deposit' transaction. The test cases for 'withdraw' transaction are generated on similar lines. The test cases – 9 and 10 respectively bring out the functional test-cases for the two transactions, namely: deposit and withdraw. Since there are two labels for each of these two transactions, therefore, only one combination is generated in each case. Corresponding to each of these transactions (deposit and withdraw), the rule for selected account is found to have higher priority over default account when both the scenarios hold good and accordingly, the priority relationship is identified. With the identified priority relationship, the selected account only gets affected and, not the default one.

Example 3 – Representing and Prioritizing Views of Multiple Stakeholders (Corporate Event Processing). This example scenario considers a corporate action event announced on a security. If a client is holding the security on which event is announced, then that client is eligible to get the announced benefits of the event. These benefits can either be in the form of cash or stock or both. The types of benefits disbursed to the clients vary from one event type to another; it also depends on various other factors like base country of the security on which event is announced and if the client is opting for an option etc. It is possible that the announced benefit is in the form of stock whereas, client has opted for cash. In such a scenario, client is disbursed the equivalent cash amount and vice-versa. Following the algorithm in Fig. 1, similar test cases (nullness-check, validity-check, trivial functional test case and scenario-representative functional test cases) were generated successfully for this scenario too just as for Examples 1 and 2. We are not representing these test cases to avoid repetitiveness and space-constraints. Instead, we present below the summary of the test cases generated using our approach referred to as 'system-generated test cases' in Table 3 below:

Table 3. Summary of System-Generated Test-cases.

Scenario	Nullness test case	Validity test case	Functional test case (trivial + scenario)	Total test-case for each scenario
1.	7	7	4 + 11	29
2.	4	4	5 + 2	15
3.	5	5	4 + 33	47

In the above table, the number of nullness and validity test cases corresponds to the count of individual variables because similar checks for these variables need to be performed for each of the predicate in logical representation of requirements. The count of functional test-cases for scenario is governed by the number of labels present in the input requirements-set in logical form.

The case-studies as discussed above indicate that an adapted version of Shieber et al.'s NLG algorithm can be successfully applied to generate trivial as well as functional test cases from logical representation of requirements. However, it is important to study the real effectiveness of the generated test cases as perceived by practitioners and this calls for an empirical study as presented in following sub-section.

4.2   Empirical Study

We have conducted an empirical study with objective to find if the system-generated test cases are effective in terms of readability, comprehensibility and coverage of the given scenario. The subjects were carefully chosen from varying backgrounds in order to ensure the fairness of the study. 9 subjects participated in the study – 5 participants are students (indicated by 'STU' in Table 4) who have taken course in Software Engineering and worked on the project that requires them to write test-cases for the project. 4 participants are software professionals (indicated by 'SPS' in Table 4) having 2 to 4 years of industry experience. The study was designed to be conducted in two phases:

1. The subjects were presented with the scenarios and were asked to write the test cases for those scenarios just by reading the NL representation of the scenario. Next, they were asked to code the scenario and then, write the test cases.
2. The subjects were shown the system generated test-cases and their opinions were taken on the same on the four point Likert-scale of questions for the questionnaire: (1) Are the test cases readable and comprehensible? and, (2) Do you think these test cases cover the scenario exhaustively?

We first conducted an hour session to introduce the tasks involved to the participants to make sure that they are comfortable with the study and their tasks. The second phase was executed after the completion of the first one so that the subjects do not get influenced by the system generated test cases. In order to cross-check that subjects' participation is attentive and enthusiastic, we intentionally left the Example 3 ambiguous by removing few parts of it. We found that none of 'STU' participants were able to attempt the ambiguous third example, whereas 'SPS' participants raised concerns about ambiguity and attempted as much as they could. Table 4 below summarizes the number of test cases reported by the subjects. The responses for each of the STU and SPS category are averaged across their respective counts 5 and 4, dropping the fractional part.

Table 4. Summary of Test-cases by Subjects.

Scenario	Nullness test case	Validity test case	Functional test case	Total test-case for scenario
Subjects — (*STU/SPS*) — Before Coding				
1.	0/0	3/2	4/4	7/6
2.	0/2	0/2	4/4	4/6
3.	NA/1	NA/2	NA/3	NA/6
Subjects — (*STU/SPS*) — After Coding				
1.	0/2	5/2	5/5	10/9
2.	1/3	1/4	4/6	6/13
3.	NA/3	NA/4	NA/3	NA/10

For the question on readability and comprehensibility, all the participants unanimously reported complete agreement. Table 5 below indicates the responses of the subjects on Likert's scale for the second question on test coverage; the responses being averaged for respective categories:

Table 5. Summary of Responses to question – 2.

Scenario	Subjects	Completely agree (%)	Agree (%)	Disagree (%)	Completely disagree (%)
1.	STU	81	19	0	0
2.	STU	87.5	12.5	0	0
3.	STU	NA	NA	NA	NA
1.	SPS	89	11	0	0
2.	SPS	88	12	0	0
3.	SPS	84	16	0	0

4.3   Observations - Empirical Study

We have interesting observations from the summary of results displayed in Table 4, namely:

1. The number of test cases reported by both the categories of the participants is very less as compared to the system generated test cases.
2. The focus of the participants is more towards the functional test cases as opposed to the possible null checks and validation checks.
3. The number of reported test cases increases consistently for both scenarios after coding.
4. Though experience helps but the familiarity of the domain plays a role in designing test cases. The 'STU' participants are more familiar with scenario-1 and they perform a bit better than 'SPS' participants, whereas, the situation is opposite for scenario-2.

None of the participants identified negative test-cases in scenario-1. In case of scenario-2, the participants could not identify the possibility of both the default account and selected account option existing simultaneously. The test-case corresponding to this possibility is reported by 'SPS' participants after coding though. None of the participants are in disagreement with the coverage of the test cases. However, few participants are not found to be in complete agreement with (possibly extra) negative test cases and the trivial functional test cases as evident from the summary of responses in Table 5. We had a post-study session with the participants where the common queries were regarding these two types of test cases. After the discussion, the participants realized the importance of negative test cases and the trivial functional test cases which need to be carried out for unit testing a component.

The above-mentioned observations strengthen the need of formal representation of requirements as well as an automated approach towards generating the test cases.

4.4   Mitigating Threats to Validity

The subjectivity of the participants may influence any empirical study. We, therefore, tried to mitigate the possible threats to validity of our study by choosing the participants from differing backgrounds and explaining the details of the study beforehand. A quick random test was taken during the introduction session for the book-borrowing rules illustrated in Sect. 2.1 to ensure that participants have a fair idea of writing test cases. We also presented scenario-3 was given with ambiguous statements to cross-check that participants are actually following the given scenarios and working accordingly and we observed that concerns were raised by the participants for this particular scenario.

5   Discussion and Conclusion

In this paper, we have presented an approach to automatically generate trivial as well as functional test cases from courteous logic representation of the requirements. The approach borrows from semantic head-driven approach for NL Generation proposed by

Shieber et al. The advantage of our approach is that courteous logic representations have English-like constructs and easy to process. Secondly, we are generating these representations from NL requirements, therefore the courteous rules representing requirements become self-explanatory and with limited set of support words, we have been able to generate the functional test cases automatically. We have validated the applicability of our approach to various business scenarios through different case-studies. We show the usability and effectiveness of the test cases generated through an empirical study that indicates that the generated test cases are comprehensible and good in terms of functional coverage. We further intend to refine our algorithm to include semantic and sequential information too.

References

1. Ammann, P., Offutt, J.: Introduction to Software Testing. Cambridge University Press, USA (2008)
2. Incomplete List of Testing Tools. http://research.cs.queensu.ca/ ~ shepard/testing.dir/under. construction/tool_list.html
3. Tsai, J.J.P., Weigert, T.: HCLIE: a logic based requirement language for new software engineering paradigms. Softw. Eng. 6(4), 137–151 (1991)
4. Boghdady, P.N., Badr, N.L., Hashem, M., Tolba, M.F.: A proposed test case generation technique based on activity diagrams. Int. J. Eng. Technol. 11(3), 35–52 (2011)
5. Kansomkeat, S., Thiket, P., Offutt, J.: Generating test cases from UML activity diagrams using the condition classification method. In: 2nd International Conference on Software Technology and Engineering (ICSTE 2010), pp. V1-62–V1-66, San Juan (2010)
6. Li, L., Li, X., He T., Xiong, J.: Extenics-based test case generation for UML activity diagram. In: International Conference on Information Technology and Quantitative Management (ITQM 2013), pp. 1186-1193 (2013)
7. Hartmann, J., Vieira, M., Foster, H., Ruder, A.: A UML-based approach to system testing. J. Innovations Syst. Softw. Eng. 1(1), 12–24 (2005)
8. Offutt, J., Abdurazik, A.: Generating tests from UML specifications. In: France, R.B. (ed.) UML 1999. LNCS, vol. 1723, pp. 416–429. Springer, Heidelberg (1999)
9. Heumann, J.: Generating test cases from use cases. In the Rational Edge, e-zine for Rational Community (2001)
10. Ahlowalia, N.: Testing from use cases using path analysis technique. In: International Conference on Software Testing Analysis and Review (2002)
11. Kamalkar, S., Edward, S.H., Dao, T.M.: Automatically generating tests from natural language descriptions of software behavior. In: 8th International Conference on Evaluation of Novel Approaches to Software Engineering, France (2013)
12. Sharma, R., Biswas, K.K.: A Semi-automated approach towards handling inconsistencies in software requirements. In: Maciaszek, L.A., Filipe, J. (eds.) Evaluation of Novel Approaches to Software Engineering, pp. 142–156. Springer, Heidelberg (2012)
13. Sharma, R., Biswas, K.K.: Using norm analysis patterns for requirements validation. In: IEEE 2nd International Workshop on Requirements Patterns (RePa), pp. 23–28 (2012)
14. Shieber, S.M., Noord, G.N, Moore, R., Pereira, C.N.: A Semantic-head-driven generation algorithm for unification-based formalisms. In: 27th Annual Meeting of the Association for Computational Linguistics, pp. 7–17 (1989)

15. Sharma, R., Biswas, K.K.: Automated generation of test cases from logical specification of requirements. In: 9th International Conference on Evaluation of Novel Approaches to Software Engineering (ENASE), Lisbon, Portugal (2014)
16. Reiter, R.: A logic for default reasoning. Artif. Intell. **13**, 81–132 (1980)
17. Nute, D.: Defeasible logic. In: Proceedings of International Conference on Applications of Prolog (INAP 2001), pp. 87–114. IF Computer Japan (2001)
18. Grosof, B.N.: Courteous logic programs: prioritized conflict handling for rules. IBM Research Report RC20836, IBM Research Division, T.J. Watson Research Centre (1997)
19. Grosof, B.N.: Representing e-commerce rules via situated courteous logic programs in RuleML. Electron. Commer. Res. Appl. **3**(1), 2–20 (2004)
20. Kaur, A. and Vig, V.: Systematic review of automatic test case generation by UML diagrams. Int. J. Eng. Res. Technol. **1**(7) (2012)
21. Gutierrez, J.J., Escalona, M.J., Mejias, M., Torres, J.: Generation of test cases from functional requirements, a survey. In: 4th workshop on System Testing and Validation, Potsdam, Germany (2006)
22. Pertschner, A.: Classical search strategies for test case generation with constraint logic programming. In: International Workshop of Formal Approaches to Software Testing of Software, pp. 47–60 (2001)
23. Mandrioli, D., Morasca, S., Morzenti, A.: Generating test cases for real-time systems from logical specifications. ACM Trans. Comput. Syst. **13**(4), 365–398 (1995)
24. Grasso, F.: Natural language processing: many questions, no answers. http://www.academia.edu/2824428/Natural_Language_Processing_many_questions_no_answers

Visualization, Simulation and Validation for Cyber-Virtual Systems

Jan Olaf Blech[✉], Maria Spichkova, Ian Peake, and Heinz Schmidt

RMIT University, Melbourne, Australia
{janolaf.blech,maria.spichkova,ian.peake,heinz.schmidt}@rmit.edu.au

Abstract. We present our framework for visualization, simulation and validation of cyber-physical systems in industrial automation during development, operation and maintenance. System models may represent an existing physical part – for example an existing robot installation – and a software simulated part – for example a possible future extension of the physical industrial automation setup. We call such systems cyber-virtual systems. Here, we present our VxLab infrastructure for visualization using combined large screens and its applications in industrial automation. The methodology for simulation and validation motivated in this paper is based on this infrastructure. We are targeting scenarios, where industrial sites which may be in remote locations are modeled, simulated and visualized. Modeling, simulation and the visualization can be done from different locations anywhere in the world. Here, we are also concentrating on software modeling challenges related to cyber-virtual systems and simulation, testing, validation and verification techniques applied to them. Software models of industrial sites require behavioral models of both human and machine oriented aspects such as workflows and the components of the industrial sites such as models for tools, robots, workpieces and other machinery as well as communication and sensor facilities. Furthermore, facilitating collaboration between sites and stakeholders, experts and operators is an important application of our work. This paper is an extension of our previously published work [1].

Keywords: Cyber-physical systems · Virtual interoperability testing · Simulation · System modeling · Formal specification · Visualization

1 Introduction

Operation, development, maintenance (including modifications and extensions) of industrial automation facilities such as factories or mining sites profit from software support. This comprises software based monitoring, controlling and collaboration tools. The software support requires visualization capacities as well as software models of the physical entities involved and ways to reason about them. Industrial automation facilities typically comprise machinery like robots and their components. Components may serve as actuators: tools, conveyor belts,

© Springer International Publishing Switzerland 2015
J. Filipe and L. Maciaszek (Eds.): ENASE 2014, CCIS 551, pp. 140–154, 2015.
DOI: 10.1007/978-3-319-27218-4_10

work pieces or pipes, valves and pumps in cases were fluids or gases are processed. Sensors can be found throughout industrial automation sites. The data gathered from the sensors may be stored in a central facility.

Hardware-in-the-loop (HIL) approaches [2] are now standard in the development of system components in domains such as automative systems, e.g., [3], avionics and also in industrial automation. In HIL, parts of a system are simulated in software to test a distinct system component. In this paper, we are going one step further and aim at simulating different parts of an industrial site. We do not restrict our approach to the development, but also aim at supporting operation and maintenance of industrial automation facilities. Furthermore, we aim at visualizing remote facilities or parts of them. This is especially crucial when developing, operating or maintaining industrial sites located in areas that are difficult to access such as mines in the Australian outback and oil rigs. It facilitates collaboration between these different sites and sharing knowledge between them.

In the case where components of a system are manufactured at different places, transport from component development and production locations to integration and deployment sites can significantly increase the whole development costs as well as time. Integration can reveal additional work tasks and further transportation of the system's parts may be necessary. If a system's components are bulky or heavy, this may also delay optimization and correction.

For this reason, we present our existing visualization infrastructure - the "x" laboratory (VxLab). We aim at enabling decision making and collaborative work among leaders, experts and technicians distributed globally. Our facility addresses multiple use cases (signified by the "x" parameter). These comprise scientific computing, gaming, software development, engineering and architecture. VxLab is a generalization of x = "Interoperation Testing" realized in the VITELab, the Virtual Interoperability Test Lab (VITELab)[1] a global laboratory connecting industry and university sites and providing a collaboration platform for experimental design and testing of cyber-physical systems. Among its aims are to reduce development costs by simulating and virtually testing possible deployments before the system is actually physically set up. We also present the corresponding new and ongoing research directions towards combining visualization and software support for reasoning about industrial automation facilities. The ideas featured in this paper comprise the following ingredients:

- The use of VxLab/VITELab, and in particular the Global Operations Visualization (GOV) Lab, a high resolution multi-screen visualization facility.
- Software models for system components that comprise spatio-temporal information about a component's behavior and ways to reason about them, testing and simulation.
- The combination and integration of these for industrial automation.

---

[1] VITELab is an eResearch facility of the Australia-India Research Centre for Automation Software Engineering (AICAUSE), a partnership between RMIT University and the ABB Group (Australia and India) with support from the VIctorian State Government, http://rmit.edu.au/research/aicause.

Our work is a step towards software solutions facilitating global collaboration between developers, operators and maintenance of industrial sites. This paper is an extension of our previous work [1].

2   Related Work

Different languages exist for the modeling of embedded and automation systems. Standards like IEC 61131-3 and IEC 61499 target the software part of control systems and thus specify the behavior of machinery. In the scientific community different modeling languages such as the Petri-Net semantics based BIP [4] for distributed asynchronous systems and Modelica, providing means for modeling and simulation of systems have been established, cf. [5–7]. Modelica is object-oriented and its latest extensions allow modeling of system requirements [8] as well as simulation of technical and physical systems [9]. Modeling theories for distributed hybrid system such as SHIFT [10] and R-Charon [11] guarantee a complete simulation and compilation of the models, but do not support verification or analysis of the system on the modeling level. Same limitations also apply to the input language of the model checkers UPPAAL [12] and PHAVer [13]: the verification capabilities do not match the whole expressiveness of the modeling languages.

Assigning semantics to logical entities for categorizing and reasoning about them is a one goal of our models for industrial automation facilities. The general underlying concept has been made popular in the context of the semantic web [14] and ontologies [15].

The modeling of industrial automation sites involves spatial aspects. For example, robots must ensure a behavior that guarantees collision avoidance and the correct handling of workpieces. Systems that comprising thermal aspects like heat exchangers need adequate models to cover their behavior. SpaceEx [16] allows the modeling of continuous hybrid systems based on hybrid automata. It can be used for computing overapproximations of the space occupied by objects. In [17] a process algebra for 3D objects is provided. [18] provides and explains results on spatial interpretations. A quantifier-free rational fragment of logic suitable for describing spatial scenarios has been shown to be decidable in [19]. Logics for spatio-temporal reasoning go back to the seventies. The Region Connection Calculus (RCC) [20] includes spatial predicates of separation. RCC features predicates indicating that regions do not share points at all, points on the boundary of regions are shared, internal contact where one region is included and touches on the boundary of another from the inside, overlap of regions, and inclusion.

Many approaches on mechatronic/cyber-physical systems omit an abstract logical level of the system representation and lose the advantages of the abstract representation. The work presented in [21] defines an extensive support to the components communication and time requirements, while the model discussed in [22] proposes a complete model of the processes with communication. In traditional development of embedded systems e.g., [23], the system is usually separated into software and hardware parts as soon as possible, at an early stage of the development process. This does not always benefit the development process, because when using an abstract level of modeling the difference in the nature of components does not necessarily play an important role. [24, 25] independently suggest to use a platform-independent design in the early stages of system development. The approach presented in [24] introduces the idea of pushing hardware- and software-dependent design as late as possible, however, the question of the current practical and fundamental limitations of logical modeling in comparison to cyber-physical testing, is not completely answered. In comparison to [24], the focus of [25] is on reutilisation and generalisation of two existing software systems development methodologies (both elaborated according to the results of the case studies motivated and supported by DENSO Corporation and Robert Bosch GmbH) for application within the cyber-physical domain to benefit from the advantages these techniques have shown. The question, how deep we can go on the modeling of cyber-physical systems on the logical level is still open in both approaches. The goals presented here are also related to hybrid commissioning [26].

The idea of early analysis of critical system faults has the goal to identify faults which mutate the safety critical behavior of the system, and to identify test scenarios which can expose such faults from an abstract modeling level, i.e. by generation of tests (both for real system and its model) from formal specifications or from the CASE tool models (cf., e.g., [27–29]). The approach has certain limitations due the abstract nature of the formal model serving as a base for the test generation as well as an underlying assumption of existence of a precise formal model of the system being developed. Even when taking into account these limitations and assumptions, these approaches allow automatization of test case design and make the design process more stringent. VITELab and the described research complements commercially available visualization software for collaboration purposes in industrial automation such as DELMIA[2]. The approach described here, is building on (semi-)formal models which carry semantic meaning and are suitable for automatic interpretation and processing, whereas the DELMIA focus is even more on visualization.

3 From Cyber-Physical to Cyber-Virtual Systems

Let us discuss an example scenario based on the ideas of the virtual interoperation testing. In an industrial plant we require the integration/interoperability of $n + 1$ bulky/heavy robots (cf. Figs. 1 and 2): a robot of the type $AType$ (lets call it robot A) is assembled in location L_A, the n other robots are of a different type $BType$ and are assembled in a different location L_B. The robots are in different locations and making them work together in a different shared deployment location requires extensive simulation, testing and collaboration.

Assuming in addition that the n robots of type $BType$ perform simultaneously similar movements and actions (e.g., they stamp similar details on workpieces on a conveyor belt and are doing the same movements, even in the case their stamps are different), we can simulate their behavior using a single robot B:

---

[2] http://www.3ds.com/products-services/delmia/products/all-delmia-products/.

its actuator information will be replicated to obtain n virtual models $B_1, \ldots, B_n$, and its sensor information will be extended by the composition of the modeled sensor information from $B_1, \ldots, B_n$. The sensor information of the robot A will be a composition of the real sensor data and the sensor data modeled according to the actions of $B_1, \ldots, B_n$.

Thus, to check the interoperability of the robot A and n robots of the type $BType$ on the level of virtual interoperability testing, we need only two real robots: a robot A and a robot B. Moreover, they could be located in L_A and L_B respectively, because the simulator and visualization facility may take the role of a physical medium between them, allowing to ignore the real distance between robots and also allowing to have a visualization of the test and simulation not only at L_A and L_B, but also on the third place L_C, where the corresponding laboratory is located.

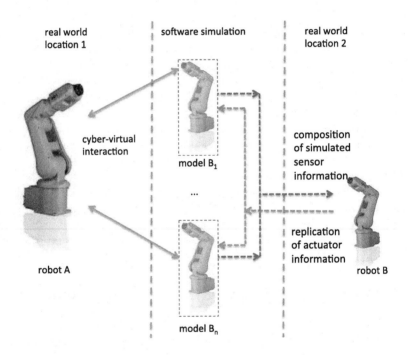

Fig. 1. Cyber-virtual communication.

General ideas for using the virtual interoperability test lab (VITELab) for the use of remote cyber-physical integration/interoperability testing in a virtual environment as a middle step between an abstract modeling and real testing were presented in [30]. Figure 3 shows the VITELab facility in operation, viewed from the GOV Lab. VITELab gives a platform for a new level of simulation and integration: interoperability simulation and testing is performed early and remotely, for example while cyber-physical components are in the prototyping

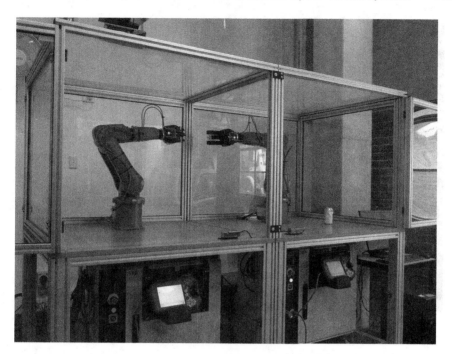

Fig. 2. Real robot setup offered by VxLab using an ABB IRB 120.

stage i.e. on the workbench: individual components (e.g., robots, manufacturing cells), are connected in a suitable virtual environment, without being deployed at the same place physically. Successful testing and simulation could significantly reduce the well-documented costs arising from discovery of design faults after implementation.

Research connected to VITElab is influenced by larger cooperations in the industrial automation domain. Remote integration and testing allows for an integration and testing phase of a real system assuming a certain level of abstraction where the network, the virtual environment and the remote embodiments may be abstractions themselves. This level of abstraction includes real physical components of the system (in the case of the VITElab project, e.g., real robots and production plants) and more characteristics of the network, environment and embodiments. Our models and their visualization can give us the possibility to identify:

- a number of problems and inconsistencies on the early stage of system development and verify especially important system's properties before the real system is build and integrated, and
- possible weak points in the system (such as some timing properties, feature interactions, component dependencies) which we should focus on, during the testing phase.

Fig. 3. VITElab in operation.

4   Research Challenges and Corresponding Projects

This section presents research challenges connected to cyber-virtual systems, VITELab, simulation and validation in more detail. We have identified the following research challenges in our scenario:

- Simulation and the visualization of simulation runs. Including the interaction with the simulation and visualized output.
- Testing, verification and validation of cyber-virtual scenarios.
- Gaining expertise and knowledge from joint work using visualization and simulation.
- Sharing and making expertise and knowledge available for similar development projects and for related operation and maintenance tasks in related facilities.

In our work, we propose two ingredients related to software models for addressing these challenges:

- (Semi-)formal descriptions based on human factors approaches to achieve better readability/usability and understandability.
- Spatial behavioral models that capture the characteristics of entities and components in industrial automation. We are interested in establishing a type system for these components.

4.1   Existing VITELab Projects

The research challenges identified in the context of VITELab fall into the network, cloud and distributed computing areas, and are covered by the following ongoing projects:

- *Network Connectivity* between sites with specialist equipment is supported by dedicated links and research software stacks.
- The *Cyber-physical Simulation Rack (CSRack)*, is a multi-node cloud server rack with attached RAID storage provides parallel cloud computing capability to support modeling and simulation and the capability to act as a 'cloudlet' gateway to major national and international cloud facilities such as NeCTAR[3].
- The *Global Operations Visualization (GOV) Lab* project, provides videoconference and streaming capability to remote sites combined with a large high resolution tiled display wall.
- The *Advanced Manufacturing Robot Interoperation Test (AMRIT) lab* provides industrial robots connected to the GOV lab. The robots comprise arms, sensors and cameras as "eyes on the robots".

Furthermore, research challenges have been identified in our existing projects:

- Collaborative engineering [31] aims at facilitating collaboration for maintenance, services and operation between distributed sites. Such sites can comprise manufacturing, mining and oil facilities, and operation centers. Visualization is an important part of this project.
- Additional challenges can be found, in the connection of software based development tools for industrial automation systems to the described infrastructure. Such tools may need to undergo a redesign of the software architecture to enable this, cf. [32].

4.2   Interacting with Robots and Their Simulations

Simulation and visualization requires adequate ways to interact with the simulated and visualized cyber-physical system. To exemplify this and in addition to classical input devices, one way of interacting with simulated and physical facilities is shown in Fig. 4. Interaction is done in a hand-movement-based[4] way that allows the manipulation of robots and their simulated counterparts which is part of our VxLab infrastructure. In the picture, a human (on the left) is interacting with a simulated robot (middle). The position of the hands is detect and visualized on the right.

---

[3] National eResearch Collaboration Tools and Resources Project, https://www.nectar.org.au.

[4] Realized using a LeapMotion https://www.leapmotion.com device.

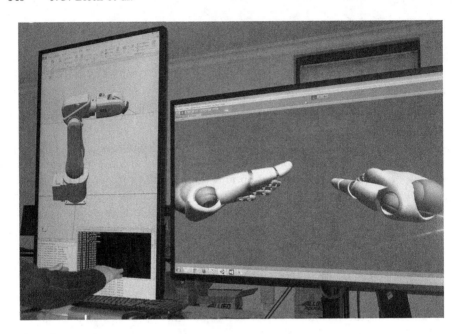

Fig. 4. Interacting with the simulation using free-hand movements.

5 From (Semi-)Formal Methods to Visualization and Validation

A starting point for our work is a HIL approach and is depicted in Fig. 5. Here, the interplay of a physical robot with a virtual simulated robot is shown. The actions of the physical robot to the environment are observed passed to the robot simulation and reacting actions are calculated. These actions are (by)passed to the sensors of the physical robot to simulate the interplay.

The interplay can be analyzed both by software tools as well as human inspection. The human based analysis profits from visualization capabilities for the display of the simulated robot and the monitoring of the physical counterpart.

5.1 Human Factors and Formal Models

To enable simulations we need (semi-)formal descriptions of robot behavior, which should not only fit for the simulation purposes but also be readable for system/verification engineers. In our approach we follow the ideas based on human factor analysis within formal methods [33,34]. This allows to have short and readable specifications of component behavior. It is appropriate for switching between different modeling, specification and programming languages and is suitable for the application of specification, reasoning and proof methodology [35,36].

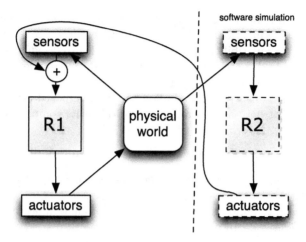

Fig. 5. Robot in the loop.

5.2 Formal Proofs and Verification

In the case of formal proofs, one of the main points of this methodology is an alignment of the future proofs during the specification phase to make the proofs simpler and appropriate for application in practice. One direction for reasoning about a system represented in a formal specification framework, is the verification of its properties by translating the specification to a Higher-Order Logic and subsequently using the theorem prover following [37].

5.3 Spatial Behavioral Types

Our (semi-)formal models comprise spatial behavioral. This can be assigned to both physical and virtual simulated robots, their components and other entities interacting with them as shown in Fig. 6. Following the ideas presented in [38] these spatial behavioral models can serve as a type system similar to types systems in higher programming languages like C and Java which come with basic types like integers, Strings and floating point values as well as composed types like records or classes. Here, we regard (spatial) Behavioral Types (BT). BT act as types for virtual or physical entities in our automation scenarios. They are characterised by the following core concepts:

- *Abstraction.* BT represent aspects of robots, robot components and other entities in industrial automation. BT abstract from details concerning interactions and internal structure.
- *Conformance.* Type conformance of BT is used to relate entities in industrial automation correctly to a BT.
- *Refinement.* BT should comprise a notion of spatio-behavioral refinement that allows replacing a component by a refined one. For example, the concept of

refinement shall allow replacing a robot by a newer version that essentially provides the same functionality plus some new features.

- *Compatibility.* Compatibility checking of BT is used to decide whether a component does indeed match required needs based on provided and expected BT. It should be decidable and automatic.
- *Inference.* A BT framework should allow to infer composed BT. For example, the BT of a robot may be inferred from the BT of its components.

5.4   Spatial Behavioral Types for Simulation and Validation

BT can serve as a specification basis for the components of robots and the robots composed of them.

BT can be used to build models of industrial automation facilities. Using BT based specifications, we can perform:

1. Simulation and *visualization* for human inspection and collaboration between developers, operators and maintenance personnel.
2. Automatic spatio-temporal reasoning for *collision detection* of robots and other entities.
3. Checking automatically the required *sensor ranges* and regions affected by physical entities.
4. Guaranteeing correct *interplay of tools and workpieces* in time and space.

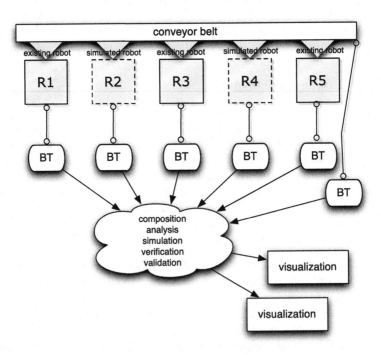

Fig. 6. Combining virtual and physical robots for simulation and validation.

5. Simulating the replacement of an entity such as a robot arm by another (refined) version.
6. Documenting behavior of system installations and sharing this for collaboration.

The BT concept is following the idea of interface automata first presented in [39]. It has been proposed as a type system for OSGi systems in the past [38]. Theorem prover export and interactive verification of properties were studied in [40] and may be an issue for future work together with human-factor analysis. Checking compatibility and means to make behavioral system descriptions compatible were examined in [41]. For checking the spatio-temporal properties in our scenarios we incorporate the BeSpaceD [42] tool. Checks in BeSpaceD are done by converting spatio-temporal models or BT and required properties into SMT and SAT problems and applying suitable solving techniques such as the z3 SMT solver [43]. Another formal methods based approach aimed at combining human factors with formal methods for reasoning about space in an automation context was presented by us in [44].

6   Conclusions

The presented research is ongoing work and part of larger cooperations with an industrial automation company. In this paper, we presented an overview on the existing VxLab/VITELab infrastructure facilitating remote collaboration by large screen/multi screen visualization. The aim of this infrastructure is to reduce the development costs by simulating and virtually testing possible deployments before the system is actually physically set up. We have highlighted connected research questions, as well as explained the VITELab applications in operating, developing and maintaining industrial automation facilities. The connection to spatial behavioral models and a related type system for the simulation of industrial automation facilities and the connection to visualization capacities was presented in more detail.

Acknowledgements. We would like to thank staff from RMIT ITS, PropertyServices, eResearch and the VxLab/VITELab team, in particular Lasith Fernando, Ravi Sreenivasamurthy, Garry Keltie, and Nicolas Vergnaud.

References

1. Blech, J.O., Spichkova, M., Peake, I.D., Schmidt, H.W.: Cyber-virtual systems - simulation, validation and visualization. In: Filipe, J., Maciaszek, L.A. (eds.) ENASE 2014 - Proceedings of the 9th International Conference on Evaluation of Novel Approaches to Software Engineering, Lisbon, Portugal, 28–30 April 2014, pp. 218–225. SciTePress (2014)
2. Schlager, M.: Hardware-in-the-loop simulation (2008)
3. Isermann, R., Schaffnit, J., Sinsel, S.: Hardware-in-the-loop simulation for the design and testing of engine-control systems. Control Eng. Pract. **7**, 643–653 (1999)

4. Basu, A., Bozga, M., Sifakis, J.: Modeling heterogeneous real-time components in BIP. In: 4th IEEE International Conference on Software Engineering and Formal Methods (SEFM), pp. 3–12. IEEE (2006)

5. Donath, U., Haufe, J., Blochwitz, T., Neidhold, T.: A new approach for modeling and verification of discrete control components within a modelica environment (2008)

6. Fritzson, P.: Principles of Object-Oriented Modeling and Simulation with Modelica 2.1. Wiley-IEEE Computer Society Press, New York (2004)

7. Anderson, A., Fritzson, P.: Models for distributed real-time simulation in a vehicle co-simulator setup. In: Nilsson, H. (ed.) Proceedings of the 5th International Workshop on Equation-Based Object-Oriented Modeling Languages and Tools. Linkoping University Electronic Press (2013)

8. Tundis, A., Rogovchenko-Buffoni, L., Fritzson, P., Garro, A.: Modeling system requirements in modelica: definition and comparison of candidate approaches. In: Nilsson, H. (ed.) Proceedings of the 5th International Workshop on Equation-Based Object-Oriented Modeling Languages and Tools. Linkoping University Electronic Press (2013)

9. Fritzson, P.: Introduction to Modeling and Simulation of Technical and Physical Systems with Modelica. Wiley-IEEE Computer Society Press, New York (2011)

10. Deshpande, A., Göllü, A., Varaiya, P.: SHIFT: a formalism and a programming language for dynamic networks of hybrid automata. In: Antsaklis, P.J., Kohn, W., Nerode, A., Sastry, S.S. (eds.) HS 1996. LNCS, vol. 1273, pp. 113–133. Springer, Heidelberg (1997)

11. Kratz, F., Sokolsky, O., Pappas, G.J., Lee, I.: R-Charon, a modeling language for reconfigurable hybrid systems. In: Hespanha, J.P., Tiwari, A. (eds.) HSCC 2006. LNCS, vol. 3927, pp. 392–406. Springer, Heidelberg (2006)

12. Behrmann, G., David, A., Larsen, K.G.: A tutorial on UPPAAL. In: Bernardo, M., Corradini, F. (eds.) SFM-RT 2004. LNCS, vol. 3185, pp. 200–236. Springer, Heidelberg (2004)

13. Beek, D.A.V., Man, K.L., Reniers, M.A., Rooda, J.E., Schiffelers, R.R.H.: Syntax and consistent equation semantics of hybrid Chi. J. Logic Algebraic Program. **68**, 129–210 (2006)

14. Berners-Lee, T., Hendler, J., Lassila, O., et al.: The semantic web. Sci. Am. **284**, 28–37 (2001)

15. Staab, S., Studer, R., Schnurr, H.P., Sure, Y.: Knowledge processes and ontologies. IEEE Intell. Syst. **16**, 26–34 (2001)

16. Frehse, G., Le Guernic, C., Donzé, A., Cotton, S., Ray, R., Lebeltel, O., Ripado, R., Girard, A., Dang, T., Maler, O.: SpaceEx: scalable verification of hybrid systems. In: Gopalakrishnan, G., Qadeer, S. (eds.) CAV 2011. LNCS, vol. 6806, pp. 379–395. Springer, Heidelberg (2011)

17. Cardelli, L., Gardner, P.: Processes in space. In: Ferreira, F., Löwe, B., Mayordomo, E., Mendes Gomes, L. (eds.) CiE 2010. LNCS, vol. 6158, pp. 78–87. Springer, Heidelberg (2010)

18. Hirschkoff, D., Lozes, É., Sangiorgi, D.: Minimality results for the spatial logics. In: Pandya, P.K., Radhakrishnan, J. (eds.) FSTTCS 2003. LNCS, vol. 2914, pp. 252–264. Springer, Heidelberg (2003)

19. Dal Zilio, S., Lugiez, D., Meyssonnier, C.: A logic you can count on. ACM SIGPLAN Not. **39**, 135–146 (2004)

20. Bennett, B., Cohn, A.G., Wolter, F., Zakharyaschev, M.: Multi-dimensional modal logic as a framework for spatio-temporal reasoning. Appl. Intell. **17**, 239–251 (2002)

21. Vogel-Heuser, B., Feldmann, S., Werner, T., Diedrich, C.: Modeling network architecture and time behavior of distributed control systems in industrial plant. In: 37th Annual Conference of the IEEE Industrial Electronics Society, IECON (2011)
22. Hadlich, T., Diedrich, C., Eckert, K., Frank, T., Fay, A., Vogel-Heuser, B.: Common communication model for distributed automation systems. In: 9th IEEE International Conference on Industrial Informatics, IEEE INDIN (2011)
23. Berger, A.: Embedded Systems Design: An Introduction to Processes, Tools, and Techniques. CMP Books, San Francisco (2002)
24. Sapienza, G., Crnkovic, I., Seceleanu, T.: Towards a methodology for hardware and software design separation in embedded systems. In: Proceedings of the Seventh International Conference on Software Engineering Advances (ICSEA), pp. 557–562. IARIA (2012)
25. Spichkova, M., Campetelli, A.: Towards system development methodologies: from software to cyber-physical domain. In: First International Workshop on Formal Techniques for Safety-Critical Systems (FTSCS 2012) (2012)
26. Dominka, S., Schiller, F., Kain, S.: Hybrid commissioning from hardware-in-the-loop simulation to real production plants. In: Proceedings of the 18th IASTED International Conference on Modeling and Simulation (MS 2007), pp. 544–549 (2007)
27. Hazra, A., Ghosh, P., Vadlamudi, S.G., Chakrabarti, P.P., Dasgupta, P.: Formal methods for early analysis of functional reliability in component-based embedded applications. Embed. Syst. Lett. 5, 8–11 (2013)
28. Broy, M., Jonsson, B., Katoen, J.-P., Leucker, M., Pretschner, A. (eds.): Model-Based Testing of Reactive Systems. LNCS, vol. 3472. Springer, Heidelberg (2005)
29. Pretschner, A., Philipps, J.: Methodological issues in model-based testing. In: Model-Based Testing of Reactive Systems, pp. 181–291 (2005)
30. Spichkova, M., Schmidt, H., Peake, I.: From abstract modelling to remote cyber-physical integration/interoperability testing. In: Improving Systems and Software Engineering Conference (2013)
31. Blech, J.O., Schmidt, H., Peake, I., Kande, M., Ramaswamy, S., Sudarsan, S.D., Narayanan, V.: Collaborative engineering through integration of architectural, social and spatial models. In: Emerging Technologies and Factory Automation (ETFA). IEEE Computer (2014)
32. Peake, I., Blech, J.O., Fernando, L.: Towards reconstructing architectural models of software tools by runtime analysis. In: 3rd International Workshop on Experiences and Empirical Studies in Software Modelling (2013)
33. Spichkova, M.: Design of formal languages and interfaces: "formal" does not mean "unreadable". In Blashki, K., Isaias, P. (eds.) Emerging Research and Trends in Interactivity and the Human-Computer Interface. IGI Global (2013)
34. Spichkova, M.: Human Factors of Formal Methods. In: Proceedings of IADIS Interfaces and Human Computer Interaction, IHCI 2012 (2012)
35. Spichkova, M., Zhu, X., Mou, D.: Do we really need to write documentation for a system? In: International Conference on Model-Driven Engineering and Software Development (MODELSWARD 2013) (2013)
36. Spichkova, M.: Specification and seamless verification of embedded real-time systems: FOCUS on Isabelle. Ph.D. thesis, Technische Universität München (2007)
37. Spichkova, M.: Stream processing components: Isabelle/HOL formalisation and case studies. Archive of Formal Proofs (2013)
38. Blech, J.O., Falcone, Y., Rueß, H., Schätz, B.: Behavioral specification based run-time monitors for OSGi services. In: Margaria, T., Steffen, B. (eds.) ISoLA 2012, Part I. LNCS, vol. 7609, pp. 405–419. Springer, Heidelberg (2012)

39. de Alfaro, L., Henzinger, T.A.: Interface automata. SIGSOFT Softw. Eng. Notes **26**, 109–120 (2001)
40. Blech, J.O., Schätz, B.: Towards a formal foundation of behavioral types for uml state-machines. ACM SIGSOFT Softw. Eng. Notes **37**, 1–8 (2012)
41. Blech, J.O.: Towards a framework for behavioral specifications of OSGI components. In: 11th International Workshop on Formal Engineering approaches to Software Components and Architectures (FESCA), pp. 79–93 (2013)
42. Blech, J.O., Schmidt, H.: Towards modeling and checking the spatial and interaction behavior of widely distributed systems. In: Improving Systems and Software Engineering Conference (2013)
43. de Moura, L., Bjørner, N.S.: Z3: an efficient SMT solver. In: Ramakrishnan, C.R., Rehof, J. (eds.) TACAS 2008. LNCS, vol. 4963, pp. 337–340. Springer, Heidelberg (2008)
44. Spichkova, M., Blech, J.O., Herrmann, P., Schmidt, H.W.: Modeling spatial aspects of safety-critical systems with focus-st. In: Boulanger, F., Famelis, M., Ratiu, D. (eds.) Proceedings of the 11th Workshop on Model-Driven Engineering, Verification and Validation co-located with 17th International Conference on Model Driven Engineering Languages and Systems, MoDeVVa@MODELS 2014, Valencia, Spain, September 30, 2014. Volume 1235 of CEUR Workshop Proceedings, pp. 49–58. CEUR-WS.org (2014)

Mobile Application Estimate the Design Phase

Laudson Silva de Souza$^{(\boxtimes)}$ and Gibeon Soares de Aquino Jr.

Department of Informatics and Applied Mathematics,
Federal University of Rio Grande do Norte, 59078-970 Natal, Brazil
{laudyson,gibeon}@gmail.com

Abstract. When addressing mobile applications, it is a technological landscape that is emerging with new requirements and restrictions requires a reassessment of current knowledge about the processes of development of these types of systems. These new systems have different features, ranging from planning to completion of the design, and therefore a particular area that is being addressed differently when it comes to estimating software. The estimation processes in general are based on characteristics of the systems to attempt to quantify the complexity of the implementation. For this reason, it is important to analyze the main models currently proposed for estimating software projects and consider whether it is suitable for mobile computing. Thus, the main objective of this paper is to present an estimation method for mobile applications still in the design phase, giving basis for all the features addressed in this scenario.

Keywords: Software engineering · Software quality · Estimating software · Systematic review · Mobile applications · Mobile computing

1 Introduction

Computing is becoming increasingly present in people's lives and currently in a much more intense and accelerated way due to the rise of the use of mobile technologies in the world, such as mobile phones, smartphones and tablets, all connected to mobile networks, which are increasingly more present in many places and with better speeds. We are facing a new technological scenario that is changing old habits and creating new ways for the society to access information and interact with computer systems [24,27,34].

The ITU[1] estimates that there are more than 6 (six) billion mobile clients worldwide. According to Gartner, 1.75 billion people own mobile phones with advanced capabilities; he also foresees further growth in the use of this technology in the upcoming years [12]. There is a global trend towards the increase of the number of users connected to the network via mobile devices which, consequently, will create an increasing demand for information, applications and content for such equipments. New ways to use existing information systems are emerging.

---

[1] International Telecommunication Union.

© Springer International Publishing Switzerland 2015
J. Filipe and L. Maciaszek (Eds.): ENASE 2014, CCIS 551, pp. 155–167, 2015.
DOI: 10.1007/978-3-319-27218-4_11

In particular, systems that were once accessed via web interfaces through personal computers physically located in offices, universities or homes are providing new ways to access from mobile devices which, in turn, have different requirements and capabilities than the personal computers.

Thus, we realize that traditional information systems are undergoing a process of adaptation to this new computing context. Current developments, including the increase of the computational power of these new devices, in addition to the integration of multiple devices on a single one and lined up with the change of the users' behavior, actually create a new environment for the development of computing solutions. However, it is important to note that the characteristics of this new context are different. They present new resources and, thereafter, new possibilities [20, 26, 40, 41], as well as introduce non-existing restrictions in conventional systems [17, 37].

The fact is that this new technological scenario that is emerging with new requirements and restrictions requires a reevaluation of current knowledge about the processes of planning and building software systems. These new systems have different characteristics and, therefore, an area in particular that demands such adaptation is software estimation. The estimation processes, in general, are based on characteristics of the systems, trying to quantify the complexity of implementing them. For this reason, it is important to analyze the methods currently proposed for software projects estimation and evaluate their applicability to this new context of mobile computing. Hence, the main objective of this paper is to present an estimation model for mobile applications.

These new systems have different characteristics and, therefore, an area in particular that demands such adaptation is software estimation. The estimation processes, in general, are based on characteristics of the systems, trying to quantify the complexity of implementing them. For this reason, it is important to analyze the methods currently proposed for software projects estimation and evaluate their applicability to this new context of mobile computing. The fact is that this new technological scenario that is emerging with new requirements and restrictions requires a reevaluation of current knowledge about the processes of planning and building software systems. Hence, the main objective of this paper is to present a partial validation of the proposed model estimate.

2   Estimation Models

In order to identify how the estimation methods in accordance with ISO could address the characteristics of the systems, a literature review on the estimation methods was performed. The methods identified in the survey can be seen in Table 1. All methods identified with their features can be accessed at the Following address: http://www.laudson.com/methods.pdf.

Table 1 displays in chronological order the estimation methods in accordance with ISO, showing the year of creation, the name of the method and the author of it. At first glance, one realizes that the main existing methods were not designed to consider the requirements of mobile applications. Indeed, the very creation of

Table 1. Estimation methods.

Year	Method	Author
1979	Function Point Analysis (FPA)	Albrecht [35]
1981	COnstructive COst MOdel (COCOMO)	Barry W. Boehm's [5]
1982	DeMarco's Bang Metrics	Tom DeMarco [18]
1986	Feature Points	Jones [39]
1988	Mark II FPA	Charles Symons [39]
1989	Data Points	Harry Sneed [25]
1990	Netherlands Software Metrics Users Association (NESMA) FPA	The Netherlands Software Metrics Users Association [8]
1990	Analytical Software Size Estimation Technique-Real-Time (ASSET-R)	Reifer [36]
1992	3-D Function Points	Whitmire [29]
1993	Use Case Points UCP	Gustav Karner [23]
1994	Object Points	Banker et al. [4]
1994	Function Points by Matson, Barret and Mellichamp	Matson, Barret e Mellichamp [28]
1997	Full Function Points (FFP)	University of Quebec em cooperao com o Software Engineering Laboratory in Applied Metrics [29]
1997	Early FPA (EFPA)	Meli, Conte et al. [30]
1998	Object Oriented Function Points – (OOFPs)	Caldiera et al. [32]
1999	Predictive Object Points – (POPs)	Teologlou [6]
1999	Common Software Measurement International Consortium (COSMIC) FFP	Common Software Measurement International Consortium (COSMIC) [7]
2000	Early & Quick COSMIC-Full Function Points (E&Q COSMIC FFP)	Meli et al. [31]
2000	Kammelar's Component Object Points	Kammelar [19]
2001	Object Oriented Method Function Points – (OOmFP)	Pastor and his colleagues [1]
2004	Finnish Software Metrics Association FSM	The Finnish Software Metrics Association (FiSMA) [11]

most of them precedes the emergence of mobile devices as we know today. This suggests that the use of these methods to estimate the effort of the development of projects involving systems or applications for mobile devices would cause a possible failure to quantify the complexity of some features and, therefore, would not produce adequate estimates.

3   Characteristics of Mobile Applications

In order to identify characteristics that are inherent to systems and mobile applications, a surveying of the characteristics of these types of software was accomplished through a systematic review. Conducting a systematic review is relevant
because most searches begin with some kind of review of the literature, and a
systematic review summarizes the existing work fairly, without inclinations. So
the surveys were conducted according to a predefined search strategy, in which
the search strategy should allow the integrity of the research to be evaluated.
The planning and accomplishment of the methodology discussed were directed
by *Procedures for Performing Systematic Reviews* [21].

In the context of the research questions, the following research questions were
formulated: "What are the characteristics of mobile applications" and "What
are the main differences between the Mobile Applications and other Applications"?. Procedures for The Evaluation of the Articles: the articles will be analyzed considering its relation with the issues addressed in the research questions,
inclusion criteria and exclusion criteria, and their respective situation will be
assigned with either "Accepted" or "Rejected". The evaluation will follow the
following procedure: read the title and abstract and, should it be related with
the research question, also read the whole article. The implementation of the
systematic review was performed almost in line with its planning, except for
the need to adjust the syntax of the proposed search string due to the particularities of the research bases. 234 articles were analyzed, of which 40 were
selected and considered "Accepted" according to the inclusion criteria; 194 were
considered "Rejected" according to the exclusion criteria. The list with all the
articles Inclusion and Exclusion Criteria and Criteria can be accessed at the
following address: http://www.laudson.com/sr-articles.pdf. The 40 articles that
were accepted were fully read, thus performing the data extraction. All of the
features found during this phase extraction are described below.

Given the results extracted from the systematic review, it's is possible to
identify 29 kinds of characteristics in 100 % of the articles evaluated and considered accepted in accordance with the inclusion criteria. However some of these
are a mixture of characteristics of mobile devices and characteristics of mobile
applications, such as the characteristic called "Limited Energy", which is a characteristic of the device and not the application, however the articles that mention
this type of characteristic emphasize that in the development of a mobile application, this "limitation" must be taken into account since all the mobile devices
are powered by batteries, which have a limited life, depending completely on
what the user operates daily. Applications requiring more hardware or software
resources will consume more energy. The 23 types of characteristics mentioned
the most in the selected articles can be observed following. There is a description
of each characteristic identified in the review:

o Limited energy [38]; Small screen [38]; Limited performance [33]; Bandwidth
[33]; Change of context [33]; Reduced memory [38]; Connectivity [9]; Interactivity
[33]; Storage [33]; Software portability [33]; Hardware portability [33]; Usability

[9]; 24/7 availability [9]; Security [9]; Reliability [22]; Efficiency [2]; Native vs. Web Mobile [9]; Interoperability [33]; Response time [15]; Privacy [9]; Short term activities [3]; Data integrity [15]; Key characteristics [3]; Complex integration of real-time tasks [16]; Constant interruption of activities [3]; Functional area [14]; Price [14]; Target audience [14]; Provider type [14].

After this survey, a refinement was made and a mix of characteristics was elicited with the purpose of defining which characteristics would be emphasized. Of a total of 23 types of characteristics that were most mentioned in the selected articles, a common denominator of 13 characteristics was reached, some of which had their names redefined, like "Interactivity", which became "Input Interface".

With the conclusion of the systematic review, a survey was carried out among experts in mobile development with the purpose of ratifying the characteristics previously raised and to prove their respective influence on mobile development. The disclosure of the survey was conducted in more than 70 locations, among them universities and businesses, through e-mails, study groups and social groups. In general, of all 117 feedbacks received through the survey, 100 % of the experts confirmed the characteristics; among them, an average of 72 % indicated a greater effort and complexity regarding the characteristics during development, an average of 12 % indicated less effort and complexity and, finally, an average of 16 % indicated they did not perceive any difference in mobile development, even though they confirmed the presence of the characteristics.

4   Problem Addressed

As noted in Sect. 2, there is no estimation method developed for mobile applications projects. Moreover, some of the characteristics elicited in Sect. 3 aggravate the complexity and, thereafter, the effort in the development of mobile applications. From the analysis that follows, with the characteristics of applications on mobile devices elicited in Sect. 3, it is clear that they are different from the characteristics of traditional systems and directly influence its development. A clear example, which is different from the information or desktop systems, is the characteristic that the mobile devices have "Limited Energy". As mobile devices are powered by battery, which have a limited lifetime period, the applications must be programmed to require the minimal amount of hardware resources possible, since the more resources consumed, the greater amount of energy expended. This characteristic makes it necessary for the solution project to address this concern, generating a higher complexity of development and, thereafter, a greater effort and cost. All other characteristics that tend to influence the development of a mobile application and its attached thereto analyzes can be accessed at: http:// www.laudson.com/characteristics.pdf.

From the survey of the most popular estimation methods cited in Sect. 2, it was found that these characteristics are not covered by the current estimation methods for two explicit reasons: first, none of the existing methods was designed to perform project estimation in mobile applications development; and second, all the characteristics discussed in this section are exclusive to mobile applications, with direct interference in their development, thereby generating a greater complexity and, thereafter, a greater effort. However, to consider any of the existing estimation methods to apply to the process of development of mobile applications is to assume that this kind of development is no different than the project of developing desktop applications, in other words, an eminent risk is assumed.

5   Estimation in Mobile Application Design Phase

The approached proposed is an adaptation of an existing method, which was named the "MEstiAM (Estimation Model for Mobile Applications)", based exclusively on methods recognized as international standards by ISO. Among the most popular estimation methods mentioned in Sect. 2, the method used to base the proposal below on is known as "*Finnish Software Metrics Association* (FISMA)". The model is one of the five methods for measuring software that complies with the ISO/IEC 14143-1 standard, is accepted as an international standard for software measuring [11] and nowadays over 750 software projects are completed being estimated by FISMA. However, the difference between this and other methods that are in accordance with the above standard, which are the *Common Software Measurement International Consortium Function Points* (COSMIC FP) [7], the *International Function Point Users Group* (IFPUG) FPA [35], *MarkII FPA* [39] and the *Netherlands Software Metrics Association* (NESMA) WSF [13], is that the method used is based in functionality but is service-oriented. It also proposes in its definition that it can be applied to all types of software, but this statement is lightly wrong since in its application, the method does not take into account the characteristics elicited in Sect. 3. Finally, other methods were analyzed tested, become unfeasible a possible adapto of them because mostly has its year of creation before the FISMA itself.

The COMISC FP [7], the MarkII FPA [39] and the NESMA [13] were created based on the FPA [35], in other words, they assume the counting of Function Point (FP), but considering the implemented functionality from the user's point of view. With this, it is clear that the methods mentioned above do not take into account the characteristics of mobile applications because they are not noticed by the user. The methods are independent of the programming language or technology used. And, unlike FISMA, they do not bring in their literature the information that they can be applied to all types of software.

Overall, the FISMA method proposes that all services provided by the application are identified. It previously defines some services, among which stands out the user's interactive navigation, consulting services, user input interactive services, interface services for other applications, data storage services, algorithmic services and handling services. Finally, after identifying all the services, the size of each service is calculated using the same method and thus obtaining a total functional size of the application by adding the size of each service found [10].

5.1   Approaching the Chosen Model

The FiSMA method in its original usage proposes a structure of seven classes of the Base Functional Component or BFC (Base Functional Component) type, which is defined as a basic component of functional requirement. The seven classes used to account for the services during the application of the method are [10]: interactive navigation of the end user and query services (q); interactive input services from end users (i); non-interactive outbound services for the end user (o); interface services for another application (t); interface services for other applications (f); data storage services (d) and algorithmic manipulation services (a).

The identification for each class name BFC previously mentioned, with a letter in parenthesis, is used to facilitate the application of the method during the counting process, because each of the seven classes BFCs are composed of other BFC classes which, at the time of calculating, these BFCs "daughter" classes are identified by the letter of their BFC "mother" class followed by a numeral. The unit of measurement is the point of function with the letter "F" added to its nomenclature to identify the "FiSMA", resulting in FfP (*FiSMA Function Point*) or Ffsu (*FiSMA functional size unit*). The measurement process generally consists of measuring the services and end-user interface and the services considered indirect [10]. Briefly, the process of counting should be done as follows. Identify: ○ How many types of BFCs does the software have? ○ Which are they? (identify all) ○ What are they? (provide details of each BFC identified). After doing this, it is necessary to add each BFC root using the formulas pre-defined by the method and their assignments. Finally, the formula of the final result of the sum is the general sum of all the BFCs classes.

5.2   Applying the Chosen Model

The FiSMA method can be applied manually or with the aid of the Experience Service[2] tool, which was the case, provided by FiSMA itself through contact made with senior consultant Pekka Forselius and with the chairman of the board Hannu Lappalainen.

When using the tool, it is necessary to perform all the steps of the previous subsection to obtain the functional size. Figure 1 shows the final report after the implementation of the FiSMA on a real system, the Management of Academic Activities Integrated System (Sigaa) in its Mobile version, developed by the Superintendence of Computing (SINFO) of the Federal University of Rio Grande do Norte (UFRN).

After the application of FiSMA, the functional size of the software is obtained and from this it is possible to find the effort using the formula: Estimated effort (h) = size (fp) x reuse x rate of delivery (h/fp) x project status; the latter is related to productivity factors that are taken into account for the calculation of the effort. However, of the factors predefined by the FiSMA regarding the product, only 6 (six) are proposed, in which the basic idea of the evaluation is that

---

[2] http://www.experiencesaas.com/.

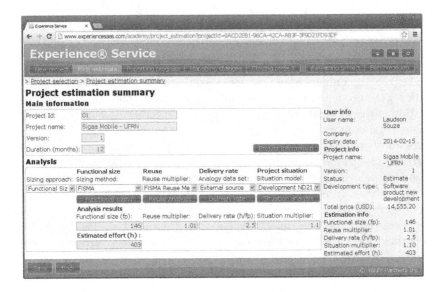

Fig. 1. Final report of FiSMA applied to Sigaa Mobile.

"the better the circumstances of the project, the more positive the assessment". The weighting goes from $--$ to $++$, as follows:

Caption: ∘ $(++) = [1.10]$ Excellent situation, much better circumstances than in the average case; ∘ $(+) = [1.05]$ Good situation, better circumstances than in the average case; ∘ $(+/-) = [1.0]$ Normal situation; ∘ $(-) = [0.95]$ Bad situation, worse circumstances than in the average case; ∘ $(--) = [0.90]$ Very bad situation, much worse circumstances than in the average case.

Productivity Factors: ∘ Functionality requirements $\rightarrow$ compatibility with the needs of the end user, the complexity of the requirements; ∘ Reliability requirements $\rightarrow$ maturity, tolerance to faults and recovery for different types of use cases; ∘ Usability requirements $\rightarrow$ understandability and easiness to learn the user interface and workflow logic; ∘ Efficiency requirements $\rightarrow$ effective use of resources and adequate performance in each use case and under a reasonable workload; ∘ Maintainability requirements $\rightarrow$ lifetime of the application, criticality of fault diagnosis and test performance; ∘ Portability requirements $\rightarrow$ adaptability and instability to different environments, to the architecture and to structural components.

Among the productivity factors mentioned above, only the "Portability Requirement" factor fits in harmony with the "Portability" characteristic regarding both hardware and software. However, none of the other factors discusses the characteristics of mobile application, in other words, after obtaining the functional size of the software and applying the productivity factors related to the product to estimate the effort, this estimate ignores all of the characteristics of mobile applications, judging that the estimate of traditional information systems is equal to the mobile application. However, with the proposal of the creation of new productivity factors, which would be the specific characteristics of mobile applications, this problem will be solved, as presented below.

Performance Factor: ∘ (−) The application should be concerned with the optimization of resources for a better efficiency and response time. ∘ (+/−) Resource optimization for better efficiency and response time may or may not exist. ∘ (+) Resource optimization for better efficiency and response time should not be taken into consideration.

Power Factor: ∘ (−) The application should be concerned with the optimization of resources for a lower battery consumption. ∘ (+/−) Resource optimization for lower battery consumption may or may not exist. ∘ (+) Resource optimization for a lower battery consumption should not be taken into consideration.

Band Factor: ∘ (−) The application shall require the maximum bandwidth. ∘ (+/−) The application shall require reasonable bandwidth. ∘ (+) The application shall require a minimum bandwidth.

Connectivity Factor: ∘ (−) The application must have the maximum willingness to use connections such as 3G, Wi-fi, Wireless, Bluetooth, Infrared and others. ∘ (+/−) The application must have reasonable predisposition to use connections such as 3G, Wi-Fi and Wireless. ∘ (+) The application must have only a predisposition to use connections, which can be: 3G, Wi-fi, Wireless, Bluetooth, Infrared or others.

Context Factor: ∘ (−) The application should work offline and synchronize. ∘ (+/−) The application should work offline and it is not necessary to synchronize. ∘ (+) The application should not work offline.

Graphic Interface Factor: ∘ (−) The application has limitations due to the screen size because it will be mainly used by cell phone users. ∘ (+/−) The application has reasonable limitation due to the screen size because it will be used both by cell phone and tablet users. ∘ (+) The application has little limitation due to the screen size because it will be mainly used by tablet users.

Input Interface Factor: ∘ (−) The application must have input interfaces for touch screen, voice, video, keyboard and others. ∘ (+/−) The application must have standard input interfaces for keyboard. ∘ (+) The application must have any one of the types of interfaces, such as: touch screen, voice, video, keyboard or others.

The proposed factors take into account the same weighting proposed by FiSMA, but only ranging from − to +, in other words: ∘ (+) = [1.05] Good situation, better circumstances than in the average case; ∘ (+/−) = [1.0] Normal Situation; ∘ (−) = [0.95] Bad situation, worse circumstances than in the average case. The functional size remains the same, thus affecting only the formula used to obtain the effort, which will now consider in its "project situation" variable the new productivity factors specific for mobile applications.

Table 2. Analysis of estimates of Sigaa Mobile.

Real effort spent	MEstiAM model	FiSMA model
860 h	792 h	403 h

Table 3. Analysis of estimates of SigRH Mobile.

Real effort spent	MEstiAM model	FiSMA model
103 h	115,2 h	152 h

The validation process was as follows, was raised the total effort expended in developing the Sigaa Mobile project, i.e., we obtained the actual effort. After we applied the method of estimation FISMA, in his original proposal thus obtaining an estimate of effort. Then we applied the method MEstiAM also generating an effort estimate finally the comparative analysis between the three estimates generated was performed to verify which method is closer to the actual effort spent. As can be seen in Table 2.

As can be seen in Table 2, the proposed method, MEstiAM, which is closest to the actual effort spent. You FISMA model, it was very much desired for the new model and the actual effort expended.

As it was also performed, the validation process was as follows, was raised the total effort expended in developing the SigRH Mobile project, i.e., we obtained the actual effort. After we applied the method of estimation FISMA, in his original proposal thus obtaining an estimate of effort. Then we applied the method MEstiAM also generating an effort estimate finally the comparative analysis between the three estimates generated was performed to verify which method is closer to the actual effort spent. As can be seen in Table 3.

As can be seen in Table 3, the proposed method, MEstiAM, which is closest to the actual effort spent. You FISMA model, it was very much desired for the new model and the actual effort expended.

6   Conclusion

Given the results presented, based on the literature review of estimation methods and on the systematic review of the characteristics of mobile applications, it was observed that this sub-area of software engineering still falls short. Basically, it's risky to use any existing estimation method in development projects for mobile applications, as much as there are some models already widespread in industry, such as the Function Point Analysis, the Mark II and the COSMIC-FFP, which are even approved by ISO as international standards. They all fall short by not taking into account the particularities of mobile applications, which makes the method partially ineffective in this situation. Based on this study, it is concluded that the proposal presented in this work is entirely appropriate and viable and that this proposal should take into account all the peculiarities of such applications, finally creating a belief that there actually are considerable differences in the development project for mobile applications.

With the common emergence of new systems, experts always find a barrier when using one of the current methods of software measurement. This barrier can be on the effectiveness of the method, on what type of method should be used, when it comes to a software that is considered unconventional and, mostly, when it is required to apply it in completely atypical scenarios. This whole situation is aggravated further when it comes to mobile applications.

Based on this study, it is concluded that the proposal presented in this work is entirely appropriate and viable and that this proposal should take into account all the peculiarities of such applications, finally creating a belief that there actually are considerable differences in the development project for mobile applications.

References

1. Abrahão, S., Poels, G., Pastor, O.: A functional size measurement method for object-oriented conceptual schemas: design and evaluation issues. Softw. Syst. Model. **5**(1), 48–71 (2006)
2. Al-Jaroodi, J., Al-Dhaheri, A., Al-Abdouli, F., Mohamed, N.: A survey of security middleware for pervasive and ubiquitous systems. In: 2009 International Conference on Network-Based Information Systems, NBIS 2009, pp. 188–193. IEEE (2009)
3. Rogov, I., Erlick, D., Gerbert, A., Mandadi, A., Mudegowder, D.: Mobile applications: characteristics and group project summary. Mobile Application Development. Google (2009)
4. Banker, R.D., Kauffman, R.J., Wright, C., Zweig, D.: Automating output size and reuse metrics in a repository-based computer-aided software engineering (case) environment. IEEE Trans. Softw. Eng. **20**(3), 169–187 (1994)
5. Boehm, B., Valerdi, R., Lane, J., Brown, A.: Cocomo suite methodology and evolution. CrossTalk **18**(4), 20–25 (2005)
6. Caldiera, G., Antoniol, G., Fiutem, R., Lokan, C.: Definition and experimental evaluation of function points for object-oriented systems. In: 1998 Proceedings of the Fifth International Software Metrics Symposium, Metrics 1998, pp. 167–178 (1998)
7. COSMIC-Common Software Measurement International Consortium: The cosmic functional size measurement method-version 3.0 measurement manual (the cosmic implementation guide for ISO/IEC 19761: 2003) (2007)
8. Engelhart, J., Langbroek, P., et al.: Function Point Analysis (FPA) for Software Enhancement. NESMA (2001)
9. Feng, H.: A literature analysis on the adoption of mobile commerce. In: 2009 IEEE International Conference on Grey Systems and Intelligent Services, GSIS 2009, pp. 1353–1358. IEEE (2009)
10. Finnish Software Measurement Association FiSMA. Fisma functional size measurement method version 1-1 (2004)
11. Forselius, P.: Finnish software measurement association (FiSMA), FSM working group: FiSMA functional size measurement method v. 1.1 (2004)
12. Inc. GARTNER: Gartner says worldwide mobile phone sales declined 1.7 percent in 2012. Gartner, Egham (2013)

13. Gencel, C., Heldal, R., Lind, K.: On the conversion between the sizes of software products in the life cycle

14. Giessmann, A., Stanoevska-Slabeva, K., de Visser, B.: Mobile enterprise applications-current state and future directions. In: 2012 45th Hawaii International Conference on System Science (HICSS), pp. 1363–1372. Google (2012)

15. Hameed, K., et al.: Mobile applications and systems. Google (2010)

16. Hayenga, M., Sudanthi, C., Ghosh, M., Ramrakhyani, P., Paver, N.: Accurate system-level performance modeling and workload characterization for mobile internet devices. In: Proceedings of the 9th Workshop on MEmory Performance: DEaling with Applications, Systems and Architecture, MEDEA 2008, pp. 54–60. ACM, New York (2008)

17. Husted, N., Saïdi, H., Gehani, A.: Smartphone security limitations: conflicting traditions. In: Proceedings of the 2011 Workshop on Governance of Technology, Information, and Policies, GTIP 2011, pp. 5–12. ACM, New York (2011)

18. Jones, C., Jones, T.C.: Estimating Software Costs, vol. 3. McGraw-Hill, New York (1998)

19. Kammelar, J.: A sizing approach for oo-environments. In: Proceedings of the 4th International ECOOP Workshop on Quantitative Approaches in Object-Oriented Software Engineering (2000)

20. Ketykó, I., De Moor, K., De Pessemier, T., Verdejo, A.J., Vanhecke, K., Joseph, W., Martens, L., De Marez, L.: QoE measurement of mobile youtube video streaming. In: Proceedings of the 3rd Workshop on Mobile Video Delivery, MoViD 2010, pp. 27–32. ACM, New York (2010)

21. Kitchenham, B.: Procedures for performing systematic reviews. Keele, UK, Keele Univ. **33**, 1–26 (2004)

22. Maji, A.K., Hao, K., Sultana, S., Bagchi, S.: Characterizing failures in mobile OSes: A case study with android and symbian. In: 2010 IEEE 21st International Symposium on Software Reliability Engineering (ISSRE), pp. 249–258. IEEE (2010)

23. Kusumoto, S., Matukawa, F., Inoue, K., Hanabusa, S., Maegawa, Y.: Estimating effort by use case points: method, tool and case study. In: 2004 Proceedings of the 10th International Symposium on Software Metrics, pp. 292–299 (2004)

24. Liu, T.C., Wang, H.Y., Liang, J.K., Chan, T.-W., Ko, H.W., Yang, J.C.: Wireless and mobile technologies to enhance teaching and learning. J. Comput. Assist. Learn. **19**(3), 371–382 (2003)

25. Lother, M., Dumke, R.: Points metrics-comparison and analysis. In: International Workshop on Software Measurement (IWSM 2001), Montréal, Québec, pp. 155–172 (2001)

26. Lowe, R., Mandl, P., Weber, M.: Context directory: a context-aware service for mobile context-aware computing applications by the example of google android. In: 2012 IEEE International Conference on Pervasive Computing and Communications Workshops (PERCOM Workshops), pp. 76–81 (2012)

27. Macario, G., Torchiano, M., Violante, M.: An in-vehicle infotainment software architecture based on google android. In: 2009 IEEE International Symposium on Industrial Embedded Systems, SIES 2009, pp. 257–260 (2009)

28. Matson, J.E., Barrett, B.E., Mellichamp, J.M.: Software development cost estimation using function points. IEEE Trans. Softw. Eng. **20**(4), 275–287 (1994)

29. Maya, M., Abran, A., Oligny, S., St-Pierre, D., Desharnais, J.-M.: Measuring the functional size of real-time software. In: Proceedings of 1998 European Software Control and Metrics Conference, Maastricht, The Netherlands, pp. 191–199 (1998)

30. Meli, R.: Early and extended function point: a new method for function points estimation. In: Proceedings of the IFPUG-Fall Conference, pp. 15–19 (1997)

31. Meli, R., Abran, A., Ho, V.T., Oligny, S.: On the applicability of COSMIC-FFP for measuring software throughout its life cycle. In: Proceedings of the 11th European Software Control and Metrics Conference, pp. 18–20 (2000)

32. Morisio, M., Stamelos, I., Spahos, V., Romano, D.: Measuring functionality and productivity in web-based applications: a case study. In: 1999 Proceedings of Sixth International Software Metrics Symposium, pp. 111–118 (1999)

33. Mukhtar, H., Belaïd, D., Bernard, G.: A model for resource specification in mobile services. In: Proceedings of the 3rd International Workshop on Services Integration in Pervasive Environments, SIPE 2008, pp. 37–42. ACM, New York (2008)

34. Naismith, L., Sharples, M., Lonsdale, P., Vavoula, G., et al.: Literature review in mobile technologies and learning (2004)

35. Oligny, S., Desharnais, J.-M., Abran, A.: A method for measuring the functional size of embedded software. In: 3rd International Conference on Industrial Automation, pp. 7–9 (1999)

36. Reifer, D.J.: Asset-R: a function point sizing tool for scientific and real-time systems. J. Syst. Softw. **11**(3), 159–171 (1990)

37. Shabtai, A., Fledel, Y., Kanonov, U., Elovici, Y., Dolev, S., Glezer, C.: Google android: a comprehensive security assessment. IEEE Secur. Priv. **8**(2), 35–44 (2010)

38. Sohn, J.-H., Woo, J.-H., Lee, M.-W., Kim, H.-J., Woo, R., Yoo, H.-J.: A 50 Mvertices/s graphics processor with fixed-point programmable vertex shader for mobile applications. In: 2005 IEEE International Solid-State Circuits Conference, Digest of Technical Papers. ISSCC 2005, vol. 1, pp. 192–592 (2005)Google

39. Symons, C.: Come back function point analysis (modernized)–all is forgiven!). In: Proceedings of the 4th European Conference on Software Measurement and ICT Control, FESMA-DASMA, pp. 413-426 (2001)

40. Yang, C.-C., Yang, H.-W., Huang, H.-C.: A robust and secure data transmission scheme based on identity-based cryptosystem for ad hoc networks. In: Proceedings of the 6th International Wireless Communications and Mobile Computing Conference, IWCMC 2010, pp. 1198–1202. ACM, New York (2010)

41. Yang, S.-Y., Lee, D.L., Chen, K.-Y.: A new ubiquitous information agent system for cloud computing - example on GPS and bluetooth techniques in google android platform. In: 2011 International Conference on Electric Information and Control Engineering (ICEICE), pp. 1929–1932 (2011)

Author Index

Printed in the United States
By Bookmasters